A Quiet

Revolution

D0168472

A Quiet Revolution

Revolution

THE CHRISTIAN RESPONSE
TO HUMAN NEED . . .
A STRATEGY FOR TODAY

John Perkins

Word Books, Publisher
Waco, Texas

First Printing, December 1976
Second Printing, April 1977

Printed in the United States of America
ISBN 0-87680-793-7
Library of Congress Catalog Card Number: 76-48541

All Scripture quotations, unless otherwise marked, are from the
Revised Standard Version of the Bible, copyrighted 1946, 1952,
© 1971, 1973 by the Division of Christian Education of the
National Council of the Churches of Christ in the U.S.A., and
used by permission. Quotations marked Phillips are from *The
New Testament in Modern English*, copyright © 1958, 1959,
1960 by J. B. Phillips.

I dedicate this book to the people of the Voice of Calvary community who have committed themselves to make the vision a reality, and to the many faithful friends and supporters around the country who have sacrificed over the years to make pursuit of the vision possible, and to emerging community groups around the world who are making the Body of Christ come alive in their local neighborhoods.

Contents

Preface

The call to remember the ways in which God has acted for and among his people is one consistently sounded throughout both Old and New Testaments. God's acts point to his unique position as the one true and living God, the Lord of all life.

This book is intended to follow the biblical principle of remembrance, to recall the unique ways God has worked among us and faithfully kept his promises. I say *unique* because this is an account of what God has done through and among black people in Mississippi in the past sixteen years.

Statistics show that blacks in Mississippi have been subjected to the most prejudiced legislation and traditions, have lived in the most desperate poverty, and have migrated since 1930 out of the state at one of the fastest rates ever recorded. Never in the state's history has there been a comprehensive plan to evangelize people in the black community.

Yet God brought my family back to Mississippi. He raised up strong black Christian leaders in the midst of an oppressive society—people like Mr. R. A. Buckley, Jesse Newsome, and Mrs. Lillian Fletcher. God changed young people through Christ, made ways for them to get their education outside the state in Christian colleges and Bible institutes, and, what's even more unique, sent men and women like Dolphus and Rose Weary, and Artis and Carolyn Fletcher, back to make up a strong wave of black college graduates returning to Simpson County. God has worked through his people to give them the vision and then the skills to carry out the vision of his ministry—unique blessings in a society which has deferred the dreams and withheld the skills from the black segment of its people.

The format of this book reflects the fact that God has done a unique work through the *many* lives of those "called according to his purpose." The story of the Voice of Calvary Ministries is not the story of one man's personal struggles but of how a group of people have struggled together to know God and make him known, right down to the very basic needs with which they wrestle every day. So I have used interviews with the Wearys and the Buckleys and Herbert Jones and the Fletchers, and the other people who have given their

9

energy and sweat and hearts to what the Lord has done here. The format of personal testimonies, interviews and then my own interpretation of our history will, I hope, reveal that a good story does tell itself best from the lips of the people who wrote it originally with their lives.

I believe our story is unique also because it is a testimony to the ministry of reconciliation between white and black people carried on today by God's Holy Spirit. Over the past years I have seen Paul's words given flesh: "For he [Christ] is our peace, who has made us both one, and has broken down the dividing wall of hostility" (Eph. 2:14). Back in the 1960s I can remember seeing that the poverty and racism and the deep spiritual needs which we faced were greater than we were going to be able to confront with local economic and human resources. I can remember a sermon I preached to our staff then saying, "God will probably have to bring in outside people to work with us." And this has happened with nurses, teachers, and doctors, social workers, students and carpenters and almost every kind of skilled person imaginable (and some not so skilled). God has brought together over the years from almost every Christian denomination and background—Baptists, Quakers, Brethren, Mennonites, Catholics, Episcopalians, Presbyterians, and many more—black and white men and women in a relationship of commitment and love and power that is a witness to the "ministry of reconciliation" given to us by the Lord Jesus, through whom God has reconciled us all to himself.

This book also reflects the unique way in which God has called people to do his work. In writing, I have worked jointly with a young man, H. P. Spees (known as H.), who was called to the Voice of Calvary over three years ago. Since that time we have worked closely together. From the first thing we wrote together God has enabled H. to communicate my thoughts and the vision of our work. My dream has become his dream, my vision, his vision—and that is the secret strength that the Lord has given all of us throughout this ministry. In this case it has allowed H. and me to put words to biblical concepts that have been borne out as truth during the last sixteen years and to interpret this work of God to the outside world.

Finally, this story is unique in the same way Christian works should be unique—the yoking of the faith relationship with God and the creative work of ministry. Faith and works have been separated many times by theological differences. But there is a need today and in all days to put faith and works back together.

Voice of Calvary Ministries has not sacrificed one for the other. A small group of people decided that their faith and their Bible and their love of God was relevant to every human need, and, knowing this, knew the responsibility of applying the resources of faith to the needs. They had to do it, as well as teach it. To do both is hard, but to have courage to do both is what is necessary. So this book is about a group of people who decided to put faith and works together, made the sacrifices necessary to do it, and then discovered that it works.

Because this is such a basic element to the whole nature and history of our work, I have tried throughout this book to show how biblical principles are practical and can be used to develop a whole community, no matter what the needs and, more importantly, can be duplicated in other places. Voice of Calvary is one small way in which God is working. Many people have looked at us and said VOC is a model. That startles and frightens me a little. But in a way this book is a test of that statement. For if Voice of Calvary is a model for biblical community development among poor people, then the concepts within these chapters should be relevant to any group of people seeking to mobilize their faith around human need anywhere in the world. A model is little good if it can't be duplicated somewhere else.

I hope that this book will serve as a testimony of hope for black people who see the massive problems in their communities and wonder, "Can anything really be done?"; a testimony of encouragement to white people, that "yes, you can do something; yes, there can be racial reconciliation"; and a testimony of power to all people of the grace of the Lord Jesus Christ.

1655 St. Charles St.   JOHN PERKINS
Jackson, MS 39209   January 2, 1976

Acknowledgments

I would like to acknowledge the help of several people who made it possible for this book to be written: H. P. Spees, for hours spent interviewing and writing; Lisa Hendricks, Jewel Adams, and Becky Hernley for their professional typing; Mary Quinlan for her research assistance; and Mary Ruth Howes for her expert editorial assistance. And a special thanks to Ms. Colleen Karcher Stone for her gracious support of this book.

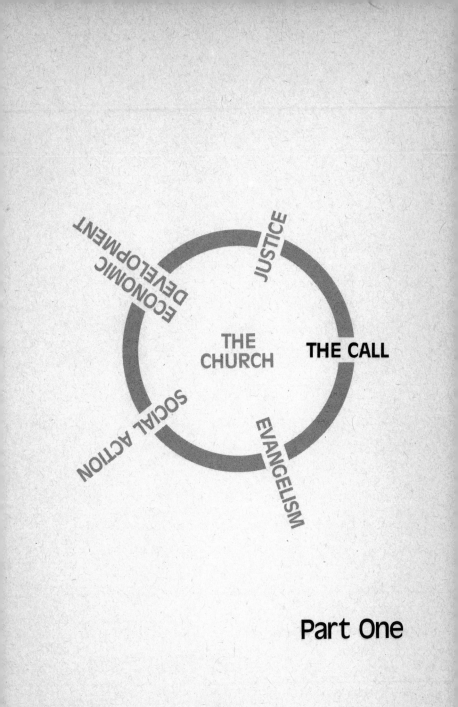

Part One

1.

A Personal Testimony

As I look back at my family history, I am the first person I know of in the Perkins family to receive Jesus Christ as personal Savior. My people in Mississippi were bootleggers and gamblers as far back as I can go.

My grandfather, who died before I was born, raised his sons as bootleggers. Our family never owned a home, but were always moving from one plantation to another, choosing them on the basis of how close they were to town and how much freedom they would allow to practice the family trade. Mississippi at this time was a dry state and most counties, including Simpson County where we lived, are still dry today. Selling whiskey was a way to make extra money. My people understood the economics of the day, and tried to beat the system.

My mother died when I was seven months old, and my father gave us to his mother who had been the mother of nineteen children. So, as far back as I can remember, there were eight of us together on a shuck bed.

In my first seventeen years in Mississippi I never heard the simple truth of the gospel, the fact that Jesus Christ can live his life in a person. I'd been to religious services and I'd heard people go through emotional discourses, but I never heard that simple truth: that you can have the power of God in your life, and that can make a difference in society. I never heard that once. I dropped out of school somewhere between the third and fifth grade and took a job.

I guess what really began to shape my life in the area of economics happened when I was a boy of about eleven or twelve, and away from home. To go away from home back then was to go twelve or fourteen miles from your community. It was a custom then to buy something to show our friends in the community that we had, in fact, been away someplace. So I was away to visit a friend, and needed some money, and a white man from a plantation was hauling hay and needed help. I thought this was a good chance to make a dollar and a half or two dollars. That's what you could get for a day's work, and that's what I expected to get. But at the end of the day he gave me fifteen cents—a dime and a buffalo head nickel. Here I was, a twelve-year-old boy and I didn't know whether to take it or not. It

was a white man handing it to me, and I was in his house, and I had
worked for him. I was afraid that if I didn't take it, he would say I
was an uppity, smart nigger. And if I did take it I would feel completely dehumanized.

Well, I took that fifteen cents, but that started me thinking about
economics. From that day on, I began to understand something about
the economic system and how it works. I understood that you had to
have money to get the mules and wagons and land, and then you had
the means of production. But all I had was my labor and so I was
exploited.

Violence is another thing which shaped my childhood. When I was
a boy, Saturday afternoon was when all the people would come to
town. But three Saturday afternoons I will never forget. On one Saturday a black man who had accidentally run over a white man with
his car was in jail. A big mob of white people went to the jail and
took this man out and tied a chain around him and dragged him up
and down the streets of the town behind a car until he died.

On another Saturday afternoon during World War II, a young
black sergeant was home on leave and in uniform. He had been
drinking heavily, and a group of white men got hold of him and
almost beat him to death with clubs and axe handles.

Then there was the third Saturday afternoon. At one point when
we were coming up, my grandmother had to give three of us children
away. She kept me and my oldest brother, because Clyde was old
enough to plow and because I was the youngest. I would see my
father only about once a year, so you can see how I became attached
to Clyde. He, too, went into the service during World War II. Clyde
was wounded in Germany, and when he came home with a purple
heart and battle scars we were really proud of him.

He was home about six months when he was killed, shot down in
an alleyway of New Hebron, Mississippi. It happened like this: On
Saturday at a certain time, blacks would have to leave town or be
very quiet. The marshal, "Uncle Bud" Thurman, had a way of walking the streets and coming up behind black people and hitting them on
the head with his stick. This Saturday afternoon, my brother and
some others were waiting at the back entrance of the Caroline Theatre
which led to the balcony or "colored section," when Uncle Bud came
up behind my brother and hit him on the head. When Clyde turned

and grabbed the club in self-defense, the marshal stepped back and shot him twice in the stomach. Clyde rode in my arms to the hospital in Jackson, and died a few hours after we got there.

James Silver, former professor at the University of Mississippi, wrote a book called *Mississippi: The Closed Society*.[1] As I look back, that really describes the society in which I grew up. Silver said that for a black in Mississippi, everything in his environment was designed to make him feel inferior, like a nigger. Once he accepted that, then he could appear to be happy. The white man could say then, "See, our blacks are very happy with the life they are living."

As blacks after World War II we had just three choices: We could stay in the state and become dehumanized niggers and accept the existing system. We could go to jail or be killed. Or, we could leave rural Mississippi and go to one of the big cities. My family decided it was no longer safe for us in Mississippi, so most of us left and went to California.

I never expected to go back to Mississippi. I left with some awareness. The work I did had shown me how economics worked. The situation of violence gave me a keen awareness and interest in politics. And I also had an awareness of the church and religion. Since we were bootleggers, we did a pretty good business with a lot of the church people, both white and black. Since I had never heard the central message of the gospel, I did not see the black church as relevant to my needs. I always looked at things economically, and it was hard to see how the shouting and turning over benches in black churches at the time was giving any kind of incentive to people to develop. In fact, I always looked at these black Christians as sort of inferior people whose religion was keeping them oppressed by making them submissive to an oppressive structure.

I did not see white Christianity as meaningful either, or relevant to my needs. It was part of the system that helped dehumanize and destroy black people. Many of the outstanding killings and murderings right down through history had white ministers involved in them. This was even true with the killing and secret burying of the three civil rights workers in Philadelphia, Mississippi. And it is still true. A pastor who participated in the killing is still the pastor there.

Because I had boiled all my problems down to economics, when I

---

[1] New York: Harcourt Brace, 1966.

got to California my basic concern was to make it economically for myself. I thought of most of my life in the framework of what happened to me back on the plantation, especially how I had been exploited. Well, I got a job at a steel foundry, where there was no union and most of the workers were black. When union people began to talk to us about exploitation and how if we organized we could get a certain amount of economic justice within the foundry, I understood what they were saying. Even as a boy I had understood a little of the power of labor if it could just be organized. Me and my cousin Jimmy were cutting sugar cane for a man who was one of the few fair white men. He always gave those who worked for him a good meal. But his wife's mother didn't feed us the meal that we had agreed on (we had agreed to work for one gallon of syrup and dinner per day). She gave us the trimmings and scraps off the table. So we would not go back to work. The man came and worked it out and we finally went back to work.

We did organize a union at the foundry, and at nineteen I was one of its leaders. After that I was drafted into the service where I had lots of time to think. I began to think about the system and I was pretty well convinced that for real change to take place, in order for black people in the South to break free, there was going to have to be some kind of revolution. But all this time I had never been confronted with the claims of Jesus Christ.

In '53 I got out of the service, got a good job with a company in California and began to make money. I understood the system and I was trying to make it for myself. (By this time, I was married and had a family.)

All this time I had an inward desire for a deeper and greater life. After my army service I began to search in earnest. I joined a church. I joined Jehovah's Witnesses. I became involved with Christian Science and Science of the Mind. And through this I began to associate religion with success. Success and money and "making it" were my religion, but I was not happy. I had no peace inside.

Then my son began to go to a little Church of Christ Holiness Mission that was teaching him the Word of God. He would come home and say verses before we began to eat, which was something new for us. I could see something beautiful developing in him that I knew nothing about. I had had no experience of seeing Christianity in a personal life that was beautiful and good. He would always ask me to go with him to the church, and finally, because I liked him so much, I decided to go.

At the Bethlehem Church of Christ Holiness, they put me in the adult class where they were teaching the life of the Apostle Paul. This was my first encounter with the Bible, which I had always looked at as a superstitious book only for old ladies. As I said, I looked at religious people as being inferior people. Most of the successful people I knew in the company that I worked for were just so-so religious. They would not be the people who had Bibles in their hands, giving out tracts. I looked on the real religious people as not being able to make it in society.

But in this Sunday school I began to enjoy the Bible because of what I was learning about the Apostle Paul, how he endured so much for religion. This really was something for me to look at. I didn't see anything in religion that would cause a man to want to give up his life and endure suffering. When I learned that the Apostle Paul was the writer of most of the New Testament books of the Bible, I began to study the Bible myself for the first time.

Then one night for the first time the Holy Spirit was able to take the Word of God and apply it to my own life. I was reading the Book of Galatians where Paul said, "I have been crucified with Christ; it is no longer I who live, but Christ who lives in me; and the life I now live in the flesh I live by faith in the Son of God, who loved me and gave himself for me" (Gal. 2:20).

Trying to find what made Paul tick, I could hear him say that he had another life—it was Christ's life—in him and that his motivation and his drive were coming from Christ who was in him. Now I always had economic motivation. But I could see that here was one with a greater, deeper motivation who gave himself. I knew that I didn't have this kind of life.

The next Sunday morning the minister was speaking from Romans 6:23, "The wages of sin is death, but the free gift of God is eternal life in Christ Jesus our Lord." That verse spoke to my whole experience. I understood wages and gain, profit and loss. I knew what a gift was. For the first time I understood that my sin was not necessarily and altogether against myself. My sin was not necessarily and altogether against my neighbor. But my sin was against a holy God who loved me, who had already died on the cross. I hadn't known that. I was sinning against his love. I didn't want to sin anymore.

And then, of course, I found out how I could give my life to Jesus Christ and he could take care of my sin. For the first time I had inward deep peace. I didn't have any solutions to what I'd been struggling with in my life, but I did have an inward peace.

I began to share this inward peace with people in the area where I lived. In about six months' time I was sharing my life and my testimony in many churches—white and black—in Southern California where, at that time, a real biblical movement was in progress. Right away I became sort of a Christian celebrity. You know, every Sunday night, every Sunday morning, through the week, some place, some church, was asking me to speak. Christian businessmen were asking me to share my testimony here and there. And I was also teaching children's Bible classes four or five nights a week. The result was that I didn't have time really to look at the system around me, and I forgot my upbringing.

Then I was asked to speak at a prison camp up in the San Bernardino mountains. California has several prison camps where they keep boys from thirteen to seventeen who have committed serious crimes. The boys take care of the firebreaks across the mountains. On Sunday mornings, Christian businessmen would go up and conduct worship services for the prisoners. I found out later why they asked me to go. The prison population was something like 60 to 70 percent black, and they had no blacks who had any knowledge (as they understood it) of salvation, who were able to articulate their faith in Christ and give a solid evangelical testimony.

As I shared my testimony and spoke from the Scriptures every Sunday, I began to see young men's lives change. When I talked with them, I soon discovered that their lives were just like mine. There was absolutely no difference. It seemed like it had just been an accident that I had become successful, had a good job and good opportunities, and my wife had a good job, while here they were in jail, in trouble. As I began to look at their lives, I began to remember my own past experiences and my own upbringing.

It was through that experience that I began to think of going back to Mississippi and starting a ministry. I remember the night when God spoke to me through his Word about it. I was giving my testimony to an all-white church in Arcadia, California, and I used for my scripture Romans 10:1–2, where Paul expresses his strong yearning and desire for the salvation of his people, the Jews. "I bear them witness," he says, "that they have a zeal for God, but it is not enlightened."

Paul's love for his people shot through me, as God said to me, "John, my desire for you is that you go back to Mississippi, because I bear your people witness that they have a zeal for God, but it is not enlightened." I was never satisfied in California after that.

2.

Two Sides of the Mountain

It was one thing to think about going back to Mississippi myself. But I had a family to take care of. And it would be hard to have an effective witness if Vera Mae was unwilling to work with me. I'd like her to tell her story of her own struggles with my call. Her account will also show what a difficult decision it was for me.

"When did *we* feel the call to go to Mississippi? *We* never did. Or I should say, I never felt it. He felt it. When Toop—'Toopy' is what everybody called John—started going to the prison camps and saw that most of the young fellas in the prison were black and a great number of them were from the South, he came under conviction.

"He could identify with these young prisoners. Though for them the problems were bad in California, their roots were in the South. He knew that there were more of his black people back in Mississippi just like these young men in prison, and just like he had been, who had not yet gone North or East or West and who had never heard the real gospel; who didn't know what life was all about, true life, real life.

"So coming back to Mississippi was a must for him. But I didn't want no part of coming back home, and I rebelled against it, from the time he started talking about it until November of 1959.

"What changed my mind was that Toop got sick. The burden was on him so heavily until he lost about forty pounds. I tried to think that it wasn't related to going back to Mississippi. But I knew it was. It was something that he had to do. I carried him down to doctors at Long Beach Veterans Hospital many times.

"When he first got sick, it was ulcers. Then the ulcers were cured, and they couldn't find anything wrong with him. They checked his heart and all his other vital organs. Everything was O.K., yet he was wasting down to nothing, getting weaker and weaker. And the Lord showed me that unless I would give in to his calling, what the Lord was calling him and us to do, that I wouldn't have no husband, that he would take him away from me. And the thought of having to raise five children alone . . . now, that was a frightful thing!

"One morning he went to get up out of the bed and he was so

weak, he couldn't stand up. I could see it just as plain as day. Oh, I was rebellious whenever I thought about going back to Mississippi! You see, that was the farthest thing from my mind. I didn't have any experiences back in Mississippi to entice me to return. Anyway, I went into the bedroom, and I got down on my knees by the bed, and I told Toop, 'I'm going to pray for you.' I prayed, and in my prayer I said to the Lord, 'I'm not going to rebel any longer, I'm going to say "Yes, I'll go." '

"And do you know, it wasn't just like a popping of the finger, but the next day the brother was up and walking around, and he told me that he was going to Mississippi to check things out. He got ready to leave and he hasn't been sick like that a day since.

"That was in November, just before Thanksgiving. By Thanksgiving he was already in Mississippi. That was hard! I was seven months pregnant with Debbie, and we had just moved into a big, twelve-room, two-and-a-half bathroom house that we were going to fix up. But the hardest thing for Spencer and Joanie and Phillip and Derek and I, was carrying him down to the little bus station there in Monrovia. I'll never forget how hard it was to put him on that bus. And doing this just for the sake of yielding to God's will.

"You know, sometimes, if you don't yield to God willingly, he has his own way of leading you to yield to him. Like it says in the Book of James (1:2–4): 'Count it all joy, my brethren, when you meet various trials, for you know that the testing of your faith produces steadfastness. And let steadfastness have its full effect, that you may be perfect and complete, lacking in nothing.' As I look back, this little trial of separation was just the beginning, just a taste of some of the bigger trials we would soon face. It makes me happy when I look back and see that God was preparing us all the way along.

"So Toop came down here to pave the way for moving the family back to Mississippi. He came back to preach, which he did all during December, to share the Good News and to work with our people. Although I had left the bus station lonesome and depressed, like I just couldn't make it, that time with the kids was one of the smoothest times I ever spent.

"Back home in Mississippi they didn't have phones, and Toop couldn't write worth anything, so I don't think I heard from him for six weeks. Then, on Christmas Eve, the phone rang. It was Toop, asking me to come down to pick him up at the bus station. I was happy!

"Debbie was born on the twenty-sixth of January, 1960, and later in the year Toop left his job in good standing, and we prepared to leave. During this time God met all our needs. The Christian Business-men's Club gave us a farewell gift. We left on June 6, 1960, and arrived in Mississippi, June 9.

"I didn't feel called, but I had agreed to go. Yet, as I look back on it, I had been called, because our ministry, from the word *go,* was a family ministry. We had been called as a family, and from the first day in Mississippi, I realized that God had given me special skills and talents that he was ready to unleash. Over the years I was to lead flannelgraph Good News Clubs with the children, I was to direct the first local Headstart Program in Simpson County, I would become bookkeeper for the growing ministries, and counselor and mother not only for my own family but for other families and the many volunteers that would join us through the years. So God had called me through the family, through our marriage.

"I first met John Perkins in 1949 when he came home to Mississippi from California to visit. That's when we started courting. We met on the church grounds, which was where girls and boys met their future spouses most of the time, 'cause there was no other place to go back then. There were few cars, so you couldn't just go into Jackson. You could go to the movie, but church people thought that people who went to movies all the time were outlaws and whoremongers and the like.

"After he went back to California, we wrote letters, then met again in 1951, just before he was to go into the service. We had good times together then. Then when he got through with his basic training, that's when we got married, on his twenty-one-day furlough just before he went overseas.

"Relatives tell me that we used to play together when I was a little girl. Our daddies gambled and were good friends. But I didn't know much about John Perkins until I was about fifteen. My grandmother, who raised me, knew all about the Perkins—everybody talked about them. The first time I saw him was at his sister's funeral—she had been killed by her boyfriend. When I got back home, my grandmother was telling about how sad this young boy was, how he had been standing under a tree in the middle of the graveyard crying after the burial.

"But sensitivity wasn't what the Perkins family was known for. They were one of the toughest families around. Everybody was afraid of the Perkins, even some of the white folks. The Perkins just wouldn't take nothing off of nobody. They were bootleggers and gamblers, known to fight and carry on incidents on the church grounds. Toop's Uncle Bill Perkins sure enough didn't care who he got into it with. Whenever the time came for a confrontation, he would have it.

"I remember once when I was a little girl, we had gone over to Galilee Baptist Church, a few miles east of New Hebron, over in the Perkins's territory. I was standing outside, and I saw Uncle Bill, who had been drinking pretty heavy, coming across the church grounds, slinging his pistol and cursing: 'I'll kill you white folks, I'll kill you white folks.' I should have been in the church in the beginning, but now I ran inside, I was so scared. I heard later that Bill ran down in the woods and that the law was afraid to go back into the woods after him.

"Another of Toop's uncles, Uncle Sam, was killed on the church grounds over at Taylor Hill Baptist Church.

"Besides showing how the Perkins were one of the toughest families around, these incidents also show some things about the black church. During the 1930s and '40s when we were growing up, there wasn't too much going on inside the church house. All the action was on the outside. The most action took place at the big meetings, like church revivals, where people from all over the town would come, or at Association Meetings, where people from churches all over the county and surrounding parts would come. These meetings were Disneyland, vacation, the state fair, and the Friday night date all rolled into one.

"So most people came to church to eat, court, drink and gamble, not worship. These type of meetings lasted until about the early 1950s when black people went North by the thousands after World War II and when there were a lot more cars and mobility was a lot easier. But this was the religious heritage that we would face over two decades later in the 1960s—a lot calmer, but still a religion without a consistent grasp on the truths of the Bible.

"One of the things that really made the Perkins different was that they were almost against religion. I guess they had to be, the way the religious people would talk about them. But it made them different, because the religion in the churches made you a coward. All my folks were religious back in those days. And I saw again and again how their religion made them humble down to the white structure, with all of its injustice. The Perkins were not like that.

"Besides religion, the two things that had most to do with shaping our lives were the economics of Mississippi and the racial situation. These two things were never spoken of openly or consciously labeled. But as I look back, they molded and formed everything, what we ate, what we thought, how we acted, how we prayed.

"Almost every black person's upbringing was about the same when it came to work. In fact, almost everybody ate the same food, almost everybody had the same things in their garden.

"One difference economically among black people was sort of a difference between two different shades of gray: the small farm owners and the sharecroppers, those who we said 'farmed on halves.' My people were fortunate enough to own their own farm. But if you farmed on halves, like Toop and them, you would live on this plantation for a year, then move over to that plantation for the next crop year. A lot of people just kept moving from plantation to plantation year after year. We were able to be more stable and stationary.

"Everybody worked. We would get through with our own crops, then go up to the Delta to pick cotton. From September to the beginning of November we'd pick, coming home on the weekends. We went on big, open-bodied trucks, just like hogs and cattle.

"I remember living on Mr. Dockery's farm out from Cleveland, Mississippi. The first thing we'd do is drive up to the store and get all squared away about where we were going to live, and everybody wanted to get some groceries on credit. Mr. Dockery owned the store, so you can see how the economics of the situation were at work.

"Usually we'd be ready to go on Sunday afternoon, right after church and we'd get up there late Sunday night. If it was the first time, though, we'd wait until Monday to go, 'cause we would have to go into one of them old, dilapidated houses and sweep out a corner and pick us some cotton and make a bed mattress, and spread some linen over the mattress. We'd carry our own quilts. I wouldn't want my kids to go through that for nothing in the world, those rat-infested houses. It wasn't bitter cold at that time of year but there were no lights, water or gas. We had a two-burner oil stove so we could never eat baked stuff, always fried. I didn't realize until about 1969, when I took a neighborhood health survey in Simpson County, how this type of diet and nutrition, brought about by economic necessity, could really create a lot of problems in a person—like diabetes, high blood pressure, and heart disease—later on in life.

"We'd get something like $2.00 or $2.50 per 100 pounds in the beginning of the season. This was because the cotton was thick—it was new, young, fresh-opened, and heavy. By ten o'clock in the morning we'd have 100 to 150 pounds. We'd be dragging a nine-foot sack. Those were the kinds of sacks we wanted 'cause we could put 75 pounds in them. And, oh! we picked, just kept picking and pushing. Those were some days I'd like to forget.

"Yet, hearing this from me you're still getting sort of a 'view from the top,' because although we were affected, we were never wiped out. We owned a little land. We had more stability and more freedom. We could leave the west side of New Hebron and go to the Delta if we wanted to work. But on the other side of town, where Toop lived, they sharecropped. When the people who owned their own places got through paying bills they had their own money. But sharecroppers almost always came out in the red. And as soon as he was done cropping, a sharecropper had to scramble to do something else just to keep things going. That's one of the reasons why Aunt Babe, Toop's grandma, sold whiskey.

"Because of the heavy need to work, black children didn't start school until November. I bought school clothes from money we made up in the Delta. I'd walk about a mile and a half to catch the school bus then ride twenty miles to the school in New Hymn around by Pinola. In rain or shine, snow or sleet, sick or feeling well, I never missed a day of school.

"I was fortunate. My Grandma encouraged me to go to school. One of the outstanding years of my life was when, after my grandfather died, I was eleven years old and Grandma asked the principal of the high school at New Hymn to let me live there with them in the dormitory. The principal, Rev. C. H. Harper, and his wife had such a love and compassion for the students. They were some of the few people who knew the importance of all black people getting an education. I can remember Grandma paying the bill for my staying there with peas and corn and hogmeat.

"There were only a few in my own family who had a high school education. Grandma was going to see to it that I was going to get a college education if I wanted to, I think. I don't know where the money would have come from, but she would have done all she could. Again, it was many years later, as I was raising my own children and as we started the tutoring program in Mendenhall, that I saw the real lack of encouragement in so many homes in the black community.

"Nobody in Toop's family had an education. He's got a cousin, Rosie Lee, in California now, who went back to school and passed her high-school equivalency test and went on to nursing school. But there was no one else. Toop caught a little bit of a couple of grades, but he had no one to encourage him to stay in school. Big boys, they would go to school as much as they wanted to, or as little. It would be even later before they'd get in off the farms. They'd already be behind. They'd go just a little bit and then get out, start cutting briars, fixing fences and getting ready for farming, especially those folks, like Toop, who lived on plantations. Toop never has been good at writing but he learned to read on his own, first the newspaper, I guess in the service, and later the Bible.

"This was the basic upbringing of all the kids around that time. Things haven't changed much now, from plantations to industrial plants, from segregated poorer quality schools to schools where the children flunk out and are not required by law to go, the same diets, the same churches, the same racial attitudes, just more covered up than when we was coming up.

"But, in fact, I didn't even know there was a bad racial situation, until I was up past high school. My folks just accepted it. I remembered how I used to have to walk a long ways to school and I'd see this big, beautiful, yellow bus pass every morning filled with white kids. We were not enlightened to know that things like that were really wrong. The kids in the bus would throw spitballs out the window at us. I'm glad I didn't get any malice in my heart toward them— I could have been damaged much more.

"When Toop's brother was shot, in the black community it went something like this: 'Well, another one of those Perkins got shot today.' It was just something that seemed like the black folks thought ought to happen because the Perkins was so bad. It shouldn't have been, but it seemed like most of the black folks, as far as I know, were 'tomish' type people, sort of cowered down. Toop and them, and people like my Grandma, weren't like that, but most of the other folks around were. I think it had to do a lot with security. Those who had a little something wanted to keep it. It seems funny now how some of the people most oppressed by the system were some of the greatest defenders of it, just in order to protect their little piece of the action. But it was also something in the people that made them feel inferior. Religion played a part in the whole way that the society would make black people feel inferior and coward. Religion was just the melody to the beat that everybody walked by.

"I didn't really see the depths of the situation until I married Toop. Even then, we were in California and really making a good life for ourselves. There wasn't a lot of bitterness. We didn't want to remember all the bad encounters and incidents that happened back home. We tried to push that back, and we did. It became the furthest thing from our minds—first, because it was something we didn't think we could do anything about, and second, because, although we never forgot, our minds were filled with so many things better than that: like trying to make it in life, trying to bring up our kids in a far better state. We'd go all the way for our kids, every mile of the way.

"As I look back, those years in California gave us a unique time to be developed and prepared by God without the pressure of hatred and malice. It also gave us exposure to a world much bigger than the one we grew up in. We later found this essential in our development of strong, black, Christian leaders in Mississippi and we began to send our young converts outside the South for education and experience so that they could come back as more fully developed and mature believers.

"I suppose the first step in our spiritual development, although it looks like a step backward, was our involvement with some black religious cult groups. We were both searching for something deeper in life, and Toop's energy would take him looking into a lot of things. He had always had that enthusiasm. Any group he was a part of he became a leader, even though he was slow in speech and stuttered a lot, not like he is today. He used to be a little bit shy, but what he said was always worthwhile. His enthusiasm spread to politics and sports, which he always kept up on in the newspaper. In recent years he has worked side-by-side with men who were black Muslims and I have often thought if he had never become a Christian, he would have been a Muslim, with their strict devotion and discipline and he would have risen right to the top.

"While he was looking into these cults, he was attending the Second Baptist Church and even did some ushering. After we were married, we still went to church haphazardly. Then one of Toop's buddies from work, Calvin Bourne, asked him to go to church with him. Toop put it off for a long time. At about the same time, Spencer, our oldest son, was going to the church and asked his daddy to go too. So we went to Calvin's church, Bethlehem Church of Christ Holiness in Pasadena. These were some really solid Christians, folks you could lean on, people who loved and cared.

"The Sunday that Toop was saved, he came home and told me about it. But it didn't even phase me. I wasn't thinking anything about the brother getting saved. I was a Christian from a long time back, but I didn't even have enough sense not to yoke myself with an unbeliever or even to pray for him that the Lord would save him. That shows you how far away we were! But it was true, he was genuinely saved that Sunday morning and it caused me and the whole family to really dedicate our lives to the Lord.

"Three things happened then that changed our lives. First, Toop began to go to the local Christian bookstore, and his speech began to get better. I really think Mary Feastal, the bookstore manager, prayed for him, but she also told him how to pronounce his words, and how to practice not stuttering. This was a real change.

"The second thing is we became involved in Child Evangelism Fellowship, sharing Jesus with little children. We began teaching classes—five a week, one each evening—and going to the training every Tuesday night. That was one thing about us, when we got involved in something, it was all or nothing. We made flannel scenes for nearly every lesson, up to fifty backgrounds.

"But the third and great thing was the way Mr. Leitch of Child Evangelism Fellowship began to teach Toop. He saw some great potentials in the brother. I don't know whether anyone else could see them or not. But he would teach Toop the Bible several days a week after work. This went on for two years, and this is where Toop got the foundation in the Scriptures that has been the basis for all our work. Little did we know how much we would use those flannelgraphs speaking to ten thousand children each month in the public schools here in Mississippi, or how we would use Mr. Leitch's strategy of discipleship as we taught one after another of our young converts about the Lord through one-to-one study of the Scripture.

"In 1958 John and a few others formed what they called the Fishermen's Mission. Soon, all Monrovia knew about the Fishermen. And the relationships that were soon formed in this group have lasted until this day and have been the foundation to the support of all the ministries we've ever been involved in here in Mississippi. And as John went out, more and more groups asked him to come and teach the Bible. It was a very intensive time of learning and speaking and developing and witnessing for us both.

" 'The Lord knows the way through the wilderness!' That's all I can say as I consider where he has brought us. As I look back at that wilderness and our getting ready for our ministry in the South, our forgotten home, I see something like a mountain. God was leading us up one side of the mountain, out of our past, bringing us to him, preparing us with skills we would need in his service. At the same time, in the South, there was a real unsettling atmosphere, especially after the desegregation of the 1950s. Up the other side of the mountain, although we never saw it then, was coming history itself, at least for black people. And in 1960, we got to the top of that mountain as God called us forth to do his work. Little did we know that that call would bring us face to face with a very violent time in history."

3.

The Will and Call of God

As I look back over my life prior to 1960, I can see how God was leading me and Vera Mae even before I entered a personal relationship with him. My upbringing and later experiences, the search for meaning and peace, the climactic end of that search with the discovery of Christ, my Lord, and his will for the world, all led to a concrete call for what has become my life's work here in Mississippi.

Even so, there have been many times when I have wondered why God called me to work in Mississippi. Many people have asked me, "How did God call you?" or "How do I find God's will for my life?" or "How do I know when or whether or not I've been called by God to do something?"

To me these questions are central to understanding God's movement in history today. I could never have survived the ministry we've had in Mississippi without the knowledge of God's will and the confidence of his call upon my life and the life of my family.

It is my conviction that God's specific summoning to service in our world involves two steps: learning God's will and hearing his call upon our lives.

Learning God's Will

God's will is in his Word, the Bible. Learning God's will began for me when I first heard the claims of his Word upon my life.

My life is much like Paul's letters. Paul usually takes the first part of his letter to affirm Christian truth, to re-lay the foundations of faith. The second part of the letter concerns the practical implications of faith for daily living. The first step for me was seeing that I was lost and in sin and then trusting Christ as God's payment for that sin. But it was not until I lived out what the Scriptures said that I really knew God's will. In other words, God's will is in the Scriptures, yes, but after my mind is transformed by God's Word, then the Scriptures have to be put into practice. That's when I "prove what is the will of God, what is good and acceptable and perfect" (Rom. 12:2). A transformed mind without any practical life attached to it is worthless.

This is important, because the implication of making faith practical is that my faith in Christ is relevant to every problem, personal or societal, which I face. I meet so many people who don't think their faith is relevant to anything but heaven and hell.

This idea of relevance becomes clearer when we see that *God's will is summed up in the two Great Commandments:* to love God with all that we have and are, and to love our neighbor in the same way we love ourselves (Matt. 22:36–40).

After I accepted Christ and got settled down in my relationship with him, he immediately called me to relate my faith to others. A principle that Jesus used over and over again was to find the need and fill it. Now, I was called to find the same need in others and fill it. For me to love others like I love myself was to share that which had given me the deepest contentment in my own life, the good news that Jesus could live his life through me. But I loved myself in other ways than seeking out a relationship with the Lord. I loved myself enough to want a good job, a safe home, and healthy food. As I began meeting people without these basic things, I saw that God's love in me wanted them to be healthy and not retarded also. But wanting these things for them was not enough. My faith had to relate to their needs, if for no other reason than that Jesus had told me to love others like I love and care for myself.

This principle of the relevance of God's will has always been a part of the Voice of Calvary. But, I have just recently found out something that really blows my mind. If you take all of the verses in the Bible and organize them under themes, the two major themes with the most individual verses supporting them are God's hate for idolatry and God's concern for the poor and the oppressed. But when I think about it, it isn't so strange. It makes sense that if the first thing God wills is that we love him with all that we are, then his chief concern must be what happens when we don't do that and instead worship things. And it also makes sense that if the second thing God wills is that men and women love their neighbors with the same love they have for themselves, then his second biggest concern must be what happens when we don't do that and damage our brothers and sisters.

So, the biblical evidence overwhelmingly states that the will of God is to love him in a way that leaves no room for idols and to love our neighbor in a way that liberates him from poverty and oppression, either spiritual or physical.

Most of us don't even see the commandment to love our neighbor as having anything to do with dealing with his physical needs. But this is primarily because we have allowed the culture in which we live to redefine the word *love* for us. The love that we talk about now is a lollipop, it's a smile and a "God bless you"! But the love of Jesus, the love he intends for us to show to our neighbors, is much tougher than this. In his first epistle, the Apostle John says that our love should be of the same quality as Jesus' love for us, that we get our definition of love not from our feelings or our culture but from the cross: "By this we know love, that he laid down his life for us; and we ought to lay down our lives for the brethren" (1 John 3:16).

God's will is plain. We are to love him and are to love people. But when it comes down to loving people, we hedge. Jesus says, "Greater love has no man than this, that a man lay down his life for his friends" (John 15:13). People say, "Sure, I'm willing to die for you." But the point is are we willing to *live* for our neighbor? To love people is to spend my energy and resources and time to serve them. To love people in practical ways that have impact on their whole being— their spirits, their economic situation, their health, their minds—that's God's will (Neh. 8:10; Prov. 21:13; Prov. 19:17; Matt. 25:35–40; Luke 6:38; Luke 14:12–14; James 2:15–17).

God's will has objectives. And one of God's main objectives is liberation, to liberate the oppressed, to offer new and more abundant life. Here again, the theological and the practical are two sides of the same spiritual reality. As we look at Scripture, especially in the Old Testament, apostasy almost always resulted in economic oppression. The Book of Judges shows that Israel's spiritual enslavement to idols resulted in their own physical enslavement by their neighbors. In the prophets the cycle was a little more complex. The people of Israel would worship other gods and end up oppressing their own brothers and sisters. This always brought God's judgment, their own collapse, and sometimes captivity. A total liberation, spiritual and physical, that is the objective of God's will.

Another principle is that *God's will works from the inside out.* This is assumed in the order of the commandments, that we love God first with all our heart, then we can express our love outwardly toward people. That's energy! That's power! But it also means that if I have not dealt with God's will practically in my life, I cannot be used by him as a vessel for his love to others.

Up until the time I was saved I had always interpreted my problem as a completely economic problem. I thought, "If I can just make it in business, then I will be set." God couldn't use me to really share his gospel with my people in Mississippi until he had shown me how my evaluation of my need was wrong. Even after I was saved, I could have continued working on the assumption that I had to make it economically instead of seeking first God's kingdom. If God hadn't dealt with us inside, with our values, we never could have been used by him to develop cooperatives, the health center, and other projects that express his love and deal with people's physical needs. We would have been too busy "making it."

Finally, *God's will is to work through broken vessels*. When I think of heroes like Samson and Gideon and even David with all their flaws, I wonder at the way God has committed himself to shooting his power through and revealing himself in human beings. One of the really great things about God is that he arranges the broken fragments of our lives together in a beautiful mosaic that exhibits his glory. Paul knew this when he said, "We have this treasure in earthen vessels, to show that the transcendent power belongs to God and not to us" (2 Cor. 4:7), and "[The Lord] said to me, 'My grace is sufficient for you, for my power is made perfect in weakness.' I will all the more gladly boast of my weaknesses, that the power of Christ may rest upon me" (2 Cor. 12:9). If you are a human being, it is God's will to work through you. That's Good News.

What God's Will Isn't

One big problem I see, especially in young people who are enthusiastic about their faith, is that many ask, "What is God's will for my life?" rather than thinking about God's will, period. I have people say to me, "I want to know God's will for my life." Then I find out that they have already decided what careers they are going to pursue, who they are going to marry, where they are going to live, how much they will earn in salary, how many children they will have and what kind of car they are going to buy. This happens with people preparing for full-time ministry as well as for secular vocations. It is not God's will that these people are looking for, it is their own will. They are not asking, "What is God's program on earth and how do I fit in?" Their question is more like, "How does God fit into my life?"

God's will for our individual lives must be found within his overall will which exists separate and apart from me and does not depend on me or my response to him. It's my responsibility to find out what that will is, adjust my will to it and do it. As I find God's will, I can find the most perfect will for my own life. But we live in a society where individualism is held up in honor, where the rugged individualist is the person who makes it. Our whole teaching, our environment, our culture are permeated with an individualism that is increased by the competition in our society.

God's will is not my culture, it is not individually tailored to fit the assumptions I hold dear in life, like getting an education or going to a particular church or treating a certain group of people different because of their skin color or their salary.

God's will does not just ratify my present lifestyle. I can't know God without having to at least question and maybe change my present patterns of thought and attitudes. Lustful desire for things, a need for personal acceptance or status, tradition and environment—all can keep a person from hearing the will of God and its claim upon his life, all can maintain a person's individualism and keep her from accepting the responsibility of God's work and the opportunity to be a vessel for his power (1 John 2:16–17).

Hearing God's Call

After I know God's will in the world, I can listen for his call to ministry. God's will exists whether or not I exist or respond. It is objective. But the call of God is where my feelings, my talents, my very gut response to God make a difference, because it is *a summons to a special place or situation in which I can do God's will with the special and unique equipment he has provided me.* As believers we can find complete unity in God's will (Eph. 4:1–6). But when it comes to our calling, the Spirit of God explodes into diversity in our midst by giving us different gifts (Eph. 4:11, 12; 1 Cor. 12). It is dangerous to talk about "feeling" God's will. But we are on solid ground if, knowing God's will and doing it, we are looking for *the* opportunity in which we can be of greatest use for the kingdom, and where we can, as a result, feel the greatest sense of personal satisfaction and fulfillment. One way to be called by God is to find out where God's will is being done in the world and get yourself there.

There are other principles that can help us hear the call of God. First, *God's call to ministry is usually a response to past faithfulness.* It is the formal commissioning of a person who is already functionally participating in God's will. We ought to be faithfully in a ministry where we are before we get "called" to do something someplace else. We begin to experience the call to ministry as we do his will. "He who is faithful in a very little," said the Lord, "is faithful also in much" (Luke 16:10; 19:17).

The Apostle Paul is a good example of this. After spending a year in faithful teaching at Antioch, he then was called to continue what he already had been doing but in a way that would use all of the special equipment and training with which he had been prepared. Like Paul, we don't have to worry about being adequate to respond to God's call. God will not call us to do something that he won't equip us to do.

Second, *God's call to ministry is perceived in unity,* first with the Scriptures and then usually with the fellowship or group of people to whom we are accountable. I have seen too many people who have angrily rejected the leadership of the Body just so they can go and do their own thing, even if it is their own "Christian" thing. I am not talking about total agreement here. The group of people I was most committed to, the Fishermen's Fellowship, did not want me to go to Mississippi at all. But they knew that I was submitting my life to them and God's call became plain to them as they saw me and knew my gifts. Then I could leave that local fellowship with some kind of sense of direction and support. My brothers and sisters could trust my calling, having faith in the God who had given me the gifts.

The third principle is that *God's calling is in relationship to building his Body.* It is not the ultimate purpose of God to glorify himself through individuals, but rather through groups of people who are called by his name (Eph. 1:18; 3:10). God did not intend for me to be a lone-wolf Christian. Ever since we got to Mississippi he has given us people who could support and encourage us as well as hold us accountable to doing his will.

As an individual I can be a witness. But even though I as a missionary may seem to be alone, there are always others standing by me, praying from afar off or working by my side. And this is a reflection of how God moves us out of our individuality toward a body. In the body, with all of the gifts making up the arms and the legs and other parts, we can become the actual, in-the-flesh representation of Jesus Christ, the very Body of Christ.

Paul always talks about the gifts of the Spirit in relationship to the body of believers. And I have seen this happen as God's call to us has been accompanied by his call upon the lives of many others. It has been a real confirmation to my call to Mississippi to see others called to the same vision and work.

Finally, *there is no escaping the call of God*. Responding to the call of God is like a trap. It's like walking into a closet and shutting the door and finding out that there is no doorknob on the inside. You just can't get out. Once I got to Mendenhall and began to do God's will I was trapped. Personally, I wanted to get out so much sometimes that I would have caught the first thing smoking out of town.

But I couldn't leave. For one, I had cut off all my alternatives. We had sold everything we had, left our jobs and all. But also, for me to leave would have been to deny something that I knew about the character of God himself and his faithfulness. It would have meant that I would have had to deny some of what I knew about his will and the personal way that he finally called me.

Why did I want to leave? I guess it was because God's will was not really giving me the personal gratification that I wanted in terms of popularity and acceptance. It was really tough when we were rejected by both the black and the white churches in the area. But I learned something, that once God has called you to do something and you become his person for the task, he will complete his work. God will glorify himself through you, though you are sometimes unwilling. I remember Jonah, Moses, and Jeremiah. It's a process of growth and real wrestling (Exod. 4; Jer. 1:4).

I believe in God's call, and I think it is central to making Voice of Calvary Ministries what it is today. We wanted to be here, we couldn't be anywhere else. We have cut off all the alternatives and have no choice but to plant our feet and be obedient. This kind of call—the kind that ends in a box—grinds up the individualism that destroys our witness. Through obedience and submission to the people we leave behind, through calling us to use our special gifts to continue to do his will, through calling us in bodies, God's purpose is so great and we are so frail that he pens us in and ends up using us. That's how it worked with us. The call was the beginning, just a taste of the grace that would be sustaining us as we laid the foundation for a work among black people in the poor rurals of Mississippi.

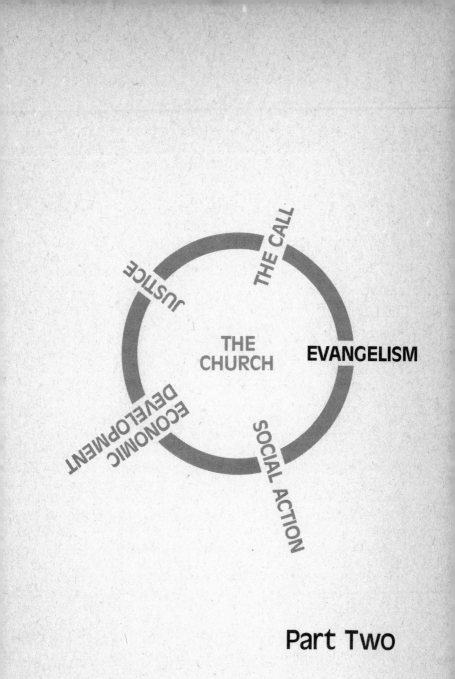

THE CALL

JUSTICE

THE
CHURCH

EVANGELISM

ECONOMIC
DEVELOPMENT

SOCIAL ACTION

Part Two

4.

Building the Base

It was June 9, 1960, when we arrived down home in New Hebron, south of Jackson. People were surprised to see us but even more surprised to see the trailer—to see that we were actually moving back. That was unheard of, especially if you had made it where you had been. It was a funny feeling—people wanted us to come back, yet in a way they didn't. There was absolutely nothing here, no future, and here we were with five children. As far as they could see we had no income, and they couldn't imagine how anybody could ever have an income if he was coming back to preach and was not the pastor of some big church.

We started off staying with Vera Mae's grandmother and right away I began working. We did have $75 to $100 per month coming to us from a few friends in California, but that was not enough to feed a family our size. So I would go out to the fields or to cut wood with the men around, like Uncle Doc Berry. I didn't know it at the time, but these times of working together would later pay off in terms of the strong relationships they helped build.

Another thing we did right away was start a relationship with Oak Ridge Missionary Baptist Church, a church near home. One of the first big breaks I got that summer was when I became good friends with Brother Isaac Newsome, who reviewed the Sunday school lesson—in many rural black churches a very important time in the service where the whole congregation listens while one man sums up the issues raised in Sunday school. He began to ask me to review the lesson, and ended up giving me his place. That was sort of the sign that the church had accepted me. Later, they ordained me as one of their ministers.

That summer I went to a Sunday school institute involving many churches down near Prentiss, Mississippi. Mr. S. L. Richman had been president of the Sunday school convention for twenty-five years, and his daddy was probably the president before him. He accepted me and put his authority behind me as a Bible teacher—he gave me his power. The older folks wanted a young person who could teach the Word and who was committed to the community.

Down in Prentiss was Prentiss Institute, an all-black, private junior

41

college. Almost all the black people in that area of the state who were trained, especially teachers, had gone to Prentiss Institute before going on to get their degrees. During that first summer I also helped to conduct a Christian camp program at the Institute. There I met Mrs. J. E. Johnson, founder of the Institute, one of the most remarkable ladies I have ever met. She had been a student of George Washington Carver and Booker T. Washington and had graduated from Tuskegee Institute. She was not only one of the last from the generation that Booker T. Washington produced, but she also was a genuine Christian. Mrs. Johnson accepted me as being her preacher and pastor, and I became the chaplain of Prentiss Institute, quite an honor for a third-grade dropout.

These relationships not only broadened my base of acceptance and credibility in the community, but also helped my financial base, because after that summer, churches began to have me come out to speak to their Sunday schools which would always mean a small offering. I depended on those offerings of eight or ten dollars to buy gas during the week. I would never take an offering at Oak Ridge— that was my home base.

The fall and winter of 1960 (and also of 1961) we got all the men of the Oak Ridge Church together every week, and I began to systematically teach them like I had been systematically taught and to encourage them to go home and teach their families. We developed some strong relationships and trust. Everything that we've done in Simpson County has been built on that base at the Oak Ridge Church. That was the first base that allowed me to venture out, to try great things. Those folks have always been my stronghold, my body.

In the fall of 1960 we put our two oldest kids, Spencer and Joanie, in school. Joanie was not quite old enough but we sent her anyway. On enrollment day I went with them to the school in New Hymn. I remember they didn't have a gym at that time, so all their big gatherings were held in the church. Mr. Gray, the principal, seemed to be having a little trouble getting the support of the parents so he took the enrollment day as an opportunity to speak to all of us. He made this long speech just like a preacher. He was trying to convince everyone to get behind the school and move ahead. Well, afterwards I met him and told him I was enrolling my kids and asked him if he would like me to come and speak to the student body. He said, "That would be great!" Although he didn't know me, he took a risk for me, and out of that generous opportunity we became friends. So I started coming to his school twice a month and sharing with the kids from the Bible using Child Evangelism flannelgraphs and materials. The church was not big enough to hold all the students, so I'd speak to all the elementary kids one time and the high school kids the next.

Later, I asked Mr. Gray about some other schools and found out that his cousin was the principal at J. E. Johnson High School in Prentiss. So we got into that school. The school ministry began to grow and by the end of the year I was speaking to about five or six different schools. The kids were fantastic. They would sit spellbound by those flannelgraph pictures and by the straightforward presentation of God's involvement with people down through history. They could see that it was more than story, and one after another they gave control of their lives over to Jesus Christ as a result of hearing God's Word in an unreligious way.

In the spring of 1961 we began to look for a place to settle down. We ended up renting one of two new little houses just built in Mendenhall along with a tin storefront, both for $60 a month. Since we had arrived back home we had never lived in a place with the plumbing for our washing machine. The storefront had the plumbing so we kept our washer there and set that up as an office and a place to prepare our lessons.

Things were pretty tight financially, but it was amazing how the Lord took care of us. I would pick cotton in the afternoons after going out and speaking to the schools, or plow and cut pulp wood. Then the people took care of whatever else we needed. They'd give us vegetables and potatoes. Later on I met Mr. R. A. Buckley, almost seventy years old then. He let me farm with him and gave us milk for our kids. As I look back at my life, it is all like that. I have always had to depend on the people and in the end, the people have always done me right.

During the summer of 1961 we set up vacation Bible schools, camps and institutes like the year before. We organized "Shepherd Leagues" in three churches at Oak Ridge, Spring Hill, and Pleasant Hill where I'd meet together with the boys in the church, teach the Bible and talk with them about the future.

In the fall of 1961, we began to localize our ministry, and adopted the area around Mendenhall, including neighboring D'Lo, as our target area. Our kids enrolled in Mendenhall schools. I recruited two disciples, Leonard Stapleton and Excel McGee, and we organized

Bible classes, first in Mrs. Effie Mae Tyler's house in D'Lo, and eventually another class down at the store front. We called the store front, "The Fishermen's Mission"! By the end of the winter both classes had filled up. I was still teaching in the schools during the days.

Then came the summer of 1962, the amazing summer. One day, out of nowhere, Rev. Wallace appeared. We had known him back in California—in fact, he had preached at Bethlehem Church of Christ Holiness, where I had been converted. He was regarded by everyone like a prophet. We still can't figure out how he found out where we were; we sure hadn't had the sense to write him. But he appeared.

And he preached. We took him around to all our churches and the different places we had gone and the people went wild over him. He was a fantastic preacher, and people just gave him an immediate reputation.

During the day, Rev. Wallace would work with me around the mission with his hands. He was almost like an Elijah or a hermit. The only difference between him and a hermit, though, was that he was always clean. He always wore white shirts and a necktie and a black suit. What would always get me is that he'd work with his hands wearing his white shirts.

That was a summer of massive public exposure. Then, as suddenly as he had come, Rev. Wallace left. But through the fall and winter, the work in the schools expanded. Both Bible classes were filled to capacity. Rev. James Howard, the man who was preaching the morning I committed my life to Christ, came down and would come several times to help us in our work.

Nineteen sixty-two had been a people year. Lucille, Sarah, and Eva Quinn, who were to be a part of the ministry for the next decade, began coming as little kids to the Tyler home. Vera Mae met Herbert Jones where he worked pumping gas and invited him to come to our mission. He has been with us ever since. Artis Fletcher, now the pastor of the church in Mendenhall, was converted while he attended Prentiss Institute. God's principle of faithfulness worked, even through those first months when there were only five of us meeting out at Mrs. Effie Mae Tyler's. God was saying, "Don't grow weary in well-doing, for in due season you will reap, if you don't lose heart" (see Gal. 6:9).

After the winter, we made plans to build a home on some land we bought. We started work on it in the spring of 1963 with the help of some of the young men in the community, and got a company to put up the outside while we finished the interior. In May, after school was out, I went out to California with the idea of raising enough money for a Bible school building. I came back with $6,000—enough money for the building.

Mama Wilson, one of the original "Fishermen," and Sister Carroway drove me back to Mississippi from the West, and we started our summer program in 1963. We had house-to-house visitation, vacation Bible schools, and kept up the meetings in the Fishermen's Mission. Mama Wilson and a team were going out into the community asking everyone they met, "Are you saved?"

Then, all at once, Rev. Wallace shows up again in his old Studebaker. We were concerned because we didn't have many places for him to speak, since we had focused locally in Mendenhall during the year. He could fill up our little mission before a cat could wink its eye. He could have just stood in the streets and hollered and the folks would have filled it up.

This put some heavy pressure on me, because Rev. Wallace was reaching people and I was the "businessman" behind the scenes making the decisions with all the money we didn't have. I was making the "faith" decisions because it seemed to me he was too foolish to be making those kinds of decisions—he was a guy who lived *totally* by faith. But I had to make sure that the message got out and that Rev. Wallace had a little money in his pocket for gas when he left. So I put faith and business together and came up with an idea.

I asked about a rodeo stadium down in the country. The owner, a white businessman, let us use it for free! It was fantastic—people came from every holler and hill to hear Rev. Wallace. The clouds were dark. There was a hundred percent chance of rain, we thought, but God held it back for us. So that rodeo meeting started the summer off with an explosion.

Then I remembered a church that had been meeting in a circus tent while they finished work on their building. They agreed to sell us the tent for $400. It would cost us about $20 to have somebody haul it to Mendenhall. Vera Mae and I had $800 in the Mendenhall Bank. We went down and got out $420 and brought the tent up to D'Lo. It was round with green and white panels, and could seat two hundred, so you could see it for miles. We used folding chairs, some theatre seats that were given to us and some benches that we made, plus apple crates and boxes.

It would take us two or three hours to set up the tent and we would leave it in the same spot for about three weeks. Herbert Jones had a job hauling hogs to market. I'd sometimes go with him, leaving about 5:00 A.M. to be in Jackson by 7:00 or 8:00 A.M. with a load of hogs. But afterward, Herbert would wash out the truck, we'd load up the tent and take it wherever we needed. Then Herbert would drive out into the country picking up people for our meeting that night. On one of those nights a young man, Dolphus Weary, gave his life to the Lord. He now directs our youth program in Mendenhall, thirteen years later, after attending college and seminary. On another night, his brother Melvin was saved.

Finally, the summer ended, the leaves turned brown, the kids started back to school, and Rev. Wallace left again in his Studebaker.

That winter things went on growing. We went to fourteen different schools, sometimes two a day. Soon we would be speaking to over ten thousand young people every month. We had moved from both the house and the storefront into our new two-story house. Herbert, who now heads up our construction team, learned how to put up sheetrock in that house. But it never was finished, and we didn't put up any insulation, so you'd almost freeze in the winter.

Then early in 1964 we opened up the Bible Institute building which we had finally gotten time to finish. We soon got hold of an old bus to replace the hog truck and began to reach out all over the county. Herbert would drive that bus anywhere, all over those dirt roads, bringing people in to the Institute. Three other people besides me taught. Rev. James Spencer, a white Presbyterian minister from Crystal Springs taught all that winter and into the next. Rev. Kenneth Noyes from up north helped teach. And Mrs. Annie Bell Harper, the retired principal of the local high school that has since been named in her and her husband's honor, came to teach English and public speaking.

In the summer of 1964, we prepared for the same strategy of tent meetings. But this time, Rev. Wallace didn't show. He never returned and we never saw him again. (He has since died.) Talk about pressure. That summer I took over the teaching and preaching, all the time aware that I was walking in some pretty big boots. But that was a fantastic summer.

In the winter we reopened the Bible Institute. But something was going on that had started far away like Elijah's cloud and now darkened the whole atmosphere. The civil rights movement was upon us. It had been in Mississippi for quite some time, and by 1964 the radios and televisions were constantly proclaiming the newest activities and violence. Out in the country areas like Simpson County it had gotten to the point where the tension was so high that black people almost had to whisper on the streets.

Then Rev. Spencer was forced to quit teaching at the Institute. It was subtle, but the pressure was there, silent harassment where he'd see certain people following him at night on his way home. When the people in his congregation discovered what was happening and that it was probably the Klan, they asked him to stop helping us. The closed society was tightening up.

5.

People Saved by Grace

We discovered in the early years that in laying a base for ministry in the community, the bricks and mortar for the foundation couldn't be programs. The foundation had to be made up of people who would be willing to lay down their hearts and lives for the sake of bringing the Good News to our people. Wherever I go to speak, people always ask me about our programs, and I have to keep reminding them that the programs are nothing without the right people.

So, what I'd like to do in this chapter is to introduce you to some of the people who committed themselves with us to Christ. Some of them will be speaking a foreign language to some of you. These are the country people, my people. They don't talk educated, but what they say has meant more to me than all the fundamentalist or radical rhetoric I've ever heard. First, there is Mr. Robert Archie Buckley who, along with his wife, took us in and became like our parents.

I was about eleven years old when my father died from malaria after serving for three years as a prisoner up in Parchman on a false charge. My mother was born the second year after the Emancipation and my daddy was borned right around the time of the Civil War. His folks were slave people. They lived on a plantation and got married and then were sold to two different people and were kept separate for about three years. Then they, my grandmother and my grandfather, was freed and they got back together.

I was born in our house on the farm about thirty miles south of Forest, Mississippi, on December the first, 1889. I worked with my two sisters and my brother on our farm under my mother until she finished paying off the land. School was poorly then, but I didn't get a chance to go much anyway. My mother didn't have the school interest that she should have had. She mostly wanted to get us on some free land, all paid for, so to raise us up free.

But I've come through two hard depressions, one around '29 and one in the Forties. Man, you couldn't get money for nothin'. We raised eleven children through the depressions, the oldest one now is about fifty. But during those times I did some work! I worked for fifty cents a day clearing land. But the hardest work was making them crossties for the railroads. We'd cut 'em by hand, get about thirty-five cents a tie. I'm lucky to be here after those years. I done hauled and cut and toted and hauled them crossties. I'd tote them three- and four-hundred-pound ties, get them in the wagon. I'd load twenty-five of them things on one wagon. Man, that's dangerous too, 'cause those things'll fall off and break your leg. I got my leg broke haulin' ties, yeah.

Now, in terms of my life with God, the Lord has had to deal with me in some tough ways. Several times he has had to speak to me in a vision. This weren't no dream, you're awake for a vision, you know. I'll tell ya, whenever the Lord gets a chance to talk with you in a private talk, it takes you down.

The first time was when this church I was going to wanted to make a deacon outta me. Now when I read the qualifications, I wasn't up to that standard, so I didn't want them to make me no deacon, not under no such stuff as that I was under. I was drinkin' and I wasn't livin' like I oughta. I was livin' under the law and didn't know it, but the Lord appeared to me in the field one day. The voice, I could hear it just talkin' to me just like you talkin' to me now. And it explained to me about my condition. And it said this, "When you joined the church, you said you'd be willing to be governed and ruled by that church, that's what you said. Now they want to make you a deacon, and you done said you won't let them do it. Now, if you refuse to be a deacon, you'd better take your name out of the church because you done broke the contract." It was just plain, I was just sittin' back on my plow handle listenin' at it.

Well, let me tell you how it ended. I was in a tough spot. I didn't think the Lord wanted me to come outta there, but I also knew that if I was gonna be a deacon I was gonna have to come out from under the junk I was in. Then was the time when I rode over to a church in the next county and heard this visiting preacher explain the difference between law and grace. That's how the Lord broke me up from that whiskey and stuff that I was in. Well, that night I made a vow.

Two days after I made that vow the Lord appeared to me again and showed me about the difference between his deacons and the world's deacons. So when they went to ordain me, the pastor what ordained me said, "I have ordained a whole lot of fellas," he said, "but I ain't never had my hands on a man like you." He said, "You're the first man I ever had my hands on that, really, that I could feel the Spirit of the Lord. You're something, you're somebody."

Well, I tell you my experience to say this, that there ain't much

Scripture base of knowledge out in the country churches. And when Perkins came around, he was puttin' out stuff that we all needed. He had his whole heart workin' for the black people and we all needed what he was puttin' out. He was training people in the Word and teaching about grace and faith and what "thus saith the Lord." He was puttin' out stuff I know'd was right—both the gospel and lettin' folks know what sort of shape and condition they was in. I got with him because I know'd he had it—but he was heavy.

He was so heavy that he scared some of the pastors out in the churches. I was in charge of the youth church in our church, so I asked Rev. Perkins to come and be the guest speaker. The pastor didn't like it and he challenged my choice by taking it to the folks. The folks backed him up—they didn't want to cross the pastor. Well, I knew then it was time for me to leave there, because I didn't have any protection. Rev. Perkins was forming a church, so we joined up and have been with Voice of Calvary ever since.

I'll tell you what—the vision that Perkins came back to Simpson County for was a God-given vision. He didn't think that up himself. God gave him that. Like Moses, he had a lot of trouble, but he was going by the vision. But our folk couldn't see it. Maybe they was too far back to see it. But I could see it. I knew the ignorance that I had come up with, so much that God had to speak direct to me. That's the reason I moved in here with Voice of Calvary. It was by orders. I left my other church by orders to help start this thing here because, you see, all of my folks are scared to participate in anything that's got meaning.

When you have somebody dedicate themselves to your vision and when minds come together searching to do something good, it holds you accountable. It causes you to look not only after your own interests, but also after the interests of others (see Phil. 2:1–11).

Another person with whom we shared that kind of relationship from the start is Brother Jesse Newsome.

Yes, I've always lived in Simpson County and around here. In 1927 I built my house. I had my wife and two children and we plowed up forty acres. After coming into that forty acres I went to farming and farmed for about fifteen years, up until '49. Then I was struck down with rheumatism and I went to the hospital. After that somebody helped me farm for two more years, but I didn't farm myself. I retired in 1950 and they put me on a pension. So I haven't done any farming since, but I have been working around helping people, through different folks like Voice of Calvary's health center and other community organizations.

I was born on July 14, 1896, so I am eighty years old. I've been a Sunday school teacher for forty years.

When John Perkins came back to Mississippi I was really hoping he was gonna make it. I kind of felt embarrassed in the situation, like things have been here, you know—I couldn't see how he could make no money. But when the Lord gave courage to come in, he and the preacher began to work together. I sure said it was the Lord's work.

The thing that caused him and us to keep going was that the Lord had revealed to him that he had something for him to do and he was going to do it. Then the Lord gave him a few people to support him. I'm one of the ones that stayed with him through the time he started till he left Mendenhall and went to Jackson. And I have been with him since then—we continue under his jurisdiction in the sense that he is being the leader of this community and locality.

Now, I don't want to make it sound like there weren't no problems. After a while, we discovered that as we makes the churches try to work with us and sees we weren't making any progress, we wants more and more to stay with the people that are going to contribute, and be moved by the teaching. Well, he is a good teacher, nobody can deny that because he laid his whole heart out to God and out of that come some good things. But they got to kind of fighting in the churches. They couldn't handle the teaching. So Rev. Perkins worked in the church for a couple of years and finally he said, "Well, I will build a church, get somebody to help me build a church." So that was the beginning of the Voice of Calvary, something new in the community. It started out of the rejection by so many of the set churches.

Having a home base and having people who loved us was an expression and affirmation of God's call upon our lives. Brother Eugene Walker, a farmer from the Oak Ridge Church, is a deacon of that church and president of the Sunday School Institution, a quarterly meeting of thirteen black churches.

I can remember both Rev. Perkins and Miss Vera Mae when they was children, when the Perkins moved over on the land joining mine belonging to old man Bill Turnidge. The Perkins lived over there for years. Then they went to California.

When John Perkins came back, he came back here to our

church. He taught Bible classes there for three years. I know because I went to the Bible classes at night time. Those Bible classes sort of turned our church, they helped it. We had a men's class two or three nights each week. I don't think I missed a night. I went and that's where I got most of my Bible training, under Rev. Perkins. When he went to Mendenhall, I went with him, and I'd go to the Voice of Calvary Bible Institute. Then I joined in later with him in the store, the co-op, and on those houses—I bought some shares in both co-ops. He then would come back and teach in our Sunday School Institution. But Oak Ridge was his home base. That is where he first baptized at.

I would say the biggest thing was the setting up of the Bible classes so we could know more about God, because you know we never did have any Bible classes too much. We would go to church on Sunday all right. You could go out and hear the preacher preach but if you don't know or read the Bible, it won't give you much anyway. And if the preacher don't read the Bible, well then, you're in a mess. But he gave us something to go by. Sound. And all of the other activities of Voice of Calvary begun there.

They just helped out our whole family. All of my kids, when they call from off at school or their homes, they always ask about Rev. Perkins and Miss Vera Mae. I've put ten children through college, five girls and five boys. Yes, that's about the first generation of Walkers ever to have that much schooling. In fact, I met with the Voice of Calvary board of directors the other day and they told me, "Well, you are the only person black or white that we know that college-schooled ten children."

But it was tough. Rev. Perkins, he'd go around to all these different schools and he was real good friends with Mrs. Johnson, the head of Prentiss Institute Junior College. Well, I had some of my children there and one out at Alcorn and one up at Mississippi Valley State in Itta Bena. Then in 1960 I got burned out of my house. Times were tough, and I didn't have a penny. I moved to another place across the highway and planted me a big crop, about sixty acres of cotton. But that year was a bad crop year. I got about four little bales of cotton and owed about $2,000.

So Rev. Perkins came by one day and he said, "Well, Walker. How you makin' it?"

I said, "I'm gonna have to go get my children out."

He said, "No, I wouldn't do that."

I said, "Yes, I have to go. There is no other way under the sun for me to keep those kids in there now."

"Well, why?" he said. I told him. He said, "Let's pray that the devil won't deny them now."

I said, "Yeah, pray. But it's also gonna take some financing."
He said, "Go see Mrs. Johnson."

So I went to see Mrs. Johnson over to Prentiss and come to
find out she had a son-in-law in the administration at Alcorn and
a nephew at Valley State. So before I knew it, she was saying to
me, "Eugene, you let those children stay."

Now, Rev. Perkins wasn't like most preachers who had about
four churches. And a lot of times at Oak Ridge folks would say
something like, "But I can't understand that he isn't going to take
up an offering." Most preachers take up offerings, but he didn't
and that had the people spellbound. They said, "Well, how is he
gonna live?" Sometimes someone would give him a few dollars
for gas, but people would wonder how in the world he was gonna
make it. I would have to say he made it by the help of God, that's
all I know.

Then, every now and then over here at my farm—well, we had
watermelon, a garden full of greens and stuff, pea patches. I gave
him stuff and told him if I wasn't here to just go on in and get
him some greens, peas, eggs, anything he wanted. That's how we
made it—together.

The struggle for development in the black community in Mississippi has been shared by many. And in southern Mississippi, when
it comes to discussions of educational, economic, or just general
community development, it would be rare if Prentiss Institute didn't
come up. I had the privilege to serve as chaplain at the Institute and
the great opportunity to make friends with Mrs. J. E. Johnson, one
of its founders, and then later her son, Dr. Al C. Johnson. Dr.
Johnson and I have become good friends and colaborers in the real
struggle to make education a tool through which black people can
turn to their communities and make an impact. It was always exciting for me to see the way that he saw the Christian faith as being
able to mobilize young people.

The most memorable occasion on which Rev. Perkins shared
with us on the campus was when he came to conduct a series of
talks with our young people during religious emphasis week. He
was not just preaching at them, but went with them into the
dormitories and into their rooms and out on the campus—walking, talking, counseling. And we had a very remarkable thing
happen. You know that this is a Christian institution, but like
many nonsectarian institutions, the religion on campus can wear
pretty thin. But at the end of this week of religious emphasis there
were about forty of our youngsters who came down the sawdust

trail. Yes, I mean they came forward to accept Christ. We never had that happen here before. That was a remarkable thing.

It was not just one of those fired-up experiences where a person gets happy and joins the church. It wasn't that. You could see that this commitment operated in the lives of these youngsters throughout the year.

But this concept of commitment must be deep. Like I heard Rev. Dolphus Weary preaching over the radio that the type of revivals run in the country churches says nothing about salvation of souls and the redirection of lives but only about how much money was raised. "We took in $1500 at this revival!" He went on to say that a good revival should produce an increased attendance regularly, an increased visitation of the sick, a better relationship with those who are in jail, and so on.

I've been to some of the functions at the Voice of Calvary. In fact, I was asked to speak at the dedication of their new gymnasium and vocational facilities. They have had a great effect on the community at large. But the greatest impact has been the inspiration to our young people here. I'm speaking personally now. The kids coming into Prentiss Institute are coming with a hate for people, not only white people, but black people too. And they hate themselves. They depreciate their own potential. They come in here fighting the world. Nothing is right. That's the kind of thing Rev. Perkins has been able to help us with, and that's what I feel to be the impact of Voice of Calvary Ministries: helping to teach people to love people as the first step to loving God, that they are one and the same drive.

Perhaps the greatest power base in the world was described by Jesus when he said, "Where two or three are gathered in my name, there am I in the midst of them" (Matt. 18:20). I think the working element here is the unity Christ can develop between people, a unity where people can agree never to divide, where they can covenant with each other around an objective so that nothing can come between them and no one can divide them. That was the dynamic developing at this stage of our growth. And it was nowhere more evident than in my relationship with Brother Isaac Newsome.

Well, I'm much older than Brother Perkins and I've been knowing him ever since he was a boy. I knew him before he began his ministry. When he came back from California he was an altogether different man. He was preaching and in the ministry, and missions was on his mind when he came back. He had totally changed his mind. He grew up in a rough family, you know. But when he returned, all he wanted to do was teach Bible lessons.

He and I got together and made friends, new friends. I was teacher here at Oak Ridge and he came in and we worked together, we had an agreement. People kind of thought we probably were going to go apart and that we wouldn't say just the same words. We'd have the same meaning about explaining about the Bible, but they would think we were going to differ. Well, we just got together and I talked it over with him and told him, "Now, if I don't put the same words that you have it in, just know that I'm not trying to contrast you or betray you or anything, I don't mean that."

You see, people would try to divide us. Yes siree! Not only just in the community. It was around two or three years after he came back. He would teach stuff that was so strong until, well, you know people, lots of them didn't like him and they tried to criticize him. They'd talk to me about it and I'd always give them my side of it, the way I saw it. Then I wouldn't say anything bad what they wanted me to say, only just for right. I'd say, "That's what I see. Don't misunderstand him, but that's the way he talked." So we was never divided.

Now, going back to before I was a dedicated Christian, I was rough. I said I was *rough!* I drank terrible. But once, when I was about half-drunk, the Holy Spirit convicted me. I was under the influence of whiskey and the Holy Spirit made me see what kind of mess I was in. My buddies thought I was down drunk, the reason I was cutting up. I was crying, just crying like a baby. One Saturday night I began crying and I viewed my own condition I was in, coming home and telling my wife big tales about where I'd been. I got ashamed of it. I began to start to have some strength to overcome it, when I dedicated my life to the Lord. He came with soul-searching force but I had power. Day by day I've grown a little stronger in the love of God.

The furthest thing back I can remember? Oh, my mother. I was a dedicated child to her. Seven and eight years, she would always carry me along with her to where she washed and cleaned for a white lady. Then, on a Christmas Eve when I was eight or nine years old, she passed. Well, you know about how I felt. Quite naturally it left me lonely. I remember one day going off on a hillside and laying down crying and out of the depth of my heart, I asked God to be a mother for me. It's been a mystery. I hadn't ever heard them pray and had never been to a prayer meeting or anything. That's the truth. I can remember just as well as can be of asking the Lord to be a mother for me, and I can say he's been that. I haven't acted like his child all the way. But he certainly has been a mother and a father to me.

But back to Brother Perkins and our times together. In about 1960 he came back and set up Bible classes all across the community. I followed him from one place to another. We reached not just the "good" folks, but people who was just drunkards and gamblers too, young folks who would just walk the streets. Some of them have become missionaries.

Also we stirred up in the people the whole idea of helping the poor, seeking out those that were hungry and didn't have sufficient clothes. He stirred up the spirit in a lot of people, not only at Voice of Calvary, but out in these community classes. And also people like me who didn't have much schooling. I had more since I've been grown than I did when I was a child coming up. Night school at Voice of Calvary helped me so much.

Well, I was born in 1900 and if I live to see the 3rd of July of 1976 I'll be seventy-six. About my growth, I'm not full grown yet. I'm not perfect, but it's my desire to be more like Jesus. He gives me strength and knowledge how to do it.

6.

Working God's Will

When I think about the great people God has given us, I am reminded of the Book of Acts. Luke begins it by referring to his Gospel and "all that Jesus began to do and teach," implying that Jesus' work was not finished. In Acts he describes how Jesus through his Holy Spirit continued to act out and teach the gospel through his people. Then it is amazing to me the way in which the Book of Acts ends so abruptly—just cut off. But it's because the activity of the Spirit of God had not ceased, and he is writing history through us today, the twentieth-century volume of the Book of Acts. I believe Christians in every age and generation are to continue to write church history. We become the history.

As we have seen God move in our midst, we have come to recognize several basic principles. The first is that *God's work is anticipated by prayer*. All of the big decisions and moves Voice of Calvary has made over the years have been surrounded by prayer. I'm not talking about only emergency praying, but also that regular prayer that seeks direction from God on a daily basis. The result has been that we, like King David, have found that the Lord has gone out to battle before us (1 Chron. 14:15). There have been plenty of times when, through prayer, we have sensed the Lord going out before us to meet our requests, and even more times when, looking back, we have seen that he went before us.

There was a Tuesday morning prayer meeting started in Monrovia on Mama and Papa Wilson's porch two years before I left California. When I left it became *the* prayer meeting for us and later for Voice of Calvary Ministries. It's still going on today, and this Tuesday people from around the neighborhood will be gathering on that porch.

Prayer is the kneeling and praying, the action itself, but it is also just the coming together for the seeking out of God's will. Sometimes the morning prayer meeting we have at VOC in Jackson consists mostly of discussion and just short prayers at the end. But sometimes that discussion is just an extension of our prayer, that through it we can sharpen each other's senses to what God's will really is on a certain issue.

Prayer is aligning ourselves with God's will, not trying to change God's mind. There is a real unity as we interact together to change our minds collectively to what God's mind is. Prayer develops the unity needed to move people out.

Prayer is the sincere desire of the heart, that which we desire fervently and are willing to put our energy behind. I believe God hears prayers that are on the verge of leading us into action, prayers that reflect how we want to be used by God in practical ways. And if prayer is our sincere desire, God will answer it. Our words are not always the prayer, because God intercedes through his Spirit for our words and sifts them out. I believe many times the only thing from me that really reaches the throne of God is my desire, my yearning. In prayer God's Spirit molds my desires into the pipeline through which God pours his power. We not only accomplish things through the Spirit, but the Spirit himself is the guarantee that God's will will be accomplished. God doesn't give his Spirit and then pull him away and say, "Hey, I couldn't use my Spirit to accomplish my will through you." No, the promise we need to act on is that "God is at work in you both to will and to work for his good pleasure" (Phil. 2:13). Prayer is our most dynamic interaction with the Holy Spirit and so also God's will.

Prayer, then, is for people who are hard working, it is the end of their work, it is the guarantee of accomplishment at the point of my inadequacy. "Work out your own salvation with fear and trembling" is our side of our partnership with God (Phil. 2:12). Prayer isn't for people who sit down and wait for God to do it. Prayer is for people who are willing to use up all their energy and still see needs that need to be met and then seek God to meet them.

Another principle in doing God's work is that *God's work is affirmed by his provision* (see 2 Cor. 9:8). There have been so many examples of how God has provided "in abundance" for the continuing of our ministry. Some of the first were the rodeo stadium, and the tent, and Rev. Wallace himself. Herbert's hog truck was another example. The power of faith is that as we move out the provision will be there.

God has provided us with people. One day in August of 1974, when our last volunteer doctor had left, everyone on our staff fasted and prayed all day for a full-time doctor. That was on a Friday.

On Monday we received a letter postmarked Saturday from a young doctor from First Presbyterian Church of Colorado Springs, Dr. Eugene McCarty. By January 1975, the McCartys were in Mendenhall practicing medicine.

To me it's been a lot like Israel's crossing the Jordan under Joshua. It was not until the people got in and got their feet wet that the waters parted. Here is a principle we can lay hold of: that as we actively engage in doing God's work, our needs—physical as well as spiritual—will be met.

God's work is aggravating to the system. After a certain period of time the gospel we preached in the schools and in Mendenhall became offensive to many of the black churches, the black religious establishment. Kids began to go back to their home churches and talk about the new birth and righteous living and wouldn't take the hypocrisy and double standard of the old system of religion. Starting about 1965, pastors began to encourage their kids not to come to Voice of Calvary. And here VOC began to have an impact I never expected. When we came to Mendenhall, none of the churches met except on Wednesday nights for prayer meeting and on Sunday mornings. But to keep up with the competition, the churches began to have youth meetings and usher board meetings, and all of a sudden the lights were burning in these churches almost every night. Now up to this time, Voice of Calvary had been having little effect on the business of the three honky-tonks in town. But with this heightened religious activity in the churches, the honky-tonks were out of business by 1968. So, in the end, even indirect aggravation and response caused some good in the community.

The same thing happened when we began to threaten the economic system in Mendenhall. Later I will talk about that and the civil rights struggle and how we had much more to face than rejection from the white community—there was also the violence.

So, part of God's work is to irritate the system. Just like light irritates your eyes when you've been in the dark for a long time, so we in being God's light will irritate the system. There is fear involved in a call like that.

We see this in the life of almost every Old Testament figure. Moses, Isaiah, Elijah, Jeremiah, David, and Paul—all the great men of God feared because they knew that the call of God to do his will was abrasive to the systems which they had to face (Gen. 26:24; Exod. 2:14; 3:7–4:17; Judg. 6–8; Isa. 8:12–13; 1 Kings 19; Jer.

1:4–8; Pss. 27:1; 56:3; Acts 18:9). But to every one, echoing throughout the Bible, came God's same promise: "Fear not, I am with you." When Jesus gave us the great commission and asked us to make disciples of all nations he knew that this would aggravate the system and that we would become fearful, and so we hear the great promise again, "Lo, I am with you always, to the close of the age" (Matt. 28:20).

But it might be that we live in an age where we are not really facing the systems with Jesus' threateningly new way. The conservative tells me to go out and change society without upsetting the richest men in town because that's where I'm going to have to go for support. "You have to preach the gospel without offending anybody," people say. But that's stupid! It's just not right. When Paul went to Philippi, he preached the gospel and people wanted to beat him because it messed up their economic schemes (Acts 16).

A footnote to this point is that *God's work is accompanied by rejection.* This is really a promise with a hidden blessing. Once you have aggravated the people you are called to love and carry the gospel to, and a few have responded but the rest reject you, you can lay hold of some heavy power. If you continue, God gives you the grace to keep reaching out to those who have rejected you with the intention of still winning them. And what happens is this: God is going to give you some tools that are nearly invincible. Those tools are the ability to accomplish your objectives whether people are with you or not, the ability to be your own best critic, the ability to get energy from within rather than from others.

The person who overcomes rejection receives an almost undefeatable power. It is like the power MacArthur had when he said, "I shall return." He did return and defeated his enemy. He had learned what had defeated him and conquered it. That's power! The danger is that a person with this power can use these tools to either exploit the people or to lead them.

Finally, *God's work is actualized through leadership development.* Basic to the spreading of the gospel is the raising up of leadership. This is especially important in the black community, or in any community where the gospel must address physical needs as well as the spiritual needs of people. If we are talking about seeing the whole community uplifted as a result of the gospel, then it's not a one-man show. Creative leadership must be developed. This was a part of the great commission and was basic to Paul's strategy in the early church (Matt. 28:19 ff.; 2 Tim. 2:2).

Now the business of real evangelism and real human development is so complex and difficult that the big need of a person working in the community is for endurance and just knowing what to do next. What we have seen so far through these early years of VOC's history are the roots of leadership development, that young and old people were called and responded with a basic commitment to Christ which right off the bat was a commitment to him as Lord, as master of their lives, as well as Savior. Herbert Jones, Dolphus Weary and his wife Rosie, Artis and Carolyn Fletcher were young people who responded to this call. Mr. and Mrs. R. A. Buckley, Lillian Fletcher, Jessie Newsome, Robert Clayton, and Eugene Walker were older people who responded.

As I look back and see how these people are still with us, I've come to the conclusion that God is committed to providing special leadership to carry on his work. We do not need leaders with answers that are quick and easy, or programs instead of real love. We need leaders with a burning concern, who see the depth of the problems and don't know how to deal with them but who can listen to the Holy Spirit for God's vision and listen to people, often outsiders, who have the technical skills and experience needed to wrestle with the problems and make the vision reality.

To me, all of the principles of beginning to do God's will led to developing a small group of people with a vision for the whole community. At this early stage in our development we did not know who would be in that group. Nor did we know that we would be facing in the next few years the kinds of challenges that would test the endurance, commitment, and fortitude of both young and old, and create the crucible out of which our vision could be poured.

7.

Discovering Real Evangelism

From the very beginning of our ministry there was one basic question that we were asking ourselves and being asked by others: "Is evangelical Christianity relevant to the black community?" Could an evangelistic faith have an impact on people who had been long-term poor? And as I look back, I see that we stumbled onto the answer to that question. It was like God, having trapped us with his call, was now going to allow us to live out that question until, by trial and error, we found ourselves living into the answer.

One key was that we lived in the community and we depended upon the people for our support. As we would go out into areas like "Baptist Bottom," "Sullivan's Holler," and "Rabbit Road," as we would cut wood and farm with people and speak in the schools, we could not escape seeing firsthand the desperate physical needs of many of our people. We began to discover that real evangelism brings a person face to face with *all* the needs of a person. We had to see people not just as souls, but as whole people.

Another key was that we were committed to the poor. My commitment to poverty went back much further than just the present situation. It went back to my birth. I am told that I was born sick. My mother had pleurisy and died from it when I was seven months old. Most people around us couldn't afford cows, but they tell me that an old lady up the road would come to our house every morning with a quart jar of milk for me. That old lady was poor herself. So my commitment to poverty comes out of my debt to her and to others who have taken care of me. I can say with Paul, "I am a debtor" (Rom. 1:14, KJV), and that's where I get my energy to preach the gospel.

But I could have so easily forgotten my past and my love for the people. However, by calling me back to Simpson County, God made it so I couldn't forget. To me, forgetfulness is the sign of a degenerated people. Forgetfulness and thanklessness are the great first steps to apostasy throughout the Bible. I remember a story told by Muhammed Kenyatta after he took part in the struggle resulting in the Woolworth stores beginning to hire black people. I remember how those kids who were peacefully marching with him had their heads beaten; how hundreds of blacks involved in civil rights were herded like cattle into corrals over at the fair grounds without food, sanitation facilities, or medical care; how the authorities took kids to Parchman State Prison; how Fanny Lou Hamer (one of the mothers of human rights in Mississippi) is crippled because she's been beaten almost to death because of her vision of justice and what was right.

Muhammed Kenyatta said he went back to Woolworth's just a few months later after they hired some black people to work in the Woolworth store. He was trying to buy something and one of the girls in there was a little bit pushy.

"Sister," he said to this black girl who was the clerk, "don't you recognize what this cost us together? You should be kind to me, to another black. Because you know what it cost us for you to have this opportunity to work here. It took a lot of us getting our heads crashed in and some folks have been made cripple to give you the opportunity for this job."

And she said, "No, you didn't do that for me. I got this job because I'm qualified"!

So quick to forget! Yet once you forget, you lose a sense of responsibility. And so I feel responsible. I feel a sense of responsibility that comes out of remembering what others have done for me, that everything that God has given me I must use in a creative way that other people can be blessed.

Our first response to the needs was to meet the worst ones—like relief—in whatever way we could, sort of off to the side of what we could have called our ministry. Once I visited a woman who was literally wasting away in her bed from cancer. The smell of her sores was so strong it almost made me sick. She didn't have any money for medicine or for food for her family. I gave her $5.00— the only $5.00 I had. But I knew it wasn't enough. The needs were so widespread and so deep, the more we met in a little way, the more it seemed like we were trying to lay our ministry's foundation on some light, spiritual sand rather than digging down to the deep bedrock of the issues which made up the substance of most people's lives. The whole community was suffering. And we realized that it would take more than a verbalization of the gospel and token action in our spare time to be effective. God was allowing us to take the blinders off the methodology we were using to present the gospel long enough to love people. Meeting physical needs was going to have to be right at the center of our evangelism and ministry.

We were reminded daily of where people were hurting. We would watch the roaches crawl up and down their walls. We ate their cornbread and milk even when it was the only thing in the house. We felt the wind as it came through the cracks in the walls. And what we discovered was that God's love in us created real responses: we wanted to counsel, to get food, and to fix homes.

On the way to the schools, I'd see school-aged kids in the streets, some retarded, some with orange-tinged hair and distended navels, all signs of malnutrition. There were kids in our classes who were sleepy-eyed and tired-looking all the time who I knew didn't have enough to eat. And I read medical doctors' reports about how malnutrition at certain ages can create irreversible learning problems. For our school ministry to be real it had to deal with the fact that these kids were being systematically destroyed by their environment. Our evangelism had brought us face to face with physical needs. We had been preaching the gospel according to John 3:16. Now, we were discovering that our response must be to implement the gospel according to 1 John 3:16.

The needs were not new to us. What was new was the feeling that filling those needs had to be a basic part of our strategy and that it might be the key to reaching the community. It seemed to bear itself out in terms of the trust we were feeling from the community. People were coming to us for advice and help on everything from how to make a loan for a house to getting a sick child to the hospital. With each relationship came the new opportunity to share our faith in Jesus Christ.

We had sort of stumbled on a key biblical principle: that a response to the needs which people feel most deeply fleshes out the meaning of the gospel which we proclaim. We now call this the "felt-need concept." It's based on the principle that the best way to communicate to a person's most basic, spiritual needs is through his physical needs, or the needs he can best identify for himself.

We could see in the Bible how Jesus used the felt-need concept all the time in communicating who he was to people. When he met the woman of Samaria at the well, he zeroed in on her need for water, and then moved from there to show her that she had a deeper need for the living water, a life which flows out of a relationship with the living God (John 4).

Again and again Jesus showed us the way to use opportunities, to meet people's physical needs as stepping-stones to treat their spiritual needs. In fact, Jesus often used three steps. He'd *verbalize* the Good News, usually telling who he was. He'd *actualize* his words, acting upon what he said. Then he'd *spiritualize* his actions, pointing out that they had spiritual implications upon the lives of his listeners. For instance, he said, "I am the bread of life," went on to feed over five thousand people, and then explained the spiritual reality behind his works by saying, "If any one eats of this bread, he will live for ever; and the bread which I shall give for the life of the world is my flesh" (John 6:51).

In the same pattern we hear him proclaiming, "I am the light of the world," then see him healing the darkened eyes of a man born blind, and finally after the man is rejected by the rest of the religious establishment, we hear him explaining that he was the one sent from God "for judgment . . . that those who do not see may see and that those who see may become blind" (John 8 and 9). The Gospel records that the man fell down and worshiped Jesus.

The news that we can have Jesus' same impact and an even greater impact on the world and its physical suffering (John 14:12) gives me a sense of power, a sense that my faith makes a difference and that I'm on the winning side. Jesus said, "As long as I am in the world, I am the light of the world" (John 9:5). But he promised that "he who follows me . . . will have the light of life" (John 8:12), and then gives us the same title that he gave himself: *"You* are the light of the world . . . let your light so shine before men, that they may see your good works and give glory to your Father who is in heaven" (Matt. 5:14, 16). If we are called by the same name, and if we follow his example in both proclaiming the Word and acting to meet human needs, Jesus Christ living through us will produce the same spiritual results in the hearts of men and women that were produced when he walked the earth. That's an evangelism that reaches the whole of a person's life.

When Jesus describes his own ministry, he talks about preaching and healing and releasing prisoners (Luke 4:18–21). His target is the poor, the blind, the prisoners, and the oppressed. We don't see here a theology that divides a man up into little compartments— body, mind, soul, emotions, spirit—then puts one above the other and deals with that only. No, the words have both physical and spiritual meaning which show Jesus' strategy to rescue *whole* people, and to enlist both their bodies and spirits in his kingdom. Jesus makes God's love relevant to my every need, to my whole person.

This is the ministry of Christ. What we discovered was that we had inherited the responsibility and the power to continue this ministry in our world with the same clarity and quality with which he began it two thousand years ago.

Why is this idea of the whole person so especially crucial when we are talking about sharing the gospel in the black community? It's because among the poor there is often a basic cause-and-effect relationship between spiritual and physical needs. It is somehow very cruel to share the words of life with a person without sharing also things that person needs to live (James 2:14, 17). But also we can get caught in the shallows of welfare or paternalism if we help meet people's physical needs without sharing with them the understanding that they can have a new quality of life with God that lasts forever. God wants people to develop into whole human beings.

So real evangelism brings us face to face with *all* the needs of people and then reaches out to make them whole. I did not know it at the time, but our early commitment to this vision of evangelism was grafting us into the trunk of a tree so powerful that it would result in our little mission branching into dozens of new directions.

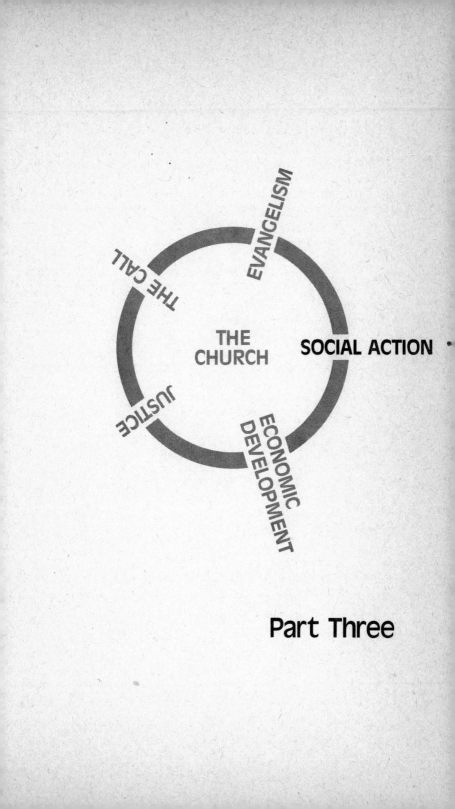

EVANGELISM

THE CALL

SOCIAL ACTION

THE
CHURCH

JUSTICE

ECONOMIC
DEVELOPMENT

Part Three

8.

Cracks in the Closed Society

As I began to visit the homes in Mendenhall and talk with the people, I was getting a close-up look at the people and their life. There were the houses—all dilapidated and falling down. And the girls—so many of them pregnant at fourteen or fifteen. And then I'd find out that so many of the kids were not going to school because they had to stay home with the younger kids who had no one else to stay home with them—their mothers worked.

Vera Mae also saw the need, since we had six kids, and she began to think about starting a day-care center in the community. We started it around 1963 in the new house we had just built and later moved it over to our new Bible Institute building. Then people from as far away as Sanatorium and Magee—about eight and ten miles away—would bring their kids to the center.

My wife sort of killed two birds with one stone through the day-care center. Besides getting the older kids into school, she tried to fix a nutritious meal for the kids who came. It would mainly be beans and some type of vegetable, and usually some cut-up wieners. A lot of food began coming from people giving us their "commodity" foods, the surplus foodstuffs given out by the government to poor people—things like powdered milk, oatmeal, and packages of grits, beans and split green peas, and raisins.

The food was how people showed their appreciation. They knew we needed food for the day-care center. But really, most of them were giving it to us for our own personal use. They were more concerned about us personally, for "the preacher and his wife," than about our ministry. Out of that concern we could spread our base of support and commitment. Unfortunately, it's that dynamic appreciation among the people that turns a lot of would-be pastors or community developers into rip-off artists. If you go into a community and want everything personally, if you even want to get rich, you can end up with all you want. But the test is whether or not you're willing to share—in our case, whether or not we would share with the kids who came.

Our day-care center was the first real social action we got into.

Later would come our Headstart program and a more comprehensive feeding program, then tutoring and recreation for the kids, then leadership development, vocational training, and adult education. In the Seventies we would get into housing and health care and counseling. But right now it was day care.

I believe that we were developing at a very crucial time in history, a time when we could learn some important lessons just because we were caught up in a unique flow of events and because we believed so much that, as Christians, we could shape the events around us and make it happen. But as we got deeper and deeper in the community through evangelism and as the civil rights movement got closer and closer to Simpson County, we saw the struggle of our ministry taking place on three different levels at once—spiritual, social, and justice. In fact, what we had was a crazy assortment of programs that to most people seemed completely nonrelated. From 1965 on through the Seventies, some thought we were civil-righters, others thought we were fanatic fundamentalists, others just thought we were "some crazy niggers."

We had a good example of this mixture in 1966. The Bible Institute was still going strong. We were still getting up at daybreak to study the Bible. But the same old bus that we used to pick up kids for Bible classes was now also picking up adults to take them to register to vote. In January my wife went to study Early Childhood Development at Tuskegee Institute so she could open up the Headstart program, our social outreach to Simpson County. Later that year, I flew to the Caribbean on a preaching mission. In between we had our eighth child, Betty. We had civil rights speakers like Charles Evers as well as great Bible teachers like John MacArthur, Jr. We continued to have the Youth for Christ meetings on Saturday nights, and we began organizing a civic league for political action in the county. I went out and spoke at the schools while Vera Mae ran the Headstart program.

That was just the way it was. We didn't plan it that way, but one thing led us to another. When the Headstart crowded our Christian youth activities in the church, we added a new wing especially for day-care right on to the church sanctuary. This all took place in '66. All the different themes were running together—concerns for the spirit, the needs, and justice. Like the clarinet, the sax, and the trumpet in some jazz band, each would have its time to shine, but all played together in harmony.

After about two years, the day-care center moved into being Headstart. Headstart came out of the poverty program, the government's attempt to deal with the needs behind the whole civil rights struggle. It came right at the height of the civil rights movement, in about 1966, and for Voice of Calvary it lasted about two and a half years until August of 1968.

One thing we found out from Headstart was that Vera Mae was a natural born organizer. She can get the folks together, especially the old folks. She got them on her side and then moved them out. She had been made director of the program for the county, mainly because of her grass-roots involvement in the schools with me in Child Evangelism. That is what made her the director. And also the fact that most people looked at us and saw that we were the only people in the black community with a facility that could meet the need. We had our own house and the Bible Institute building as well as the chapel.

We started Headstart in 1966 with over a hundred kids every day. This pushed our facilities to the absolute maximum. There had to be over twenty staff members—teachers, cooks, secretaries—to handle the kids. So, every day we had people in all of our buildings. We built little movable partitions for the chapel and, like I said, finally had to build a special wing right onto the chapel, we were so pushed.

We were pushed in other ways too. For those twenty or so positions we must have received over one hundred fifty applications. For the most part, what we had, besides unemployment was underemployment. What we found was that we, a day-care center, were really the first black business that could employ more than three black people in the county. People would work with us as volunteers just so that their names would be first on the list when a job did come up.

It was a big struggle. Here was a fundamentalist who wanted everyone to be fundamental Christians. And here were folks needing jobs. They could accept the basic ideas we stood for in Christianity. They had a great respect for Voice of Calvary, but they didn't want to make a commitment. Mostly, they needed the money.

In our early-morning prayer meetings, we'd pray that the teachers would know Christ. Mostly we communicated Christ personally and through our staff meetings and prayer meetings and Bible studies that Vera Mae and Gladys Griffin, my cousin, organized. It was a good struggle, a healthy struggle. We were meeting some needs, both physical and spiritual.

Most people criticized the Headstart program. They thought it was only an educational program. But it wasn't. A prime objective was nutrition. Kids who were being retarded by malnutrition could get good meals. Second, it was a program that gave real employment to people. Jobs are still at the heart of reaching the needs of a family. But third, the program we ran did get the kids out of their homes and into an environment that could prepare them to think and to want to learn in school. Many times it put children ahead of other kids from roughly the same environments whose families made a little more money so that they couldn't qualify to come.

The civil rights movement had brought thousands of northern whites, especially college students, down to the South during the summer. We had our first whites working full-time with us as volunteers in Headstart. This began a new phase of development. We had always had preachers, black and white, like James Howard and John MacArthur, come and be with us. But here were some people with skills that wanted to help too. We have never quit the volunteer program. Even now, we have as many as two hundred volunteers come down to help us in our work during the course of a year, some spending three or four days, others as long as a year. It is a part of the civil rights movement that we have held on to. It may be one of the most important forms of social action in any of our programs, the difficult struggle of understanding and reconciliation across racial lines that seems to take place so beautifully when people work with each other around a common objective, like remodeling a house or painting the gym floor, or tutoring.

In the summer of 1968, integration was just around the corner. Already "voluntary" integration had taken place with a handful of black students going to the white high school. Spencer and Joanie, our oldest children, were among them. We saw that a crisis would take place in black school attendance if black students were not prepared emotionally and academically for the switchover. Mississippi was now one of the few states in the union without a mandatory education law—an open door to dropping out for black kids facing a hostile, new, integrated environment with inferior training.

The result was that Dolphus and I organized the first tutoring school that summer. For Dolphus, this was a breakthrough. He had gone off to college and had returned that summer, but there were no jobs. He had an offer to drive a cab with his brother Melvin in Washington, D.C. I could see that if we were really talking about bringing trained leadership back to the community it had to begin now. So we prayed about it and decided that the ministry would try to support Dolphus working among youth that summer. I wrote a letter to all my friends and asked them to help us. The money came in.

Dolphus organized the volunteers, Doug Huemmer, Chris Erb, and Louise Fox, around a program of tutoring kids, brushing up their math and reading skills. With this program we also began to stop the Saturday Youth for Christ meetings, because we now had up to a hundred kids every day where we could share the same gospel message that we had been sharing just on Saturdays. We decided that for these older kids a good meal was important too, so we did it on our own that first summer.

Louise came back and stayed in Mendenhall from January on into the next summer, maintaining the tutoring with about ten or twelve kids. That next summer we had about one hundred twenty-five kids, and we had been given a feeding contract from the state, which had had federal money set aside for just that purpose. When the schools finally integrated in 1970, many black kids dropped out or were failed or were suspended. It was rough. We have continued the tutoring programs up until now, considering it of absolute importance. Now we have a new twist and that is the development of black Christian leadership. After students have been in our tutoring program, we ask them if they want to tutor others. We let high school kids tutor elementary school children. In addition, they take part in a special discipleship and leadership training program run by Dolphus. This has led to sending kids off to college and most recently to a whole group of VOC's graduates attending schools in Jackson, like Jackson State, Tougaloo and Belhaven and continuing to work for VOC in Jackson while in college. It may be possible to see in the next few years a significant number of college graduates, with a Christian commitment to work in their community, returning to the rural areas of Mississippi to fill the leadership gap that plagues black Mississippi communities.

Not only was there a crisis among the children, but we also saw

tremendous need in adults. Many couldn't read or fill out the forms
needed to apply for a job. Now the Bible Institute had thrived in
1965 and 1966. That had started our whole thrust toward educating
adults because Mrs. Harper, the retired principal of the black high
school, taught English and basic communications at the Institute.
But around 1968 the Bible Institute began to reach a crisis. Some
of the white ministers who were teaching dropped out—afraid of
reprisals. The civil rights movement was so strong in Simpson County
that even many of the black people were afraid to identify with us.
You see, Voice of Calvary was standing alone in the spotlight. So
in 1969, the Bible Institute was fizzling out. Since then, with the
help of black schoolteachers, like Brother Robert Clayton and his
wife, Elgin (who is Dolphus's sister) VOC sponsors adult education
classes both for basic education certificates and for those seeking to
take their high school equivalency tests.

We allowed the Headstart program to pass into someone else's
leadership in 1968 in order to do some more pressing things. Vera
Mae was asked in 1969 to do a nutritional study of Simpson County
to see if the food stamp program was being effective. She and
Dorothy Michaels and Mrs. Anna Buckley worked for a year for
the Child Development Group of Mississippi, going house to house,
collecting data. What this resulted in was a comprehensive view of
the needs out in the homes. We found people who were without
food, people who were without health care. In fact, after that, we
determined that Voice of Calvary was going to have to get involved
in health care. It would be four years before our vision materialized
in a small health center.

By now deep cracks were forming in the walls of the closed society. We discovered that the more creative the approach to human
need, the more threatening it was to the System, and the more nega-
tive the feedback. Day care, feeding, employment, education, and
health care, black and white working together—all seemed to send
tremors down into the foundations of the wall. But we were just
beginning to scratch the surface of a comprehensive approach to
apply the love of God in Jesus Christ to the poverty that surrounded
us. And the more we scratched, the more it seemed like we saw the
hostile forces of hatred and racism that perpetuated the closed society gush out of the widening cracks. Our social action had brought
us to the edge of involvement, to the point where our involvement
was going to require much more than just time and money and
energy.

Six years after that survey in 1969, in 1975, the Voice of Calvary Health Center moved into a modern clinic facility formerly owned by a white doctor and directly across the street from the Simpson County Courthouse in uptown Mendenhall. Its opening marked the high point of Voice of Calvary's social involvement, for it included the county's only pediatrician, Dr. Eugene McCarty, and would come to include social workers, nurse practitioners, nutritionists, home health nurses, and other technicians, black and white, who would be penetrating homes all over Simpson County, communicating the gospel and delivering service at the point of need.

But in 1969, looking at the doctor's office building in the shadow of the courthouse and just across a large expanse of thick, St. Augustine grass from the county jailhouse, you would never know that in the six years between '69 and '75, many of us would be locked in that jail, many of us would march around the silver rotunda of that courthouse, and some of us would be tried in those solemn chambers that protected Mississippi's justice.

9.

People of Action

Social Action has long been a controversial phrase in conservative Christian circles. It was sometimes all right referring to what missionaries did on a faraway field, but was definitely out-of-bounds when referring to gospel work being done in the black community of America, especially in the Sixties.

But breaking it down, the social action we saw at Voice of Calvary was "people action," people putting energy behind their faith and aiming it at the problems around them. Looking back and listening to the people, I can see it has had an impact—not just in the physical lives of people, but also in their hearts.

Ethel Lee, everyone calls him Ba Ba (said Bay Bay), came back to Simpson County after receiving training as an electrician from Tuskegee Institute. His wife is a nurse. Together they faced a county that in terms of incentive and hope for blacks was nothing but a wilderness. Ba Ba became the president of the local NAACP chapter and has worked alongside Voice of Calvary throughout the years. His is a testimony of hope.

You know, back in the Sixties it was tough. I had just come home from Tuskegee. I was an electrician and had a fairly decent job, but it was tough in terms of the pressure from the whites. And it was also tough because black people didn't look out for each other either. In fact, one thing that I believe the Voice of Calvary did was to show people about being concerned about not just themselves, to challenge black people to care about each other.

Now they also had an impact on the racial thing too. In fact, Voice of Calvary was the first integrated church that I ever attended. This was in a time when, because the black and white communities were so separate, many black folks thought that the white people worshiped one God and they worshiped another.

In terms of rights, before Rev. Perkins came here, if a black man went to jail you know what happened? He stayed there until he could find some good white man to get him out. And if the white people didn't see fit to get him out, then he went up to Parchman State Penitentiary, or worked on a county work farm for who knows how long.

But to me, what the Christian movement in Simpson County has meant is the difference between people working together in love or working apart in hate. For black people it was the difference between everybody struggling for their own survival or learning that it's more blessed to give than to receive.

I watched closely and as I watched what I saw was that as the Voice of Calvary preached love, it created a spiritual and an economic awakening hand in hand.

From the first revival meetings they had under a tent up until today, there is one thing that Voice of Calvary has called for and that is a personal acceptance of Jesus Christ. They never tried to get anyone to change his church or his denomination. All they wanted a person to do is to accept Jesus Christ. And that has reached out into every part of the county. I can name some people that the Voice of Calvary through the Perkins made it possible to get their education. There's a girl named Lucille Quinn. She had about thirteen in her family. Sharecroppers. She began going to Voice of Calvary and through it got a way to go to school outside the state and get her education.

Leonard Stapleton is another. The Voice of Calvary used to have a little old bus that came around every night, transporting people to Bible class. Leonard started going. You know what he is now? He's one of the first black car salesmen at one of the biggest Chevrolet agencies in Jackson. Voice of Calvary helped him get an education out at Tougaloo College.

Who do you think gave Artis Fletcher his start? Artis' wife, Carolyn, too. You know Joe Paul Buckley? How do you think his children got to go to college out in California? Through Voice of Calvary.

Go to Mendenhall right now and you'll see black children that Voice of Calvary put shoes on their feet, clothes on their backs, and food in their bellies. We saw the first Headstart in Simpson County begin at Voice of Calvary. I took my oldest daughter to it and I know they didn't get any money to do it.

I've just been happy to be associated, to have a friend like Brother Perkins. See, Rev. Perkins would tackle stuff most of the people who had been here all their lives thought was impossible. If he didn't have the know-how himself, he would find someone who did. He's the one who instituted the idea of a black co-op. And let me tell you one thing, I bought stock in that store at $5.00 a share and four years later I could sell it for $19.29 a share. Amazing! There had never been a movement like this before.

I don't have to remind myself of how much things have changed

around here since the Perkins came and we began together to try
to change some things. Every time I go to work in the adjacent
county, Smith County, I am reminded. Up there people still have
separation—in some places you still have to go around to the back
of the cafe to get served if you're black. A movement like this one
in our county has never started up there.

It amazes me how Voice of Calvary can give so freely! It doesn't
matter if you come to their Bible classes or if you were a part of
the civil rights movement or who you are—anyone can go and
get cheaper and more effective medical service than ever before at
the clinic uptown. And who ever thought they'd live to see a black
doctor and a white doctor practicing together in Mendenhall, Mississippi?

If there's one word to describe what has happened here during
the last sixteen or seventeen years with us and Voice of Calvary,
it is *inspiration*. One of our local boys is there at Voice of Calvary
now, Joe Lee Shaw. It is one of the best things that has ever
happened to him. There was no future for him without it. But
Shaw is typical of just countless numbers of black people getting
inspiration, getting a chance.

My wife and I are other examples. I remember one day Rev.
Perkins came up and talked with me. He said, "Now a man is supposed to go where he can make a better living for his family. That's
just common sense. But the county needs you." And so we stayed
here. We made a commitment. And there have been others make
that same commitment, and together we have seen miracles happen.

Biblical social action has its roots in lives changed by Jesus Christ.
To me there is no better example of this than Dolphus Weary. I had
no idea that, after accepting Christ in a tent meeting where Rev. Wallace was preaching, Dolphus would later become the director of those
programs directly related to social action in Simpson County. He
knows about how to change society because his own testimony begins
with change.

I grew up in Mississippi in a family with eight children. My
father died when I was four years old. As sharecroppers we never
could get out of debt until my brothers and sisters got a little older
and we could quit sharecropping. My grandfather provided me
with the father image I needed.

I grew up in the church, joining when I was eight and working
faithfully up until I was fifteen or sixteen. I was a good person
and I thought I was a Christian, until our minister spoke and at

the end of his message asked all those who were not Christians to raise their hands. I raised my hand. Then he said for all those people to come down front and join the church. Since I was already a member, I had a problem. Was this all there was to being a Christian?

Then one day I was getting my hair cut by a young man in the community named Leonard Stapleton. He asked me, "Dolphus, are you a Christian?" I said, "Yes, I guess so. I go to church and do right and I've been baptized and all that." He said, "But you still do not know you are a Christian?" Then he invited me to a tent meeting.

It was there that I heard the gospel of Jesus Christ preached for the first time. The message came from Psalm 116:12: "What shall I render unto the Lord for all his benefits towards me?" And as I looked back over my life—in spite of a broken home and the poverty—I realized that God had done a lot for me. I had to ask myself that question, "What can I do for him?" It was answered that what God wanted us to do was to give our lives to him. That night I went forward and received Jesus Christ into my life.

I began going to the Bible Institute over at the Voice of Calvary and Youth for Christ meetings on Saturdays. By the time I was a senior in high school I had decided that I wanted to go to a Christian college. I didn't want to go to a Bible Institute because I had seen too many rip-off preachers with no way to make a living but by taking from the people. I wanted to be able to get a skill— I thought of teaching—so that I could come back to the community and support myself and carry on a Christian ministry.

The only indigenous ministering I had seen that was wholesome was the Voice of Calvary. My own minister would come to our house during revival times. My mother would prepare food for him: meat, cakes, vegetables, anything. And we children had to wait and end up eating what was left over. She'd save up all her money and then he'd come in and eat up all the food. She'd pay her little bit of money in the church and he'd drive a big car while here we were living in a shack and sharing our money with him. Somehow this didn't jive in my mind. If things were ever going to get better in terms of the way people lived and how effectively the gospel message got out, there were going to have to be some new leaders. There would have to be some changed people in the community.

I believe that this has been the main role of Voice of Calvary— getting changed people back to the community to form an indigenous base.

The results have been other changes. Some changes have been

the direct result of our labors: new Christians through the preaching of the Word on radio, in the schools; new homes through cooperative development and pooling our resources.

But there was also the change that came from a sustained Christian witness in the area of making the system work. As a result of the marches and things that VOC participated in and gave leadership to during the civil rights movement, there is now pavement on the streets in the black community, and we have street lights. Black children can go swimming in public places and parks and have access to better schools.

VOC demonstrated that things were possible. Other towns in rural areas around are just beginning to catch on to doing it.

Today, Artis Fletcher and I form a team. He functions as pastor of the church and I direct the programs in the community. I am in charge of the radio ministry through which we preach the gospel on four radio stations in Mississippi. Then there are the educational activities beginning with day care, then our tutoring program, our leadership development program for teenagers, and finally our adult education program where adults can earn both their ABE (for basic education) and their GED (the high school equivalency program).

I also work at Piney Woods, a private black school close by, doing counseling, Bible study with the students, and trying to develop an outreach among the students.

We are launching a reading program for the city of Mendenhall centered around our library, encouraging people to come in and check out books and even using them with their children or others who need help.

Just like the preaching of the Word is tied in with Christian social action in people's activities, sometimes our own healing is wrapped up in our ministry to others. This was true with Harriet McKinnis, a mother of six children who faced the crisis of separation with her husband. Harriet came to know about Voice of Calvary through Artis Fletcher, who helped found the church she belonged to in Aberdeen, Maryland, while he attended Washington Bible College. A few years later, the Lord had moved Harriet to join the ministry in Mendenhall after a brief visit.

I first came to Mendenhall to visit in 1972 and right away I began to like the work, you know, it really interested me. I thought, if I ever get the opportunity, this is the kind of place I would like to work in. I had no idea that that opportunity would ever come my way.

But then my husband and I separated. My family was broken, and I couldn't see how the Lord was going to put my life back together again. But he did. I found that I still really had a burden for this place and the people here. After months of struggling—you know, you just can't pick up and move when you have six children—I felt that the Lord was calling me to Mississippi.

I must admit, the thought of leaving a good, new home in a nice neighborhood where my next-door neighbor was white and then moving into a poor community that was segregated worried me. But it didn't keep me from answering God's call.

When I came here to live, I was a volunteer worker. I just joined in and began to work. I saw things that needed to be done, needs that needed to be met—in the nursery, the day care center, the kitchen—and I made myself available.

The fact that I was being used by God helped. But most of all it was my friends—Carolyn Fletcher, Rosie Weary, Shirley Rivers and so many others. I'm sure that what has helped me the most is the community, the people. For one thing, they hold together, they stick together. Not perfect, but different from just the usual church. My kids and I receive a lot of Christian love from our friends and brothers and sisters. The people here are like substitutes for my family back in Maryland.

Now that the thrift store is open, I'm working there full time. For me this is not only a needed ministry for people who can't afford things like clothes and stuff, but also a real opportunity to share my faith. I keep tracts and literature and play Christian music. But also, the Lord gives me an opportunity to speak to people.

10.

The Victim and the Closed Society

To me and my wife, young missionaries just returned from California, the conditions that some of our people lived in were just pitiful. Hester Evans, for instance. It was not so much the feeling that I got when I pushed up in among those ten or twelve kids packed in four rooms. It wasn't even the feeling I got when I saw that cornbread was the only thing in her kitchen. It was more like the feeling of being trapped.

I began talking about her family's condition at the Oak Ridge Church. The church began to send food out. But a little food didn't produce much change. Again I felt trapped. "How could Christ's love deal with these needs?" we asked ourselves.

But it was one summer that put my trapped feelings into perspective —that summer when, while it was hot and humid, Miss Hester and her children tore wood off the outside of the house to use in their cook fire. You could look right through the floor and see that the wood blocks that held the house up had been cut on, time and again, to get splinters to build a fire with. Eventually you could see through the whole house.

It seemed stupid for her to tear up her house in the summer when she knew that winter was just a few months away. Many of the people in the community quit trying to be charitable. They began to blame Miss Hester for her own problems. And I suppose, to a certain extent, she was to blame. But that trapped feeling was still there. I was getting a handle on it though. It was the trap that I would later call the cycle of poverty.

For Miss Hester and many folks like her, poverty had moved beyond her physical condition to claim her whole mind. For the real poor, poverty means thinking just for the moment. It is the inability to think about the future because of the total demand to think about survival in the present. It is a culture, a whole way of life. A little money can't help much.

A teacher in San Francisco did a study with her students a few years ago. The kids, both black and white, were all the same age and were all asked if they would rather have a penny lollipop right now or an ice cream sundae tomorrow. Almost all of the black kids raised their hands for the lollipop now. Almost all of the white kids raised their hands for the sundae later. Even at an early age, that survivalist, poverty mentality was trapping the minds of black children.

So poverty is passed on, communicated through a whole culture. Mamie Smith, a daughter of Miss Hester, is a good example of how poverty is passed on from generation to generation. She lives with her six kids in a two-room shack all sharing two double beds. The kids are showing signs of malnutrition. There are rats in the house. In the winter they all huddle around a garbage can with a fire in it.

Like the shacks that Miss Hester and Mamie Smith and many others live in, built up against those deep, timeless Mississippi woods, black people in general stand against a dark background of decades of poverty and racism. We can see the depth of this in statistics collected by the U.S. Census Bureau. I get so much of my energy from remembering the people who are living in those conditions. But it's a funny thing how the dry and technical charts and graphs describing the people of Mississippi can arouse the same deep passion in me.

We can start outside the average black person's door and begin looking at the house itself. According to 1970 findings, the South in general has two-thirds of the country's poorest housing. Now in Mississippi, more than five out of every ten people (55 percent), both in the urban areas like Jackson and Meridian and in the rural areas like around Mendenhall in Simpson County, live in houses considered "deteriorating or dilapidated." [1] Most of the time we call these *shacks*. Out in the country, we find three out of every four black families living in houses lacking functional plumbing. Only a handful out of every one hundred black homes are considered "sound with all plumbing facilities."

But now, let's walk in the door and see the effects of this kind of environment on the people. In Simpson County, where our ministry began, two out of three black homes (63 percent) don't have any type of proper sanitation facilities—public sewer, septic tank, or sewage disposal. Health statistics then show that if you are a black person living in this type of home, your poor housing can create poor health. In Simpson County, two out of three of the deaths caused by "infective and parasitic diseases," those diseases especially related to poor sanitation facilities, struck among the one-third of the county's population which is black. Even more devastating is the fact that

[1] These and subsequent figures are from the 1970 figures of the U.S. Census.

almost one half of these deaths were babies under one year old. One symptom of poverty can create another and the result—babies dying because they live in places that can't be kept clean.

Once inside the door we also find out that there may not be a phone or even a car or vehicle available—an alarming pair of facts. Two out of three black families in Simpson County have no phone and about 40 percent have no transportation. An emergency hits— seizure, accidental fall, illness, stroke, broken leg—help is a long ways away, and without transportation many people, especially the old, linger at home and suffer or die of long-term illnesses which could have been dealt with.

In Simpson County about 80 percent of the deaths because of pregnancy or childbirth were among black mothers and babies. Hypertension, described by many as a symptom of oppression, killed three times as many blacks as whites in 1972. About three out of four of those dying from diseases of the skin and subcutaneous tissues were black people.[2]

Not only is the health situation in many families oppressive, but oppressive structures also create poor health care. Most of the doctors in the county, even now in 1976, maintain separate waiting rooms for black and white patients. It is rare that a black person will be seen before the white waiting room is empty. In fact, I remember as a boy seeing people with fevers stretched out on the cool tile floors for hours waiting to see the doctor.

The combination of bad transportation, poor housing, lack of health education and proper medical care, oppressive structures, bad dieting with starchy and sugary foods, and lack of money creates a situation where being black in Mississippi can be not just unhealthy but fatal.

For many it simply means seeking health care only when the crisis of pain demands it. Preventive care is almost unknown. Keep in mind that the figures for Simpson County are not even the most extreme. There are counties in Mississippi where people are suffering on an even more widespread level. The breakdown of the twenty thousand residents of Simpson County highly resembles that of the whole state with about two-thirds white and about one-third black. But in many counties of the Mississippi Delta, the black population gets up to 72 percent. In either situation, what we are facing is a

---

[2] All figures relating to deaths from Vital Statistics Records, 1972, Mississippi State Board of Health.

vast segment of the population of a state in America, masses of men, women and children, who are experiencing as much illiteracy, malnutrition, retardation, and death as some of the famine- and poverty-stricken lands of Africa and Asia. For me, knowing these people awakes the same passions as do some of the most terrible pictures of suffering from the foreign mission field.

It would be good to mention here that poverty in Mississippi, although the most dominant way of life in the black community, is by no means limited to black people. The first week our clinic in Mendenhall opened, a white man and his wife and fourteen children, all barefoot, came in for free physicals for the whole family. They try to make a living raising chickens. Though over half of the state's black people live in decayed and dilapidated housing, a large segment, fully 15.9 percent of the white population, share the same poor conditions. As much as 27.2 percent of the white rural population is without functional plumbing.

But yet, for the black community, we've still touched just the tip of the iceberg, just enough to justify some charity but not quite enough to get to the heart of the problem. The pattern of statistics continues to develop. In the rundown neighborhoods of the black community, crime is another threat to life. Shockingly, almost three and a half times as many blacks as whites died in Simpson County in one year as a result of homicide.

In one vital area after another, black people experience crisis. Another is the crisis in leadership. As a result of the beatings, the hatred, and the economic pressures, over two million black people left the South for northern cities from 1939 through 1964. Most people stand amazed at the nation of Israel and the great migration of people begun by its creation, yet fail to realize that the movement of black people from the South to the big cities of the North and West constitutes the greatest migration of human beings ever in human history. And what that did to the South was to leave it without the leadership that it needed in the black community. The very old and the very young became the main age groups left. The young adults from twenty to forty needed to organize demands for better health care and stabilize the economic situation in families and communities were simply not there.

The impact of the migration is still felt throughout the black community, especially in families and in rural areas. Between 1960 and 1970, while Mississippi sustained a net increase in population, it lost

10.5 percent of its black population. Now, with the deterioration of the northern ghettos and inner cities, the trend is beginning to reverse itself. But it will take decades to reverse its effects.

We say "money makes money." But in the black community, in terms of income, the corollary is true: "Poverty makes poverty." Poverty is not just the lack of money, but the lack of money is a good piece of the picture. Taking Simpson County as an example again, compared to $3,158 income for the average American, the per capita annual income in 1970 for a black person in Simpson County is just $907. Over half of the county's black families live below poverty level, and though they represent less than a third of the general population, black people constitute over half of all the poor people in the county. This means that roughly 20 percent or one-fifth of the total population of the county is black and desperately poor.

Now, most people, when you talk about poverty among black people say, "Well, there wouldn't be so much of a problem if poor people would get themselves a job." But although the black unemployment rates across the country are always higher than the white unemployment rates, that's not been the problem in Mississippi. Mississippi always boasts one of the lowest unemployment rates in the nation. But that's because the problem is not unemployment—it's *under*-employment, the situation in which a person gets a job, works at it, but just isn't paid enough to make ends meet at home.

Part of it has to do with skills. Without education or the long-term access to technology, a third of all the blacks employed in the state are in farming—anything from driving a tractor to chopping cotton. Another third are employed in service industries—anything from housekeeping to laborers—which offer little in terms of trade or skill. Almost 90 percent of the private housekeepers, service workers, laborers, and similar jobs are held by blacks. In Simpson County except for teachers, very few of the black labor force hold professional or technical jobs.[3]

Many people have pointed to education as the best way to break the cycle of poverty. Voice of Calvary has invested a lot of its energy in education and tutoring. But education alone is not an adequate solution, because it is actually one of the best examples of how one symptom of poverty can reinforce another.

---

[3] Estimated labor force data collected December 1973 by Central Office of Mississippi Employment Security Commission. Other figures from U.S. Census Report, 1970.

One of the greatest problems we faced after integration in Mendenhall was the dropping out and the failure of many students. The seniors in the class of 1972 were in the tenth grade during their last year, 1970, at segregated black Harper High. Of the eighty-five children in the class in 1970, sixty-five started at the beginning of the 1971–72 school year. Finally, the number of graduates at the end of the year was eighteen!

What caused this massive failure of the educational system for black kids? First there was the poor training with inferior facilities and equipment, the lower budgets. There were their own feelings of inferiority. There were the parents whose own lack of education prevented them from helping their children at home. There were poor study environments in crowded and poorly lit homes, unstable family situations, the need to earn money to support their families, and some obvious cases of malnutrition which have led to learning deficiencies. On top of all of these, there was a concerted effort by white administrators and teachers to force black children out of school. This was exposed in a memo we intercepted outlining plans of suspension, harassment, and racist policies designed to thwart the efforts of the students to get an education.

The latest figures show that the median grade level for black males in Simpson County is still just a half year beyond sixth grade, and for females the eighth grade. Less than one in ten black men in the county have completed high school. This shows the cumulative effect poverty can have, how it can program a person for failure in a particular field.

I remember that when we used to try to make houses out of playing cards, stacking and balancing just right, the least wrong movement or puff of wind or a cough and they'd fall. And for masses of black people in Mississippi, life is being lived in a house of cards. All of the things that give structure to life—education, employment, income, health, housing, leadership, transportation, and nutrition—are for the most part flimsy excuses for survival, built upon and against each other, so that when one falls they all fall, and are rebuilt only to fall again.

As we began to deal with people who were poor, as we began to see that poverty surrounded them, reached into every structure of their lives, and affected the complete psychology of a whole community, we had no alternative but to conclude that the sickness and the lack of money and the malnutrition were just symptoms of something else, something bigger. Our evangelism had led us to reaching out with charity to help, to social action. But as we helped, and as we saw the ineffectiveness of much of our help and the depth of the problems, our social action led us to see the system as it was.

We saw that the different aspects of poverty formed together into a cycle of destruction and dependence that winds itself down upon and around a person. That's the cycle of poverty, that trapped feeling I had felt at Miss Hester's—a continuous cycle of damage. Not enough food when young so that he can't think straight. No hope of education or personal development or family so she gets pregnant before she's fifteen. No education, poor jobs. Poor jobs, poor pay. Poor pay, bad housing and food. Bad housing and food, poor health. Poor health, poor performance on the job, less pay. A cycle, but at its center a captive, a mind so busy responding to the day-to-day needs that it has no time to think about the future or about those spiritual realities which give meaning to life.

And as we looked back historically, there was no way we could see this cycle as anything but sinful. First, I began to see plainly how sin had organized itself into structures and institutions of inequality and oppression. Seeing the people and looking at the statistics, the terrible poverty of my people had to be something more than happenstance. To have a victim there must be a victimizer. To have someone who is oppressed, there must be an oppressor.

I became acutely aware, as I began to ask the question, "How can we deal with the roots of poverty?" that the roots of poverty were in the system itself, growing out of the very culture and traditions and history of the South and America. Paul's words came alive to me: "We are not contending against flesh and blood, but against the principalities, against the powers, against the world rulers of this present darkness, against the spiritual hosts of wickedness in the heavenly places" (Eph. 6:12).

I could see how racism and violence in individuals with power could work their way through the basic institutions of society, and then how self-interest, especially economic self-interest, had led white people in Mississippi to develop structures to control the system and then to justify the enslavement of black people. There was the segregation—the separate rest rooms and drinking fountains, the black entrance in through the kitchen of a restaurant, the separate, lower quality schools—all self-fulfilling attempts to remind the whole society that blacks and whites were somehow basically different, that blacks were somehow less. These were daily, symbolic messages supporting white superiority and black inferiority.

There was also the religion that used the Bible to justify slavery and gave cover to people who actively initiated or participated in violence against blacks. And the fact that from the beginning of slavery, there had never been a consistent attempt by whites with the gospel to evangelize the black community. And still today, the black community in the U.S. is one of the most untouched mission fields in the world.

There was the absolute power with which the system was maintained! I remember back in the Sixties when a company which was one of the major employers of black people in the county had men working for less than minimum wage. The family that owned it was finally ordered by the government to make up the difference. The boss man simply told his employees, "I'm paying you this check but when you cash it, I want the money back in cash." He went on to say, "The plant will have to close if you don't give the money back, because we'll go broke and you'll lose your jobs." Only a handful of men refused to turn back their money.

Yet, even with all of these obvious and open instances of racism and also the continual violence, there would be few white people who would have said that they had anything against black people. The depth of the problem was that it was ingrained in the behavior of the whole culture.

This is why Mississippi has been called "the closed society." It was not so much the violence or the injustice or the poverty. It was that there was such an airtight system of values and traditions reinforcing the system that not only was there no change, there also was no questioning.

The effect of the closed society upon black people was to turn them into *niggers,* a people of dependence and submission. It was either that or leave or be jailed or killed. James Silver put it most clearly in *Mississippi: The Closed Society* (p. 84). "From birth to death," he writes, "the Negro was exposed to an irresistible pressure toward deferential behavior. When he failed to conform he was driven out or even killed. He was regarded by most whites, possibly by himself, as being shiftless, apathetic, capricious, untrustworthy, lacking in initiative, unstable, insensitive, and, for the most part, an amiable

and happy beast perfectly adapted to his wretched position. By and
large he played the role of Sambo well, giving little visible indication
of a conviction that life could be better, or any apparent hope or
desire to share in the white man's privileges."

There's one dynamic example of the effect of the closed society
that I'll never forget because it happened with a man I respect.
"Token" Jones, Herbert Jones's brother, worked at the lumber mill.
He was the chief mechanic at the mill, and a pivotal man, necessary
to the operation of many of the machines. He would work up to
eighty and ninety hours a week, barely see his family, and take home
about $400 a month—an outrageous salary for the type and amount
of work Token was doing.

In 1973, Token got a job with a ship-building firm down on the
coast paying much more—a fantastic job. Voice of Calvary some-
time later bought Token's house for our doctor and his family. Token
and I were uptown in the bank taking care of the transaction one
afternoon. The bank president, who was of course very good friends
with the owner of the lumber company, sort of cornered Token.

"Now Token," he said, "why do you want to go and leave us?
Hasn't your boss been good to you? Haven't we always stuck by
you?" Token was leaving a big hole in the program over at the mill.

Token began to prance and scratch his head, trying to think what
the banker wanted him to say. "Well, the doctor told me my wife had
to get down to the climate at the coast, that she's allergic to something in the air up here."

And I said, "Token! Why don't you go on and tell this man the
truth? That your boss wasn't paying you peanuts and you found you
a better job with a decent salary so you could raise your family the
way you wanted to!"

Oh, the bank president huffed around and got so mad at me!

But the point is that besides the economics, there is a deeper side,
a psychological side to the poverty among our black people. You can
hear it in Token's remark. It's a dependence, a cultural dependence.
And what the bank president was saying was, "I'd rather have you
dependent on us than have a chance for a better life for your family."

This is the special nature of black oppression in this country. Few
people actually realize the impact of slavery on a culture. Perhaps as
much as 85 percent of the behavior of most black Americans today
is rooted in the fact that they are only two or three generations out of
slavery.

Imagine that you are one of the first persons to be told after more than two hundred years of captivity and dependence that you are now "free." You can't read or write. You have come to know marriage as that transitory interchange between a black man and a black woman that produces children and lasts as long as "death or distance do them part." You have experienced how black men are "bred" with black women, how children are later separated from their "families." You have no money, no stable religion, no silverware, no towels, no bedsheets. Chances are your primary skill is manual farm labor. You have no land.

But, you are free. And where does that leave you? The same place you were before "freedom": total dependence. That's what the slave system created in black people. So deep is the dependence that former slaves not only relied on their white masters for their economic well-being, but also for their culture, their religion, their affirmation . . . even their names. What we ended up with was what José Miranda calls "the most perfect form of slavery" ever created, where not only do the people mistakenly think that they are no longer slaves, but they hold up as superior the very values and attitudes which oppress them.

And that's the psychology of poverty. Why do black people drive big cars? Why do black people get "pushy" when they hold the least little authority? Why do black people buy the best clothes and yet live in a dump of a house? Because we are reflecting the values that we were taught over centuries of exploitation. The American dream and dependence have been sown in black people. Now we are reaping the same behavior. While exploiting and consuming by white people could be justified from a position of power and from the position of a people who could act in their own best interest, those same traits in a people who are powerless and unable to act in their own best interest become hated and despised.

When I first came to Mississippi, I knew I was coming back to people who were disadvantaged. But I also knew that the economic and social advantages we had achieved had not met my needs, they had not given me contentment. I never believed that just preaching the gospel itself was going to free people from their economic problems. I believed too much in work and that work was identified with success. What I had was a new contentment and a new direction in my work and that was freeing. So what I really believed was that preaching the gospel would give people the kind of contentment and stability and love they needed to work for their own best interests and also the best interests of others.

But we discovered that as black people we cannot act in our own best interest. That is perhaps the saddest thing about a people who have been historically or long-term oppressed. C. S. Lewis described it when he said, "One of the worst results of being a slave is that when there is no one to force you any more you find you have lost the power of forcing yourself."

One of the main results of oppression was that black people could not see beyond the immediate. I saw it in our churches, a lollipop religion that would give me a good feeling now so I could forget my troubles. I could hear it in our songs, that if I could just get my feelings out in the blues, things would be all right. The Cadillac, the new clothes, the quick run to the little, outrageously expensive 7-11 or Stop-and-Go market, rather than the planned, long-term shopping at the supermarket, all signs of a culture that has for years been so survival-oriented that it no longer acts in its own best interests. I was beginning to feel the deep spiritual damage that accompanies poverty and wondered how the gospel of Christ could ever really develop whole people in a Southern culture which was, on one side, committed to and benefiting from the continuation of the present oppressive system and, on the other side, was damaged almost beyond the point of being able to pull off anything creative in the community.

Through our evangelism we had come to know the victim in the closed society. As we reached out in concern—in day care and feeding and tutoring and housing and health care—we began to understand the victim, to see that poverty was a cycle of destruction that oppressed a person's mind and spirit as well as his body. And as we got deeper and deeper into our work, it created a deeper and deeper bitterness in me toward the system and the people who owned the system which created these victims. At this point my call was to the victim—to my black people. I cared very little about the people uptown. The suffering I saw people experiencing was to me almost good enough reason for hatred. I never called it hatred. I knew my Bible too well to say that. But it was a knot of bitterness in my stomach, a knot that God would somehow have to remove, whether I liked it or not.

11.

The Failure of the Evangelical Church

Many years before the term *Civil Rights* was a household phrase, one Southern state was refining its penal system. The latest refinement was the installation of the state's first gas chamber. The day had come for the chamber to be used for the first time. The victim, a black man, was brought into the chamber and strapped into the chair. He became hysterical and began to scream: "Save me, Joe Louis! Save me, Joe Louis! Save me!" A few minutes later he was dead.

He was found guilty by the courts. He paid the price. I don't find any meaning in that. But his words, his last words, could be the words of a whole generation of black people, few of whom have heard the real truth about salvation through Jesus Christ. They represent the majority of black people looking for something to save them, to make them whole, to give them meaning and peace and happiness, but who are without access to the central truths of the gospel.

The bitterness I felt in seeing masses of people suffering and victimized by an unjust system, the futility and injustice I felt, were not helped by the position of the white church. For me in the 1960s that position was one of extreme negligence. But it was more than that. As I looked back at history, I couldn't help but see that the white evangelical church in America, the one group of people in this country who claimed to have an access to the "words of Life," the Word of God and the message of salvation by faith in Jesus Christ, had historically neglected and left untouched what has become one of the largest untouched mission fields in human history: the black community in America. The man in the gas chamber has paid the price for his transgressions. But who will pay the price and what is the price of a race of souls?

You see, for the most part black people in this country have never really had full and complete access to the gospel and the whole body of biblical truth. To begin with, black people were brought from sections of Africa where Christianity was virtually unknown.[1] They were separated without regard for sex or family and tribal affiliations,

---

[1] William L. Banks, *The Black Church in the U.S.* (Chicago: Moody Press, 1972), p. 10.

and generally prevented from preserving or using their native language or religious practices.[2] Any marriages were not really legal, but merely temporary relationships, "dependent upon the will of the white masters." [3] According to sociologist E. Franklin Frazier, slavery "tended to loosen all social bonds among them and to destroy the traditional basis of social cohesion." [4]

The neglect of black people by Christians began early in American history. By the time of the American Revolution, "there were nearly 700,000 Negro slaves here, and about 59,000 free blacks. The proportion of Negroes to whites was at an all-time high of 19.3% in 1790." [5] Yet, although so many of those Europeans who had come to this country had come seeking the free pursuit of their Christian faith, there was almost no attempt to share the gospel with the black man during his first hundred years in this country.[6] Only a very small proportion of slaves in the American colonies could be counted as even nominal Christians.[7]

One of the reasons for this nonevangelism was that it was believed (and in fact was law under the statutes of England [8]) that a slave was no longer a slave when he became a Christian.[9] This problem was "solved" when, in the 1700s, Maryland and Virginia began a trend by passing laws "to the effect that Christian baptism did not confer freedom upon the slaves." [10] Freedom from sin did not constitute freedom from slavery.

The first period—and high point—of the evangelization of black people came during the Great Awakening, led by men like Jonathan Edwards and George Whitefield, when large numbers of blacks were reached through revivals and tent meetings. The Baptists and Methodists, because they required no educational qualifications for their ministers, made the most headway in the black community. It was during this period that one of the first black churches in Mississippi was founded in 1805 by Joseph Willis, a free black man. It was a Baptist church located in Mound Bayou. Black people did sit in the galleries of white churches in this era, and there were black churches pastored by white ministers, but the trend from the beginning was toward separate black churches. Yet in all but a few churches, white

[2] E. Franklin Frazier, *The Negro Church in America* (New York: Schocken Books, 1974), pp. 10–11.

[3] Ibid., p. 13.   [4] Ibid., p. 11   [5] Banks, p. 12.   [6] Ibid., p. 14.

[7] Frazier, p. 15.   [8] Ibid., p. 26.   [9] Banks, p. 15.

[10] Frazier, p. 26; Banks, p. 16.

control or supervision was maintained. Early in its development, racial prejudice then set the black church apart from the white, limiting it to the educational level of its new leaders, many times not far removed from slavery themselves, and often with only verbal training in the Bible. "In the South, where slavery was the normal condition of the Negro," the status of the Negro was assumed to be inferior, or "as the Supreme Court of Mississippi stated that the laws of the State 'presume a Negro prima facie [at first sight] to be a slave.' " [11]

The period that followed the few years of evangelization was about the worst in the history of the black church. William L. Banks, former professor at Moody Bible Institute and black teacher and theologian, outlines this period perfectly in his book, *The Black Church in the U.S.* These were the pre-Civil War years. There was an increased demand for cotton and consequently an increased value on slaves. There was a change in attitudes, the North becoming more staunch in its abolitionism, the white church in the South more proslavery. And there was a growing fear of a slave revolt, fueled by actual, bloody revolts led by men like Nat Turner. The result was that great restrictions were placed on black religion in the South. Negro preachers were outlawed and it became a crime to teach blacks to read or write. Except for a few courageous abolitionists, this ended Protestant participation in the sharing of the gospel or the education of black people.

An example of some of the stringent laws enacted throughout the South is a Mississippi law passed in 1823 which made it unlawful for six or more black people to meet for educational purposes. "Meetings for religious purposes," records Banks, "required the permission of the master. Even then a recognized white minister or two reputable whites had to be present." [12] The result was that only a few blacks ever responded to the claims of the gospel. Many of these were, of course, living as free men and women in the North.

These were times of great violence, of a demand for slaves so out of proportion to the supply that many white owners developed lucrative slave-breeding practices, and of a demoralization of the black man which included the development of a white theology biblically supporting the slaves' inferiority and position of bondage.

On this very weak base, with its partial grasp of biblical truth, the black church began to develop. And I thank God for its development, for the church became one of the only institutions where black peo-

---

[11] Frazier, p. 31.　　[12] Banks, p. 29.

ple could express themselves or even meet together. The black church today is criticized for its emotionalism and for its missing emphasis on doctrine. But during the years of suffering, it became the only stronghold for a people, and possibly the only means by which black people could maintain their sanity and emotional stability in a society that threatened to crush their humanity. Frazier comments that "Negroes . . . found in the fiery message of salvation a hope and a prospect of escape from their earthly woes. Moreover, the emphasis which the preacher placed on feeling as a sign of conversion found a ready response in the slaves who were repressed in so many ways. . . . The slaves, who had been torn from their homeland and kinsmen and friends and whose cultural heritage was lost, were isolated and broken men, so to speak. In the emotionalism . . . some social solidarity, even if temporary, was achieved." [13]

We see the importance of the black church emerging during the period of Reconstruction and up to the First World War. This was also a time of white Protestant negligence and of white cruelty. In the first year of the 1900s, one hundred lynchings of black people were recorded. This was the time of the rise of the Ku Klux Klan. And yet the black church grew amazingly. Under slavery the church had had to be an "invisible institution," but now it became visible. Banks says that "through the church came social cohesion, self-expression, recognition, and leadership. Self-respect and pride were stimulated and preserved and education was promoted. As nothing else, the church became the Negro's very own. It was the most powerful organization of the black man in America." [14] "Barred from full and equal participation in any of the public institutions of the country and not permitted to develop their own in most realms of life, American Negroes were 'free'—in an ironic sense—to develop their own . . . religious life." [15]

As W. E. B. DuBois put it in 1903, "One can see in the Negro church today, reproduced in microcosm, all that great world from which the Negro is cut off by color prejudice and social condition." [16] That statement, related to most areas of Mississippi, brings us up to date with the development of the black church. There was later the mass migration to the North and the rise of the storefront churches and the cults like Father Divine and the Black Muslims. But in the

---

[13] Frazier, p. 16.   [14] Banks, p. 45.   [15] Frazier, p. 5.
[16] Banks, p. 39.

rural areas of Mississippi, there was no other institution that could afford them the basic freedom needed for social interaction.

With a few exceptions—some preachers during the Great Awakening, the small heroic minority of people involved in the Abolitionist movement, and later those few white protestants who helped develop a handful of black schools—there has been, since the original enslavement of the black man in America, no systematic, concerted effort on the part of evangelical white Christians to evangelize or to develop any sort of community uplift in the black community. This is the historic negligence which we faced as the civil rights movement spread across the country and as we prayed that it would some day come to Simpson County.

In fact the civil rights movement probably marks a low point in evangelical involvement in the black community and possibly the lowest level of evangelical conscience in this country. This happened for a number of reasons. First, there was ignorance of the situation in the black community because of long-term neglect. But on top of this there was the polarization between the white Christians who were theologically either liberal or conservative. This division had been brewing since before the beginning of the twentieth century with the rise of the Social Gospel movement and confrontations like the Scopes trial. Now, the issue of civil rights was sweeping the country, polarizing these two segments of the church even more intensely. And what happened is that the liberals got involved, and the evangelicals withdrew.

The polarization was increased by the fact that the churches in the South with the highest regard for the authority of Scripture were the white churches, the church which stood for segregation and discrimination. On the other hand, the black church, being the central institution in the black community, saw most of the leaders of the movement emerge from its membership. It was not unusual for white fundamentalist or evangelical churches to look down on the black church and fault it for its lack of scriptural background. The issue therefore shifted from justice to theological correctness.

As I saw it, the white church had traditionally thought that to speak the Word of God was more important than living it out. The black church, on the other hand, did not have the educational understanding of Scripture, but in many cases struggled to live it out. And it's very difficult for someone used to living out the gospel without an educated background to come up to the approval of those who put listening before living. The person concerned with living it out will make many mistakes. But all the person primarily concerned with listening and speaking has to do is listen for correctness.

But the issue that polarized the evangelical church away from the black community, the issue with the most emotional impact, was the fear that the black human rights struggle in America might be a communist conspiracy. This accusation originated in three main arenas. First, was what I would call the extreme racist who felt in the movement a general weakening of the position that had allowed him to feel superior. This included those business interests that could be severely set back if they lost the biggest pool of cheap labor in American history. Second, were the radical fundamentalists like Carl McIntire who merged God and country and believed that to raise questions about justice in America was unpatriotic and unchristian. And third, were many of the missionaries who had come back from the mission field after World War II. This third and unlikely group was most influenced by a pattern of thinking that affected all three groups, the idea that there was an international communist takeover in black countries all over the world.

After World War II we saw a great surge of nationalism sweep the countries of the Third World. We heard for the first time things like "India for the Indians," "Egypt for the Egyptians," and "Africa for the Africans." And many countries succeeded after the war in liberating themselves from the dependence on foreign rule. The same thing is going on currently in Rhodesia and South Africa. The foreign governments of the West had used many of these lands for their sources of cheap raw materials. The nationalists coming to power saw the missionaries from the West as a part of the whole system of exploitation. Communist governments, anxious to be a part of any movement against the West, prudently invested in the revolutionary governments of countries which, many times by the sheer weight of numbers, were eventually going to rule themselves anyway. For them it was a sure bet. But these movements themselves originated in nationalism, not communism, which was still a European and Asian phenomenon.

But the missionaries who were out of jobs and forced to come home, when faced with the civil rights movement among black people in this country a decade or so later, interpreted it in the same terms they had interpreted very different sorts of movements in foreign countries: that it was communist inspired. And in 1954, when the movement started, the country was ripe for that type of propaganda.

But the movement was not communist inspired, because justice is not communist inspired, nor is it inspired by citizenship in any country. Justice is inspired by God, and those in this country who claimed to have the truth that could reveal real justice, the white evangelical Christians, got themselves in an ideological box that left them without a witness in the black community. So many Christians that I've had the privilege to speak to, especially in the 1960s, have asked me, "Do you think Dr. Martin Luther King is a Christian?" or "Do you think Dr. King is a communist?" I could never understand these questions and have an even more difficult time now, after Watergate. It's an ironic paradox. On one hand, you have a man who speaks the truth with force and acts upon it in a way that demands that I think about what he is saying—and people try to make him a communist. On the other hand, you have a man who speaks things which are not true and who acts deceitfully, and yet people think it so important to make him a Christian. I do not know whether Martin Luther King or Richard Nixon were Christians. Only God knows their hearts. But I do know that the things which Martin Luther King talked about were true, because I saw them every day in Simpson County—the prejudice, the injustice, the suffering and beating. Whether he used it like I did or not, I had my own Bible and I could check out what he said, and to me the justice which he called for was the same justice I heard Amos and Jeremiah and Isaiah and Jesus calling for.

God gave us a few friends in evangelical churches who broke away from the popular propaganda against the civil rights movement and who joined with the Fishermen in Monrovia in support of our work. If we had not had these people, Voice of Calvary Ministries would never have been born. I praise God for these few people who as Christians, many of them white, have stayed with us and are even now stepping out in courage to influence in love their brothers and sisters.

Today the big question I am asked is, "Do you think things are changing or getting better?" I would have to say, "Yes." I think there is more energy building up now in the evangelical church around social concern and the physical needs of the poor than perhaps anytime since the early 1800s. But it's still mostly on the verbal level, especially as it relates to this country. I think we are seeing in organizations like World Vision an attempt at a comprehensive approach to poverty, and doing that as a Christian witness. That's powerful. But churches for the most part still give 90 to 95 percent of their mission budget to work in foreign missions. On the conference level or the fellowship level, I think we are beginning to see breakthroughs in relationships between blacks and whites.

But there are still many white churches today that will turn away black people. It is too bad that the church has to be the last stronghold. But in Billy Graham's 1975 Jackson Crusade, in the 1976 Mississippi Faith at Work Conference, and in relationships that Voice of Calvary is developing with local pastors, bridges are being built and relationships are developing.

The question still remains, however, whether this verbal concern can be mobilized around meeting very real needs. The twin priorities in the black community are evangelism and meeting human need. Historically the evangelical church has failed at both. One reason so much money is given to meet these needs on the foreign field and not in this country, and one reason why it will be so difficult for the evangelical churches in this country to really face the victims among black people here in America, is that in facing the victim who is near us, we are implicated by his condition and therefore can feel guilty.

There are two places where we as the evangelical church can get involved but still lose our witness in the black community. The first is cheap evangelism. If we create a style of evangelism that maintains our distance from the people and their needs—using radio or tracts on the street corner or television or even busing the folks into our comfortable churches—then we will fall short of the real evangelism we talked about. Really sharing the Good News—real evangelism—brings me face to face with whole people and all their needs and leads, without exception, to God's love in me reaching out to meet those needs.

If we make our evangelism real, we can still fall short of a real witness by participating in cheap involvement. Cheap involvement is charity, meeting some random symptoms a person has without getting down to the real needs, without asking those difficult questions about why those needs are there, what causes them, and how we get down to the root of the problems. With cheap involvement I can be satisfied by saying that "Jesus is the answer" and give a little charity. With real involvement and social action I say also that "Jesus is the question," that as Lord he can ask those heavy questions that get to the heart of the problem and ultimately lead us to deal with whole systems and structures of sin.

I heard Dr. Lewis Smedes from Fuller Theological Seminary illustrate the idea of questioning from the story of the Good Samaritan. What if the week after the Samaritan picked up the wounded man, he came again down that same road toward Jericho and found another victim? What would he have done? Well, said Dr. Smedes, he probably would have done the same thing he did with the first man: he'd treat his wounds and put him up in the local inn. But what if this happened again, and even a fourth time, then a fifth time? Don't you think that after taking care of the victims, the Samaritan would have gone down to the authorities who had jurisdiction over the road and complained that it was a hazard? Would he have asked some questions, and maybe even suggested that the road be made safer, either by straightening out some of the curves where thieves could hide, or by patrolling it with guards, or if in modern times, installing some streetlights and some emergency call boxes and asking the highway patrol to police it more carefully?

The point is that the same love that motivates us to preach the gospel and meet some basic needs should also motivate us toward getting behind the needs to their causes.

But to allow the Lord to lead us in this type of questioning is difficult, because the questions don't stop with the structures of society that make victims out of people. The questions continue right down into our lives, into our own homes, into the ways that we personally participate in and benefit from the way the structures are set up. It is painful because we might discover that we are guilty of being a part of an unjust system.

It is time now for evangelical Christians to risk that pain and move beyond cheap evangelism and cheap social action in the black and poor communities in this country. I have talked with many evangelical Christians who are on the brink of doing just that but hesitate. And the question they ask is this: "How can we reach the black community as white Christians?"

This question in itself betrays a noncommitment to the problems. Sure, the problem of reaching the black community with the gospel is massive, and the problem of reaching the black community's needs is even more massive. But the question that I have is this: Why do white people, who have access to the most sophisticated technology and the most well-developed personal and economic resources in the history of mankind, come to black people and ask them how to solve the problem? Nobody looked to the black community to come up with the answer of how to get to the moon. Yet, that was an unanswerable problem, solved only by a total commitment of resources. That same type of commitment could begin to deal with some of the problems in the black community. To say to black people, "Heal yourselves," or "How do you plan to develop yourselves and your community?" is a subtle form of blaming the victim for his own wounds. It is passing the victim on the road and saying, "I'm not responsible for him because he was stupid enough to walk this dangerous road at night."

In the late 1960s I was more damaged than I am now. The Lord has done a lot of healing in my life. We had begun a work with virtually no support, but had won the support of a few people. We saw that the depth of poverty needed some massive, multifaceted attacks with technology to back them up. We saw that we were not going to get a lot of support from people with that technology, but we determined that that was not going to stop us, we were going to do it.

At this point the deep needs of black people were my primary concern. Our whole ministry was focused on the black community. It would be several years before God would give me a burden for the deep needs among people in the white community, needs for reconciliation and love. It would be several years before I realized that it would not be possible to deal with one and not the other, and that the models of reconciliation and brotherhood that would need to be built among whites would be the basis for real community development in the black neighborhood. No, at this point in our ministry, we had come to know the depth of the problem and were now looking for a strategy through which to attack and dismantle the whole, unwieldy cycle that was destroying our people.

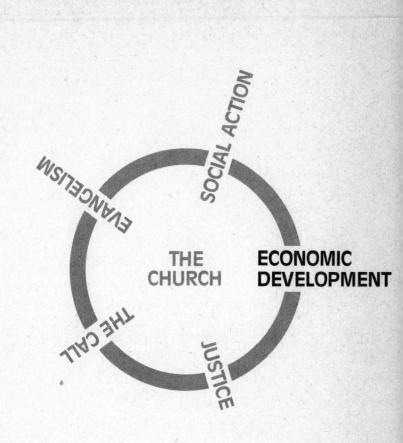

SOCIAL ACTION

EVANGELISM

THE
CHURCH

ECONOMIC
DEVELOPMENT

THE CALL

JUSTICE

Part Four

12.

The Movement

Sit-ins were· taking place at lunch counters and in public buildings all over the South in 1960, the year we returned to Mississippi. In 1961 black and white people from the North traveled south by bus during the summer, attempting to integrate the buses and bus stations. They were called "Freedom Riders." In September of 1962, James Meredith, a black Air Force veteran, attempted to enroll at the University of Mississippi. Mississippi Governor Ross Barnett attempted to prevent Meredith from entering. Rioting broke out, killing two people. President Kennedy ordered federal marshals in to insure order, and James Meredith finally enrolled.

Civil rights activities continued throughout the South, including Jackson, Mississippi, and a handful of small rural Mississippi towns. On June 11, 1963, Medgar Evers, field secretary of the NAACP, was killed in an ambush near his Jackson home. In August of 1963, two hundred thousand people from all over the country marched on Washington, D.C., in what one history book describes as "the most massive and orderly day of protest in American history."

On July 2, 1964, the Civil Rights Act of 1964 was signed into law by President Lyndon Johnson. It was the strongest civil rights act since Reconstruction and had passed with large majorities in both houses of Congress. It provided that all citizens should have equal access to public facilities such as libraries and parks and to private businesses serving the public, like restaurants and hotels and theaters. It said no to discrimination in employment or education and strengthened guarantees of the right to vote.

Later that summer of '64, in Philadelphia, Mississippi, a small town outside of Meridian, three civil rights workers—James Chaney, Andrew Goodman, and Michael Schwerner, were missing. A giant manhunt led by the FBI finally discovered their bodies. They had been buried beneath an earthen dam by members of the Ku Klux Klan led by Neshoba County sheriff deputies.

Also that summer at the Democratic National Convention in Atlantic City, Fannie Lou Hamer, Aaron Henry, and Bob Moses, all black Mississippians, led a delegation that asked to be recognized over the all-white delegation from Mississippi, bringing national attention to problems in the state.

The next summer, June 1965, President Johnson said in a speech at Hampton Institute, "In far too many ways, American Negroes have been another nation, deprived of freedom, crippled by hatred, the doors of opportunity closed to hope." In July, fierce rioting broke out in the Watts district of Los Angeles, California. By the time the smoke disappeared, 34 people lay dead, 900 were injured, 100 million dollars of damage was suffered. A growing white backlash began to whip across the country.

On April 4, 1968, Dr. Martin Luther King, Jr., was killed, shot to death on the balcony of his hotel room in Memphis.

Mississippi, during the civil rights movement, was always looked at as the most backward, the most entrenched, the most reactionary state in the South. And it was. Even today, out in the rural places, there are whole counties and communities never touched by the movement where black people still go to the back door of the restaurants for their food and still cannot hold good jobs. Black people still suffer under racism and discrimination in rural communities. Just recently, a man named Robert James Miller, a black candidate who had run for constable in Madison County, detailed a beating he said he received at the hands of Mississippi Highway patrolmen in Canton, Mississippi. An article reporting the story appeared on page 5 of the November 11, 1975, *Clarion Ledger,* Jackson's daily newspaper. "Inside the jail," the paper reports of Miller, "he was beaten and told to leave town by officers."

It was way into the movement before Simpson County began to feel the effects of any of the legislation and awareness that had been provoking the rest of the country for over ten years. But there was a terrible tension in Mendenhall, almost to the point where you had to whisper on the streets. The whole state was like a garrison, and the radio and TV were just filled with murders and police and violence.

We prayed for the civil rights movement to come to Simpson County as earnestly as we prayed for the kids and adults we shared with to become Christians. In 1964 some civil rights workers, a couple of white people, had tried to come to the county, and stayed with us for a while. But being from a Jewish background, they weren't heavily impressed with me. But it didn't matter. My meditation was on how the movement could begin in Simpson County.

Those first workers, although they knew folks needed freedom, they just didn't know what to do with themselves. They couldn't get a base in the black community, they didn't even have places to stay. Few black folks would let any white folks stay in their house. They were hearing all this stuff about people's houses getting burned down and so they were afraid.

Finally, in 1965, there was a definite program developing around voter registration. We gave John Longstreet, the white coordinator for Simpson County, free use of our facilities and house. I'd go around with him and visit. I began to bring in all of the key civil rights speakers in the state. I made friends with Claude Ramsey of the AFL-CIO and Rims Barber of the Delta Ministry and Allan Johnson, a very powerful black Methodist minister. Charles Evers came too. One thing about Charles, he could always fill up the place. We became close friends—of course, he became so popular that it was hard to maintain a friendship, especially with all his speaking. But they all came and the people began to listen.

It was frightening, though. Churches were being burned down all over Mississippi for doing what we were doing. In fact we were moving around to the churches with speakers and talking, but the insurance people throughout Simpson County told the churches that they would have to quit having the meetings about voter registration and things like that or their fire insurance policies would be canceled. So we brought the meetings back to VOC.

The voter registration really got under way in 1966. When the federal marshals came to set up an office where they could register the black citizens, nobody would rent them office space. Finally, they had to take some plywood and wall in the loading dock of the post office, which was the only federally owned property in town. So we began to bring in black voters by the van-load to register. The drivers would get threats from whites they'd meet. In fact, we'd never let someone go out to gather people alone. But our efforts were bearing fruit. One year Brother Jesse Newsome was awarded a citation for being one of the people who registered the most voters in the state— over one thousand by himself.

In 1966 we had a historic meeting. We came up with the names of the hundred most committed black people in the county, and I invited them to a meeting at my house next to the church. About sixty-five or seventy came. We talked late into the night and finally organized the Simpson County Civic League, electing Mr. Nathaniel

Rubin the chairman. That was the beginning of a real movement, a popular movement in Simpson County.

The first real sign of the movement was the integration of the theatres and cafes and public pools. Teams of people would go out, including Herbert Jones who led some. I can't explain the sense of unity and hope this "integrating" gave to the people.

By this time we had organized Headstart. Now, my wife wanted Headstart for the kids. But I wanted it for another reason. As the civil rights movement began to develop—voter registration, integration, and other things—right away I began to think of economics. I guess it was my nature. I knew that integration and voting were important. But people were suffering from poverty, and part of that poverty was a long-term powerlessness as a people. It was the economics of the society that kept black people so hypocritical, that kept them from supporting the movement with all of their strength. Economics kept people being "Uncle Toms." The "Tom" is the guy who looks out and sees the economic reality, senses his powerlessness to deal with that reality, and then decides to support the way things are and not rock the boat. And the economic reality is that the white man owns and controls the institutions. The "Tom" sees that he can only live and survive and maintain what he has if he agrees with the white man.

So *my* motive for organizing Headstart was economic—it would be the strongest black economic base in the community. But I began to see that the Headstart program itself was stop-gap. It was a program that community people couldn't control. It could be cut off by people outside the community. It had guidelines set up by people outside the community. It didn't create a sense of ownership; everything was always rented so if the funds were someday cut, it wouldn't leave anything in the community. And it did very little training in real, marketable skills. So I was struggling with this whole idea of what we could do economically. Headstart had brought an economic base into the community, and Voice of Calvary was the center of that base in Simpson County, a center for employment.

This is what I was thinking about as I'd drive around to the schools in 1967. One day that summer I picked up a flyer at the little civil rights office that we had set up in Mendenhall. It said something like, "If you are into economics, if you want to organize your own business, come and learn about cooperatives," and mentioned a meeting that Saturday in Jackson. I didn't know what a cooperative was, so I went to the meeting and met people like Jesse Morris from Jackson, Father A. J. McKnight from Louisiana, Howard Baily from Holmes County, Mississippi, and John Zippert, who would all later become some of my closest friends.

Jesse Morris had been one of the big civil rights organizers in the state. He was good friends with Rap Brown and Stokely Carmichael. And what he and Harry Bouy and some others had done was to organize Liberty House and the poor people's co-ops. First, they had recruited some of the best people out of CORE, the Congress of Racial Equality, and SNCC, the Student Nonviolent Coordinating Committee. That's one thing about Jesse, he has always been able to get the best people. Then they had gone back out into these poor rural communities and trained people out there to sew. Liberty House became a giant training organization, sending patterns for clothes and purses and handicrafts out to these folks in Canton and McComb and West Point and places where people had never had jobs before, and training them how to put them together. Then it became a massive marketing center, buying back the handicrafts from the network of co-ops and selling them by direct mail all over the country and through outlets in New York and other cities. So that was one co-op that at that time was highly successful. Changes in the market and economy have lately caused it to fold.

Father McKnight, a black Catholic leader, talked about his experience. He had gone into Louisiana about ten years earlier and had tried an educational program just like we had started, except even more with adults—like our Bible Institute. He had gone out into the community of Lafayette and had developed from high school some young blacks who would later become the leaders of the cooperative movement. He would take them out to his adults to hold educational meetings. He discovered the people couldn't read and thought all they wanted to do was to learn how to read. So he and his core of young students, now graduated from high school, began teaching people to read. He went out to teach but the people came thinking they could get jobs. Their concern for jobs overshadowed their desire to learn. So McKnight began meditating on how to create jobs, and that's when he fell upon the idea of starting co-ops. At that point in his talk there wasn't one person in the room that could have identified with him more. It was like we were wearing the same pair of shoes.

But the story went on, how they had started a co-op called

Southern Consumers, designed to help farmers buy fertilizer and
supplies. It spread swift and fast. They began making fruitcakes and
pretty soon opened a bakery. They began their own gas station.

Then early that very year of '67, the Ford Foundation gave Mac
a $700,000 grant for two years to begin organizing and developing
co-ops throughout the South. He wanted, he said, to set up pilot
programs in four or five states, and what he needed were the people
to do the organizing and the grass-roots work. He asked any of us
who were interested to come up afterwards and interview for a
workshop in Louisiana that September. I went up and interviewed.

The workshop lasted three weeks, and if it had been any other
time but early September, my commitments to the schools would
have kept me from going. They taught us all about the basic principles of a cooperative. They showed us how poor people could
organize together and have an enterprise of their own in the community. After the workshop, McKnight and the others asked me if
I would be organizer for Simpson County. I said yes. There were
seventeen workers for Mississippi. Jackson was going to be our
urban model, creating around Liberty House a model of economic
development.

As I saw it, the civil rights movement was taking a whole new
direction, a creative direction. It was moving toward development,
one whole segment investing in Headstart, another beginning to set
up cooperatives. I was seeing the roots begin to form for all the
other movements in the black struggle—all economic in nature but
with different sources and different objectives. There would be the
development of the massive government welfare programs and then
their eventual demise. There would be the rise in black, individual-
istic capitalism, good for those who could make it. There would be
the rise in black nationalism and movements like the Republic of
New Africa, calling for a whole separate national identity and economic system for black people. And there would be the movement
for wholistic community development. None would have great success. Some would fail greatly, others would provide an inspiration,
a hope for an alternative. But it was here, in the beginnings of the
black cooperative movement that I saw us standing at a very crucial
time in history.

We all went back home from that September meeting in 1967
fired up to do something in our communities. That fall was when
Spencer, Joanie, Kathy Pruitt and a couple other kids became the

first black students to integrate the public schools. It wasn't an all-out integration at first, just a voluntary integration, and most folks were scared and unwilling to make the move.

The pressure on our kids was fantastic. Spence would come home and Vera Mae would ask him how school was. He'd say, "Mama, I don't want to say much because all it would do would worry you." He'd stand in line in the cafeteria and immediately all the other students would move to a distance. He'd sit down at the library or at a lunch table and other students would get up and move to another table. He'd tell us about how, during chapel, they'd have some white preachers come and give real, down-to-earth gospel messages where kids would rededicate their lives to Christ, but it never changed their attitudes toward him or any of the blacks.

The next fall, we sent Spencer and Joanie to California for a semester. The second semester Spencer went back to Harper High, the black school, and Joanie went to Piney Woods School close by. Two years later, in the fall of 1970, the schools were totally integrated.

We had another co-op meeting in December of 1967, and they asked me if I would work full-time for the co-ops. They wanted to give me over $300 a month, which was pretty tempting. But I told them I wouldn't take the money, that I would work in Simpson County, because I had my school obligations and Bible classes to attend to. They told me that they would give me $30 a week for gas, and I began to visit different parts of the state on Fridays and Saturdays when I didn't have any classes. But as integration increased, and as Spencer and Joanie were the first to integrate, our name became identified with civil rights, and opportunities to teach the Bible in the schools, now under predominantly white authority, began drying up.

Meanwhile, I began getting together with people from Simpson County around the idea of starting some co-ops. Forty of us formed the Simpson County Development Corporation, put $10 each into a pot, and on the basis of our own resources and the fact we were a co-op, qualified for a special loan of $85,000 from the Farmer's Home Administration to build five duplex houses. So began the Simpson County Housing Co-op. The co-op has run since then, the rent taking care of the note. We still rent out a three-bedroom place for $60 a month. Our big breakthrough in housing was getting the county's first black FHA man. When we got him, it was almost like he came to work for us. It became much easier for black people to get those low-interest loans available from FHA for building and remodeling houses, and it eventually meant the construction of pretty modern homes sandwiched in between the shacks and shanties in the black section of town.

By this time Father McKnight and I were becoming close friends. He would come up and visit us from Louisiana. As they would hold more meetings of people in the state, they discovered that they needed someone to coordinate all of this. There was a lot of activity, but everybody was confused and frustrated. Many just didn't have the economic sense to put it together. They had been civil rights leaders, the most dynamic people in Mississippi, but they didn't have the management or economic know-how. They were spinning their wheels trying to get things going, but just blasting people out because they were used to high-pressure civil rights meetings. So around December of 1968, Mac asked me if I would become state director. I told him no, because of my obligations at the schools.

But then two things happened. First, Donald Jackson, who has since changed his name to Muhammed Kenyatta, joined the co-operative movement from Headstart. He had been one of the educational directors and so he knew the state real well and understood organization. But he saw that Headstart was becoming a bureaucratic institution that couldn't effect much change in the community. Second, our school work was getting shakier every month with integration. By the beginning of the 1969 school year and integration in Mendenhall, the black schools were virtually closed. So, I said I'd be co-director of the cooperative movement for the state with Donald Jackson.

Donald and Ed Coles, a graduate of Jackson State, and I began to do a lot of traveling. I had this little red Volkswagen that we just tore up during those months and years going over those highways and country dirt roads that crisscrossed the Delta and wound through the hill country. We worked with co-ops in Mound Bayou, Belzoni, West Point, Lexington, Choctaw County, just all over the state and in Tallulah, Louisiana. Most of them were farming co-ops, but there were also a catfish co-op, a woodworking co-op, a number of co-operative stores like in West Point and Lexington. We also started one in Mendenhall to go along with our fertilizer co-op. There was also a brick making co-op and a cannery. We would travel all over the state, holding meetings, staying up until late at night in some cement block warehouse with a tin roof. We really got with the people. Most of the time I would stay with folks in the community.

It was a great time in my life. It really taught me some of the harsh realities of community organizing—about how people will want to come in and pimp off of what you are doing, or how the white people in power will try to co-opt what you're doing and render it meaningless, or bad talk you or the co-op to black folks that work for them and try to put you out of business.

After about six months, Don Jackson left as director to be a part of drawing up the Black Manifesto. He was going through a lot of thoughts, leaning more and more heavily toward black nationalism. He is one of the signers of the Manifesto which called white people to pay reparations for the years black people had been enslaved. This happened in 1969, around the time when the Southern Cooperative Development Program that McKnight ran, and the Federation of Southern Cooperatives, an organization of the co-ops after they were formed, were talking about merging. The government gave the Federation a massive grant of two million dollars which speeded up the merger, and I became state director for both the Federation and the Development Program.

Then at the end of 1969, around Christmas, I was taking Doug Huemmer up to the store in Mendenhall. He was going to go back home to California for the holidays and wanted to get his mother a jar of country cane syrup. When we got in the store, we saw Garland Wilkes yelling at the cashier about a check that the cashier refused to accept. He was drunk, that was obvious. We knew this meant trouble, so we quickly persuaded Garland out to the Volkswagen and drove off. I guess the clerk had called the police, though, because before we could get very far past the tracks and down into the black community, a local policeman was behind us pulling us over. He arrested Garland for public drunkenness, even though we promised to take him home. We told Garland we'd check out about bail and stuff.

When I got back down to VOC I learned that earlier that very day a young man named Roy Berry had been dragged by sheriff's deputies out of his church, beaten up and put behind bars. They claimed he was making phone calls to a white woman, asking her for a date. We all were afraid the same thing would happen to Garland.

There were a lot of people at the church practicing for a Christmas program. About seventeen of us decided to go to city hall and find out how they were charging Garland and if he was safe.

When our cars pulled into the parking lot of city hall, the chief of police in Mendenhall came out to meet us. One of the kids said, "Where's Garland? Have you beat up Garland?" The chief pointed to Garland sitting in the squad car parked on the other side of the lot. We could tell he hadn't been beaten. Then we asked about Roy Berry. "We haven't laid a hand on him," he said. "The Simpson County sheriff arrested him, not the police. Go over to the jailhouse and see him for yourself."

So, we all went up the street to the jailhouse to see Roy Berry. When we got to the jail, the jailer felt threatened. I could see him tighten up. Later, when we finally got to see Roy Berry, I could see why. Although he wasn't cut or bloody, Roy's face was bruised, swollen and sort of pulpy. He *had* been beaten.

But because he felt threatened, the jailer did some very stupid things. After he discovered we were not going to leave until we were satisfied that Berry was safe, he told us we were all under arrest. When he opened the iron gate to the cells, Doug stepped forward a little and the man grabbed him and pushed and wrestled him into the cellblock. I was standing close to the gate and walked in after Doug. That was all the kids needed. Every one followed us into jail. The gate closed behind us. The bolt clanked into position. We were locked in.

That began the first open confrontation between black people and the white community in the history of Mendenhall. It was two days before Christmas, December 23, 1969.

13.

People Helping Themselves

In most discussions about working with the poor, self-help is usually lifted up as the key to success. And it is. Yet in the black community where ingrained economic and psychological dependence and unstable family and social structures have been a way of life for all the generations of black people in America, self-help becomes a difficult reality to grab hold of.

These interviews begin with the very old and end with one of the youngest members of the VOC family. These are people who have grabbed hold of the reality.

For a real movement of Christians to affect a community it needs the power and motivation of God, it demands a biblical strategy, it requires an economic base. But most important, the movement must have people who have invested their lives in making real their beliefs.

Mr. Buckley begins by sharing some of the dynamics of black culture and some of the experiences in his upbringing that made him a person committed to self-help.

The vision Perkins came back to Simpson County for was a God-given vision. Before black folks had only been freed by war. He came with a vision to free them by love, the love of God. But our folk couldn't see it. They was too far back to see.

In many ways our black folks is in worser shape than the white. They won't accept it but it's so. They kill more of one another than anybody. They're against each other. If the black folks had got organized when Rev. Perkins come in here they could of fell in behind. But instead they'd go with the white people, the folks that was cheatin' them and keeping them down. They always thought that the white folks were more for them than anybody. That is really what was worse than anything. They actually followed and cared more about what the white man said than about any colored.

What Rev. Perkins was doing naturally got the white folks against him. Then the white folks would go to the blacks and let them know that the thing couldn't stand cause they didn't have no money. They told 'em just someone coming in wouldn't do no

115

good. They told 'em that these white volunteers coming in to the Voice of Calvary were dangerous people, bad folks. The folks were brainwashed, white people got them brainwashed. The majority of the colored people got in their mind they supposed to be under white folks. And if white folks go and give a few blacks a little authority, that creates all sorts of jealousy and division.

Let me see if I can picture this for you from my own experience. I recollect I got hurt on a job working cutting crossties for a white man. My leg got broke real bad and I just could get around with crutches.

The man came to me and said, "Now, you look like you can sorta get about a little. I can give you a little bit, something to help you out because you got your children. I'll give you a job and all you have to do is go up and down the line."

I would stay in the yard and walk up and down the bunches of ties and number them by crew, hammering the number into one of the ties.

Well, that worked for about two or three weeks, but then they moved me out to work on the skidder lines. These were crews cutting ties out in the woods. He had me walking up and down the lines hammering ties. The job on crutches was harder work than cutting ties. It was one of those jobs where you helt a long book that had a pencil in it and I could stick it in my pocket and make me look like a big man. I worked for about a week and noticed he didn't raise my wages.

The second week when I carried the time in, I told him, "Now you done changed my job and put me back in the woods, but you haven't raised my wages back any."

When I said that he had a fit. "I tried to help you and you didn't appreciate it," he said. "I wasn't doing anything but trying to help you."

I said, "It wasn't helping me by putting me out in the woods going down those skidder lines with a broken leg. I can go out there and cut ties and make as much in two hours than I make here in a whole day. You can't raise that?"

"No," he said.

I just throwed him his book and said, "I can't work for that."

Well, a black man came and took the same job, but he gave him more money than he gave me—a little bit more. And the man stayed because I'll tell you what he was. He liked the book with the pencil. He would make those men on the skidder lines do much more work, making them cut down trees that were too small for ties just to make sure they couldn't get a tie out of 'em. He was just like the bossman. He was brainwashed. And that's

been a whole lot of our problem. We could of got someplace if
we could of got us to pull together.

I stayed with Perkins. I could see the vision. But it was because
I had always done operated my own farm. I never was handled
by white people. And the white people always have recognized
a man when he was a man, if he didn't have somebody to block
him.

You see my mother and father were born to slave parents who
had a sense of the land. My father bought him forty acres and
after he died my mother worked us and her hard to pay it off.
She was interested in us having a certain amount of independence.
We have always been on land of our own.

Now besides independence, I grew up with a sense of self-
sufficiency. My daddy farmed, taught school, was a cobbler who
could fix shoes. He would take wood and make his own pegs to
go into them shoes. He could take shucks from over the corn and
make collars for horses. If you took care you could use them for
two years. He'd make baskets . . . well, just anything on the farm
he could make it.

But my point is this: my upbringing kept me from being brainwashed.

What's happening now is that now there are more white people
than a little speaking for Perkins. I'm talking about in Mendenhall too. They think he has done a great something here in
Simpson County. And you watch, some of them black folks who
have been holdin' out will come around when they see the whites
speaking good about him. That's just the way they is.

In a poor community the motivation for helping ourselves must
come out of more than just self-interest. There must be a deep and
strong commitment to each other, to unity. If there isn't, division
will eat up any movement you try to get going. When we began to
organize ourselves around some economic project like the co-op
store and the co-op housing project, many people came together and
rallied around. But the pressure caused by doing something creative
in the area of economics coupled with the pressure of black people
getting the vote for the first time since Reconstruction caused many
to leave us and some to turn against us.

Mitchell Hayes was one of the first people involved in civil rights
who helped to form the first NAACP in Simpson County. And to use
words of his own, "he never veered, neither to the right or to the left"
from his commitment to his people and the struggle.

I don't remember when I first met Rev. Perkins. It was some-time in the late Sixties. I had heard about him all right. Some was for him and some against him just on the basis of what he preached. I remember talking with some people from one church who said, "Rev. Perkins is teaching the children idolatry." But when I asked them had they ever been to his classes, they said no.

I guess it was Brother Buckley who got me acquainted with him. After that we got closer and closer. That's what they call friendship. From that day till this we been together.

Out of all the leaders who rose up when the whole thing wound up there was only one man who had never veered and who took more punching to hold and stand as a man—that's Rev. Perkins.

Now there was a bunch of us who we thought walked hand in hand, locked together, where it looked like if one would fall the whole bunch would have to fall. Brother Buckley and Brother Newsome were two that stuck it through all the way. But some who even prayed with us later turned against us.

One of the high points for us was when we had to guard Rev. Perkins' house. Black people had just got a chance to vote and an election was coming up. We had all been working registering voters. This election was for Highway Commissioner and John D. Smith, who had been in for about twenty years was running against Shag Pyron. Well, Rev. Perkins went and talked to Smith and asked him if he would begin hiring blacks. If not, he said we would try to defeat him at the polls.

After this Rev. Perkins began receiving calls on his phone from white people. Nobody knows who the calls were made by, but it had to do with the election, there was no doubt of that. Finally one Sunday after church Rev. Perkins got a call telling him to be out of the county by 8:30 that night or they was going to kill him.

I remember that afternoon. I was on my way home from church and Rev. Perkins flagged me down on the road. He told me what happened and said he wasn't leaving. We began organizing a guard for his house that night.

There must have been thirty-five or forty men out there that night, all around Voice of Calvary. We was everywhere. There was no way somebody could have got to Rev. Perkins. We just told him, "Go upstairs and go to bed. And when it gets daylight you get in your car and go all over town—don't dodge anybody." There was some of us scattered around town the next day.

When daylight broke the next morning word of what happened had made it clear around to Hazelhurst and Crystal Springs. It was all over Magee and everywhere. And we ended up electing

Pyron who began hiring black people. After that night and some other things, people began to look up, black people began to speak.

We had decided to build a store. Actually we called it the Simpson County Civic League Building. I was in charge of getting the land together. I remember the appeal I made to the man we wanted to buy from. I said, "Uncle Dave, your children might be runnin' this place someday." Just the thought of a black-owned store was moving to people.

I became the manager of the store and of the housing we had developed. I collected rent and today we got $4,000 in the savings account of the housing. Everybody's paid up and nobody owes a cent.

In the store I remember I made change out of my pocket the first day. Since then and the time I left as manager we had $4,000 in the checking account and $3,000 in the savings. Since then the store has had to go out. It wasn't going to make it anymore and we got the health center and the thrift store now. But after our close-out sale and my last deposit of $500, we had enough money in the bank to pay off all the shareholders in the co-op. People who had bought shares at $5.00 could cash them in for $19.29.

Some joined us and stayed. Others quit. I'm just glad I stayed in this thing all the way through.

The greatest struggle in self-help development is leadership. God had blessed us with strong leadership from the older generation in the community. But I knew for change and development in the future there would have to be young leaders returning to apply their faith at home. For young people, especially educated young blacks, the big city and the high-paying job are almost too much competition for staying to minister in a rural community like Mendenhall. Two things spoke to people: the gospel and its call upon their lives, and the visible results—the Bible classes, the blocks and cement of the co-op. These two things could draw people to a commitment that went beyond their own individual goals. Dolphus Weary shares this in his testimony.

I think I was in my first year of seminary when I had an opportunity to travel with a Christian basketball team. While I was overseas it dawned on me as I was working there with people in Taiwan, the Philippines, and Hong Kong that there were people in Mississippi who needed to hear the gospel message. It was from that point that God really began to draw me back to Mississippi.

One reason I had in my mind for coming back was the vision—
that there was a place to come back to, there was a Voice of
Calvary. The second thing was the whole idea that we have a
whole segment of the people that have been overlooked. Why
should I go somewhere else? I need to start at home. It's many
times easier to look outward, to go to a faraway mission field.
For me it's been harder to be at home than it would have been
to carve out a ministry somewhere in the world at large, or say
in Birmingham or California. People know you and if they are
going to respect you you must earn it, it must be based on reality.
But once you have it you also have the trust of the people.

I think I've stayed at Voice of Calvary because I see the golden
objective of what we are about. Many times I feel like I am Voice
of Calvary. I've been through the struggles, the years, the times
when there was nothing. To see the development, to see it coming, to see hope made visible, to see poor kids have an opportunity to learn, to see people have models that they can follow,
to see people being given a chance to take part in something good
and commit themselves is what gives me motivation.

In this community apart from Voice of Calvary I see no challenge, I see no good, I see nothing that people can say "I'm going
to choose this over that." Everybody's flowing. But I think what
VOC is doing is trying to put up good models in the community.
I want to be a part of that good model. I want to be a part of
making things happen here and perhaps God could use me to
really bring them about.

Seeing young people return to the community is one way to continue self-help development. Another is to identify with people
where they are and begin to work with them on their needs as they
see them. Both of these come together in Artis Fletcher. Artis, who
is now pastor of the church in Mendenhall, was one of the first
members of the Voice of Calvary and one of the first to be sent off.
He stayed away ten years attending Southern Bible Training School
in Dallas, Washington Bible College in Washington, D.C., Moody
Bible Institute, and Los Angeles Baptist College and Seminary. He
helped found a church during this time. One young man he led to
the Lord became the first black to graduate from Dallas Theological
Seminary. Then in 1974 Artis returned with his wife to Mendenhall
where he and Dolphus form a team.

I became a Christian in 1962. I had been a church member, a
faithful worker in the church, all my life. But while I was going

to Prentiss Institute, I heard a preacher talk about knowing that you have eternal life and the assurance of knowing you'd go to heaven if you died. I began to recognize that I did not know about having eternal life or being born again. It was through that message and the Holy Spirit convicting me that I came to know Christ as my Savior.

A few months after that, Brother Perkins spoke in our chapel program. He asked if anyone wanted to dedicate their life to Christ. I raised my hand. After the program we met and later he began a Bible study on campus. Through that I came to understand the basic truths of the Bible and what it meant to really be a Christian as opposed to being religious, the difference between knowing Christ personally as Savior and having just an emotional experience.

After school was out for the summer I went back home to Mendenhall. This is also where Brother Perkins was and so I began meeting with him every morning to study the Bible. I would help him prepare his flannelgraphs and lessons and he would teach me about creation, man being a sinner, God's purpose and plan for man and the way of salvation. I remember he had some tracts with the way of salvation printed behind one of his messages. I cut that out and began using it when witnessing to people. At that time the greatest motivation for me was the joy of seeing a person come to know Christ and recognizing that I'd been used by God.

There were also the Youth for Christ meetings and the tent meetings. Then the excitement of building. I helped build the Perkins' house and then the Bible Institute building. I remember thinking how great it was to have an opportunity to work because of a commitment to Christ rather than for money, just working together with Christ being the center of it.

I eventually went off to school for a few years. But I came back, mainly because of the problem of leadership in a small town like Mendenhall. It was this crisis—the fact that strong young men and women were not always available because they had left and not come back.

To me, leadership in the community for a Christian involves commitment, skills, and identification. It costs something to live in a poor community in the rurals. I remember when I was in Chicago and we would go down to the Teen Challenge center and preach and minister to people and talk about their needs, then get back in our cars and drive for an hour to where it was all nice and clean and so forth. It was like I went down and did my duties and now I could go home and relax. That's what makes it impossible to commute to my ministry and be effective. A person needs to get down there where the people live, to know the hell the people in the ghetto are going through. If not, the people will feel you don't know what's going on. There will be a problem in them trusting you.

This is true for blacks and whites. It takes commitment. There is more of a cost, in fact, to minister to the black community here in America than to black people in Africa because money goes so much further over there. Not only will it cost more money, but for whites it may mean that they are ostracized by other whites. This wouldn't happen if they go to Kenya. But I've seen it happen when people feel called to Mississippi or Chicago. There is also the cost of crossing over in culture, the pain and struggle of learning to understand. This can happen most profoundly with whites in the black community.

Skills are an important part of leadership. I'm talking about any skill. I looked at the impact that working on putting up buildings had on a disadvantaged community and on me, and I began to get some skills. You can't do something for everybody, and sometimes the people who can afford something done by a mechanic or a repairman will come to you to get a cut price. So you want to do things for people you are trying to make contact with, the people you know are disadvantaged, and use your skills to show them the love of Christ and get to share the gospel with them. Knowing Mississippi was a poor state and that many of our people are deprived of basic, simple things I began to pick up skills in carpentry, painting and plumbing, first through Prentiss Institute. Then, while going to Bible school I worked with an electrician for nothing, learning about stoves and electrical appliances. While I was at school in California I worked with automobiles, and an electronics engineer worked with me two nights a week for about a year and a half. Then, of course, Ba Ba Lee, the electrician who has wired some of the things here at Voice of Calvary, has helped me. Now I can work on washing machines, televisions, radios, cars, houses, almost anything. And this provides an entry for the gospel.

This is the same with almost any skill—accounting, counseling, teaching—all can be part of preaching the Word.

Finally there's identification. I didn't have any trouble identifying with the people of Mendenhall because I'm one of them. But during my training, there was always the pressure in conservative Christian circles to become conservative, to support somebody like George Wallace. I felt the pressure from fellow Christians to accept ideologies that would become detrimental to seeking to minister in the black community. These included ideas like "people on welfare are lazy." Now in my community there are a lot of people on welfare who just couldn't make it any other way. I don't believe in give-away programs, but the difference is that I fault the programs, not the people who are the victims. I thought that the problem was that we needed to come up with an alternative rather than to criticize what was already going on.

To me, a key to meeting black people's needs, bringing them to Christ and discipling them is a commitment to them where they are. A commitment to their struggles, visions, hopes and dreams. This is a higher commitment than helping a person with repair work. This is a commitment to their dreams of having a better community. In their youth, young blacks deep down want to make things better than their parents. But even though it's hard for many of them to do that because of their economic situation, their spiritual condition may be making it even harder and near impossible.

. If I can commit myself to a person's economic plight, agree with him, share his or her aspirations and burdens in this area, then I have a better chance of witnessing to him. If I can commit myself to making his political situation better, then I have a greater opportunity for challenging him with the gospel of Christ. If he knows injustice is rampant in his community, but I won't take a stand against that injustice, that affects my witness to him. A real identification is the key to getting to share the gospel.

Now you can help too much and sometimes we have done this. When this happens people begin to see us as people who come to get them out of jail rather than seeing us as the Body of Christ in the community. It's important for people to know us as more than just a community organization but as a body of believers who have the keys to the kingdom of God, whose life from God makes a difference in terms of contentment, initiative, and environment.

James Batte came to Voice of Calvary in the fall of 1975. His testimony shows how God can reverse the cycles of joblessness, out-migration—that takes black young people out of their hometowns and into the big cities of the North—and sin, and turn them into creative growth and new life. He now supervises the construction and maintenance for VOC in Mendenhall.

I had left here and went to Detroit in early 1970 looking for a party life. I found all I wanted there and more that I didn't want. But a couple years after finding what I wanted, I didn't want it anymore. After roaming the streets I saw the necessity for my life to change. I saw that Detroit had no more to offer me and I wanted to take steps to change my life. One step was to go back home to Mississippi. I didn't know it then but I was looking for salvation. I had grown up in a church but had never been told how to become a Christian. I thought I had to work for my salvation, that it was something I had to do physically. I decided to go home. This was in 1974.

By the fall of the next year I didn't have a job. There was no work anywhere because I had looked, walked and asked everywhere. Then a neighbor told me about Dolphus Weary. She told me to ask Dolphus Weary if he had anything for me. I went to him and asked. He told me to check back with him. I would come around, again and again. I would get a basketball and shoot baskets all day in the gym just to be doing something. If the gym was nasty and dirty I'd clean it up. Nobody knew me. If they had they would have known that I was at the same time looking for spiritual growth.

Dolphus began giving me assignments and things to do. I lost my place to stay and they put me up in a little room that used to be a barber shop. I worked with Dolphus and Artis every day. Through that and through Bible studies they got me open to the Word of God.

Finally I became a Christian. I understood that it was something that Christ had taken care of and that I didn't have to work for it. My life has since reversed itself. Now I have something to live for. Being a Christian is beautiful.

Not putting these two men up on a pedestal or anything, but what I was looking for and didn't know how to get, these men laid out a pattern for me to follow.

People helping themselves through the power of God living in them—this is the basis for Christian community development.

14.

Organizing at the Grass Roots

A famous Chinese philosopher once wrote something that captures most of my thoughts about community organizing in a nutshell. It's almost a poem and it's called "Serving the People":

Go to the people.
Live among them.
Learn from them.
Serve them.
Plan with them.
Start with what they know.
Build on what they have.

Most people assume that the greatest need in organizing within the black community is money. "That's where to begin," they say. That idea is easy to come up with, since blacks have been economically deprived and that deprivation is at the heart of the black struggle in this country. But to give money as the answer to organizing and developing a community may often be too simple and even destructive.

There are some higher principles of organizing which, if neglected, can insure that whatever money you do get will ruin your development. On the other hand, we have found that these principles—principles of motivation and relationship—lead to structures in the community that can creatively develop and utilize resources from both inside and outside the community.

For the person working in the community, the pioneer, the groundbreaker, the leader, the initiator, strategy must begin with motivation. In scratching out a ministry in the community, a person can get rightly motivated by three things: love, power, and humility.

To love the people is the basic requirement for anyone who leads people. Only through love can I really come to know my people, their problems and failings and deep weaknesses—and not lose my energy. The prophets, beginning with Moses, had this kind of love. In fact their leadership before God was rooted in the love and compassion they had for the people, in their willingness to endure the disobedience and perverseness of the people and then to intercede and wrestle with God on their behalf. Only love will take me close enough to the people to share their real needs and to make them my own. This is important, because just as anything done in the business world is based on demand, anything done in developing a community is based on need, not just the needs projected by outsiders either, but those needs which the people can identify for themselves.

Power is another motivator. The understanding of power is, at heart, an understanding that God stands supremely in control of all history. "To all who received him, who believed in his name, he gave *power* to become children of God" (John 1:12). If I really believe that I am a child of the One who controls the course of human events, then that should have some effect on my ministry in the community.

For one thing, I can understand *the power of an idea.* One of the problems with our present educational system is that it can rob people of hope and initiative. Most people getting out of school can see the problems—they see poverty, injustice, racism, and loneliness. But they see no solution. They don't understand the power of an idea. Many see ideas in terms of textbook history, that the great ideas reaching people were somehow mysteriously created by the flow of written history itself. They don't understand that God gives ideas and has a whole book of them and that these and other ideas are not just nice things to think and debate about. An idea is something you implement, something that can create history. Ideas can shape individual beliefs. Beliefs create action. And individual action is where change begins. The roots of every great historical movement have been with individuals acting upon what they believe, working it down into their everyday life.

But an idea is something which becomes meaningful only when you tie your energy and resources to it. The power behind Voice of Calvary Ministries is what happens when a group of people get an idea, especially one that they believe is inspired by God, and put all of their little resources behind it. Now, young people gain hope when they come down and see the health center, youth center, thrift store and housing development all in the poor, black section of town, all fitting into a biblical message of concern for the poor.

I see so many students being enslaved by the mentality that the System functions on its own and that we really cannot change the way things are. What comes out of this deep sense of powerlessness is a very shaky and shady device. In the black community we call it *jive*. In the white community we call it *rhetoric*. It is the ability to surround an idea with words and the energy of talk without a plan for action.

Now anyone in grass-roots community development or in preaching the gospel knows that talk is important, but only as a means to an end. The point is that if someone comes along with an idea and talks and talks about it and knows it is going to work and all of his or her individual power and life is witnessing to the fact that this idea works, people will get excited and organize with that person around that idea and the opposition will be crushed. That's what the Apostle Paul meant when he said in 1 Corinthians 4:20 that "the kingdom of God does not consist in talk but in power."

We can be motivated by *power that wills change*. We know that there is a God in the universe who has communicated his truth and ideas to us, and we can participate in pulling them off and giving them concrete form in the community. Beyond that, we know that change will occur. We are assured that God can first make a fundamental change in the hearts of individuals that can redirect their whole lives. In his second letter, Peter assures us that God's "divine power has granted to us all things that pertain to life and godliness," and that we can lay hold of God's knowledge, his promises, and his virtues—like faith, self-control, steadfastness, and love. If we do this, we will be kept from "being ineffective or unfruitful in the knowledge of our Lord Jesus Christ" (2 Peter 1:3–8). If what we are doing in the community are attempts to flesh out God's concern for reconciling people to himself and for healing people, then we can be assured that change will take place—that's power.

We can also be motivated by a *power to persevere*. I think this can come from the basic understanding that we have power over death. We can continue to challenge cycles and institutions of sin and face hostility and rejection because we have overcome death itself, and in that there is a power. As William Stringfellow said, "In raising Lazarus . . . Jesus reveals what is implicit, but hidden, in all of the healing episodes, that is, his authority over death, his conclusive power over death, his triumph over death and all that death can do and all that death means. To so surpass death is utterly threatening politically; it shakes and shatters the very foundation of political reality because death is . . . the *only* moral and practical sanction of the State." [1] In other words, when it becomes necessary for us to witness to justice through voter registration or getting locked in jail or whatever, at a time when the ruling powers do not share that same sense of justice, we will be threatened, maybe even with death. But we can have power over all of the punishments and hostilities with which any one group of people threaten another group of people. We can have power because we can know that the ultimate threat, the threat of death, has no power over us who have eternal life. The person who has settled the issue of life with God shares with Jesus the same authority and capability over the powers of death that freed him up to complete his work and be eternally and powerfully effective.

Finally, *humility is the motivator that can balance love and power.* If your love has really boxed you into working in the community in a way that you can't leave, and you absolutely yearn to be effective, humility will come or you will be broken beyond repair. This is true because, first, you just cannot think that you know all the answers. And it takes humility to know that and then to ask the people with the necessary technology to work with you in the community. You make yourself, to a degree, dependent on them. That doesn't mean that they run the program. We've had people with massive skills come and want to take over, to change our objectives. Even the government, in its attempt to foster religious freedom, will not allow the proclamation of the gospel as an objective of a program funded by them. So there are times when you have to turn down help or ask people to leave. But once you find those people with the skills in management, Bible teaching, health care, accounting, construction and evangelism, you have to be humble enough to know that you need them and yet not to be threatened by the fact that they know more than you.

The other place where you can get humility is when you realize that the people you are working with are all you've got. There is nothing more devastating than to develop a program and find out that it doesn't meet people's needs, or that you cannot pull it off by yourself and you just need a few more hands to really do it. Or when, after you did all that you planned, you see that the people aren't any place different than before. These realizations push you

---

[1] William Stringfellow, *An Ethic for Christians and Other Aliens in a Strange Land* (Waco, TX: Word Books, 1973), p. 149.

toward relationships—the need for local people who can support you, the need to be able to listen to the uneducated advice of people at the grass roots, to their explanations and their wisdom, without comparing it to the shiny rhetoric that sounds better but doesn't work.

A commitment to be effective in changing lives creates humility. And humility causes me to listen. And once I begin listening to the people, I find out that more changes come through relationships than through the programs I create. More changes took place over the long run in Herbert's and my life because we rode in the hog truck to Jackson together and set up the tent together than because he attended our weekly meetings.

The power, again, is not in a program you get funded. The power is in the people. The rip-off artists, the pimps, say this as rhetoric, but their real motive is power for themselves. But to know, to be humbled by God enough to know, that the people you work with really have the power, frees you from the manipulation that it takes to get a program going without the people.

We discovered our need for the power in people, and that's why if I ever go to a church in the country, they will always listen to what I have to say, even my enemies. That's why I can make the people who absolutely hate me work and do things for me. That's why whenever I am at Jackson State, students I can seldom name come up to say, "Hi." And if you are humbled enough to really get yourself boxed in to living with the people, at their level, then even if the funds get cut off, you will never starve. People proved that again and again to us by giving us milk, eggs, vegetables, potatoes, everything we needed to keep the family and the ministry alive. With a base like that, you are really in a position to preach the gospel, no strings attached, and you have a constituency that will back you when you get ready to lead in creative directions—like a day-care center, a housing co-op or a health center.

So to be a leader in the community, you must first love the people, then you must understand power, and finally, you need humility to keep your love from turning into "charity" or a damaging give-away program, and to keep your power from turning into manipulation or exploitation. Humility makes you see that your programs or your "good doing" might not really be effective; it makes you see that people are the ends, not the means, and that you need them, both the technicians and the grass-roots folks.

Now, in addition to some basic principles of motivation, we've also discovered some basic principles of relating, some ground rules, you might say, for the hard-down, knuckles-in-the-grit work of organizing in the community.

We said earlier that one of the key principles to working God's will in a community, especially an oppressed community, is *the development of leadership*. This is where I begin. To me, developing creative leadership is the most essential and the most difficult part of community development. It was at the heart of Jesus' strategy. Jesus did not make the mistake of the charismatic leader who centers his programs around himself. The strategy of Jesus, which he passed on to his disciples, is simply outlined in Paul's instruction to Timothy: "What you have heard from me before many witnesses entrust to faithful men [and women] who will be able to teach others also" (2 Tim. 2:2). Out of relationships like these, Jesus knew that his ministry to the bodies and souls of men and women would be continued until he returned again to culminate the kingdom of God.

The type of leadership we develop is crucial. What the poverty programs did was to bring in outside leadership, which is always necessary in a depressed community. But their mistake was that they never extended that leadership base into the community itself. Leadership must eventually be indigenous to be effective.

It is also important for leadership to have a central unifying commitment. We have simply not found any commitment, other than a commitment to Christ and to his ministry on earth, that is strong enough to cause a person to spend the kind of time and personal resources needed for development and for effective ministry in the black community. Commitment must be developed beyond a person's natural commitment to self-interest: that means future, salary, prestige, power—everything.

Because leadership must come from the community and must have a central unifying commitment, *it is almost required that the organizer live in the community, with the people.* Commitment is more caught than taught, so association is crucial. That was the genius of Jesus' ministry. He communicated his ideas through being with his disciples and letting them follow him.

Once you are with the people, they will give you authority. I got authority because people began to trust me and to see my motives as good. They would give me their power. Now, that authority carries with it a responsibility for direction. One of our favorite verses became "Where there is no vision, the people perish" (Prov. 29:18, KJV). With the development of the vision, people can be happy, they can use their gifts behind something that is going somewhere. We found that the opposite of the proverb was true, "Where there is a vision, the people flourish."

Yet, creating a vision demands a high sense of planning and communicating. It means never assuming the way people will act, for good or bad. It means creating the situation so you know what the outcome will be. It means taking total responsibility for my behavior and calling others to do the same.

There are problems inherited with the authority people give you and the authority you get as the keeper of the vision. That's because there is always a tension between authority and freedom. For one, it might end up that your vision isn't relevant. For another, hopeful new leaders may be crushed by or resent your authority. At times I've found myself intimidating and crushing the developing leadership with my presence and my need for results and performance. The only balancing principle I can give is that a person should always maintain a high sense of freedom.

One great example of this is the black church, because it was the only place where black people could express themselves. Even today in most rural churches, at some time during the service, there will be an opportunity for anybody—visitor or member, black or white—to speak. The pastor will always ask, "Does anyone have anything to say?"

One way that this sense of freedom works itself out in organizing is allowing people to determine their own destiny by beginning with the community norms and what the community itself identifies as its needs. This means talking what people know. It is so easy to force on people what I believe their needs to be, and this happens all the time in the black community. Evangelicals come down and say, "What you need is to receive Christ into your heart and all your problems will be solved." Liberals come down and say, "What you need is tutoring and a recreation program and food stamps and all your problems will be solved." But only by beginning where people see themselves to be and leading out from there can we be effective. It might be that the greatest problem in the community is trash collection. If you address yourself to that first and

begin to move from there, leadership, energy and vision will pro-
ceed—because you haven't taken away a person's freedom to think
for himself.

It's also true that people defend what they help create. There is
a fantastic amount of freedom in ownership, and a community organizer can make the subtle mistake of taking that away even before
a program is under way by coming up with his or her plans alone.
People need to own the vision that will direct them, and for them
to own it, they must be given a chance to shape it. A good organizer
always works on the basis of consensus among the committed.

Another organizing principle that shows why people need to defend what they helped create I learned working with John Zippert
and Ed Coles: never allow people outside the room, outside
those people who have committed themselves, to affect what goes
on inside the room. Whenever something good develops, you can
count on opposition. Opposition can be felt both outside and inside
the committed consensus.

The first kind of opposition happens when a person from the
community at large comes up to one of the core group and starts
talking about the group, about one of the members in the group, or
(even more likely) about you, the organizer. If there is any doubt
or hesitation at this point, the rumor can get out of control. But people will defend each other and the group if they feel a sense of ownership in the vision.

People have to learn to defend each other, especially in the black
community where we get abuse from the white community and have
learned to cut ourselves up so much. So I always explain to people
that the defense has to be quick and powerful. "Go jump in the lake,
you good-for-nothing gossip! That stuff you're saying is absolutely
false." Then, after they've dealt with the aggravator, if there are any
questions, take them to the group to clear them up—that will give
the group a sense of self-cleansing, a sense of who is for and against
them on the outside, a sense of what real defense is, and a love for
each other. It also stops rumors dead.

The same type of dynamic works inside a meeting too, when opposition is felt without even being present. I have often been in
meetings of a local group that is struggling to get something together
and I'll hear, "So and so thinks that we are making a mistake," or
"So and so might not use the co-op if we do this," or—even more
deadly—that spoken or unspoken thought, "What will the white

man think?" But if a leader will allow criticism to be expressed only from those in the group, at the meeting, it will give people a sense of power, a sense of ownership and dignity. And it saves you as an organizer, because it begins to cause the people closest to you to begin to get tough themselves with opposition that inevitably rises up against anything creative.

When people begin to create something themselves, and when they begin to see that what other people think cannot keep them from being effective, it gives them a sense of freedom that can balance off the authority you have as an organizer. Once the vision is off the ground, this idea of letting people take part in shaping the program or project takes on the form of a question. A good organizer is always asking himself about everyone in the group, "What can this person do that will get all of us closer to our objectives?" The more creatively that question is answered, the happier people are going to be moving together toward becoming leaders. This is important because only when this leadership develops, can you get to the point where people can begin to form creative structures in their community. Why? Because any movement within a poor community must be built upon people helping themselves.

If structures are not self-helping by nature, they will not be able to provide the unique approaches to poverty needed to change patterns of thought and behavior in individuals, needed to meet the people's needs, needed to allow for joint decision-making, and needed to give people a chance to determine their own future. In short, unless people can help themselves, no structure will be able to break the *dependence* that is the hard, seemingly impenetrable reality behind poverty.

That's why we began to look into cooperatives. A cooperative is an economic structure where the people who use a service own the service. It carries in it a balance between meeting needs and developing creative opportunities for emerging leadership. A cooperative gives local people the possibility of creating their own capital. For instance, a credit union is often the most viable cooperative that a community can create, because if you create a credit union what you're doing is creating capital. A few people, once they learn to save and start looking at their savings book, quit spending. Saving becomes a fad, and pretty soon you have got an economic base.

Then the people in the community who have bright new ideas, the young man who can do good woodwork, for instance, can get enough capital to do something. Before, he could never get the $3,000 that was needed to rent a shop and buy some tools. The bank would not let him have it because he had no record of paying back a debt. He wouldn't have had a record because neither he, nor anyone in his family, had ever before borrowed money. Now he can go to the credit union that's a part of his community and knows him, and he can borrow the money to build that enterprise in his community. So, besides turning those people who were consumers into savers, the co-op is able to allow some young leadership to develop and begins to provide some job opportunities.

This is absolutely radical when talking about the black community. The system has made us black people massive consumers. Exploited people consume far more than middle-class people. We buy more furniture, more cars, more clothes. It's that yearning desire that a man has within him to own something, that deep need a woman has in her heart to call something her own. And what has happened is that, because of the fallen nature of all mankind, that need to *have* something has been confused with the need to *be* something. A cooperative can begin to meet these needs by making people owners of some of the programs in their community and giving them the responsibility for the economic stability and betterment of all the people in the community. What this does is put the "need to have" in a better perspective, removed a bit from the survival level and linked up with sharing and creating a better life for someone other than just the individual. It can be the first step to getting a hold on who a person should *be.*

Now I have formed a lot of co-ops that have failed. I'm not afraid to say that. Many have succeeded. But my point is that a cooperative is not primarily an economic structure as much as it is an educational tool. Some of the basic principles of a co-op, once they are operational, provide a climate for learning, for developing a whole new style of behavior. For instance, *open membership:* anyone can belong to a co-op, as long as they pay the dues. That speaks of freedom, of something completely opposite to the exclusiveness and privilege that mark so many of our economic institutions. Also, the principle of *one person, one vote:* everyone, no matter how big the investment or how small, gets just one vote. This speaks of equality, of a forum for free dialogue and a place where every person can have a sense of owning an enterprise and an opportunity to shape its vision. And then there is the principle of *patronage refund:*

profits of the co-op are distributed to members on the basis of how much they use the co-op. Instead of creating a flow of money upward, to those who have the most capital, and making the rich richer, the patronage refund causes the money to flow back down to the members and to the ones who, based on their consumption, would probably have the most need.

The greatest thing about a cooperative is that it changes what a man has in his head; that's why I got into organizing them. As an educational tool, it can change the basic behavior of people. I think co-ops work because they go beyond the rhetoric and actually model the truths you are trying to communicate. There was a time when we as black people were able to do a lot of talking, and the television cameras and the microphones were there. But then people found out that we weren't going to do very much. And so the administration under Nixon shifted gears, defunded the poverty programs, and all we could do was rap.

But a cooperative brings you to a practical, visible level. It brings you out of this high, sophisticated, intellectual realm and down to where something actually begins to be done. The cooperative makes money and people—black and white—work together. It is a model for the community, and because it is practical and visible it gives hope and incentive.

Models are important to people who have traditionally been without hope. A model has power because you can teach and change people so much more dynamically by putting bricks and mortar on your ideas and then communicating them to others by showing them. Isn't that what God did in Christ? "The Word became flesh and dwelt among us, full of grace and truth" (John 1:14). God planned to model his love for human beings by putting flesh on his love, someone we could see and feel and hear and know. A model has power. It can be communicated because it can be seen. It can break institutional molds of thought and power because it can, as people join together, offer an alternative institution, an alternative way of thinking, an alternative base of power.

So, beginning with motivation—from love, power, and humility—a person can begin working creatively in the community. Laying hold of some key principles—like creating an indigenous leadership, developing a central unifying commitment, balancing authority with a high sense of freedom—people in the community emerge and begin a movement toward helping themselves. And as this movement takes structure, it can develop alternative models—like co-ops that can break down old institutional molds of behavior and power.

But just as I felt a terrific sense of lethargy and negligence from the evangelical church, I also saw that the movement was not dealing with some very deep pitfalls and roadblocks which threatened to weaken and break down our efforts to develop communities. In addition, the mention of "politics" caused most people we knew a lot of discomfort. But it was nothing compared to the reactions caused by talking "economics." We began to sense, as we explored further and further what it meant to develop Christian economic models in the black community, that it was sort of like floating down the river on a raft and hearing—first from far off, but then louder and deeper— the roar of the rapids and rough waters that would threaten to scuttle and sink a tiny boat like Voice of Calvary.

15.

The Economics of Equality

Anne Moody was a young black student at Tougaloo College in Mississippi when the civil rights movement was at its peak. In *Coming of Age in Mississippi*,[1] her book about that struggle, there is a scene that I'll never forget. Miss Moody was one of three black kids who integrated the first lunch counter in Jackson, Mississippi. It was at Woolworth's. A few minutes after they sat down, the tension was rising. Waitresses, refusing to serve them and expecting immediate violence, shut down the counter and abandoned even their white customers. The three remained seated.

A white woman, standing nearby started to go, but before she did, she said to Miss Moody, "I'd like to stay here with you, but my husband is waiting." A reporter heard what she said and asked her for her name. She wouldn't give it. He asked her why she had made that statement. She said, "I am in sympathy with the Negro movement," and then walked out the door.

Within the hour, the three people at the lunch counter were beginning to receive payment for their gesture. They found themselves surrounded by more than a score of angry Mississippians. But it happened when the group began to pray. "We bowed our heads, and all hell broke loose. A man rushed forward, threw Memphis from his seat, and slapped my face. Then another man who worked in the store threw me against an adjoining counter."

By the time it was over, the three were smeared with ketchup, mustard, sugar, pies, and showered with spray paint. "Nigger" was painted on the shirt-back of one of the students. The three suffered beatings, kicks in the face while on the floor, chants of "communist" and "all kinds of anti-negro slogans." At one point, Miss Moody was dragged about thirty feet by her hair.

During this time "about ninety policemen were standing outside the store; they had been watching the whole thing through the windows, but had not come in to stop the mob or to do anything." Finally, the president of Tougaloo College escorted the students out of the building.

[1] *Coming of Age in Mississippi* (New York: Dial Press, 1968).

The scene is powerful because it draws back the curtain of Southern tradition just long enough to expose the deep emotional and fearful impact of black people expressing themselves as equals. Nothing more, just equals.

Never forget that *equality is the first and last issue between black and white people in this country*. Equality is the sun shining at the center of all the galaxy of other racial and poverty issues. You can talk about integration or fair housing or busing or voter's rights, but at the heart, your discussion turns around the meaning of equality as certainly as the earth turns around the sun. And in spite of the 1960s, real equality is still not a functional reality in the black community today.

"But," someone might ask, "what about the fact that blacks are now assured the right to vote, and that the government is strictly enforcing integration and equal opportunity employment all over the country? Is that not equality?" Now, I'm happy that black people can now register to vote and go to better schools and get jobs more easily. But as I look around in the black community, I still see masses of people that have not been touched by those programs. So I say that they are side issues. If they had worked, they would be producing human development. No, the victims that we know could not live in a society that practiced equality, because *equality produces real human development*.

But there are different kinds of equality and some are even counterfeits. There is symbolic equality—that equality which gives us the right to vote, which allows us to go into restaurants and sit anywhere we want, which allows us to drink out of any drinking fountain we want to—and there is real equality—that equality which reaches out into every aspect of our community and social life and heals people, and makes people able to be proud of what they have and who they are. To me, integration is a whole lot different from equality.

Let me illustrate. Integration always assumes that what blacks have is no good, and so we're supposed to learn white ways. Integration removes me from my community and takes me to the white community. It hardly ever works the other way around. But *equality develops what we have*. It takes what we have and makes us proud of it. It makes us well. And you can't start any more basic than making a person well.

Integration was good because it gave us symbolic equality. In giving us that symbolic equality it overcame a lot of reaction from those people, especially those poor or working-class white people, who were just one rung above or maybe even in the same positions as black people. The only thing they had was the outward symbol of inequality—the separate drinking fountains, the separate restrooms—to allow them to maintain their superiority.

So getting symbolic equality was good, but it was shallow, and that is the weakness that I saw early on in the civil rights movement. Even with Headstart, I saw that it was a shallowness of commitment, a weakness of purpose that would never allow Headstart to really create that type of development in the community that was rooted in the community itself—its leadership, its resources, and its needs.

You see, traditional approaches to the problem of inequality have not worked. Gaining symbolic equality worked because in the end those people who were against symbolic equality, those working-class and poor-white people, were overpowered by the conscience of the rest of the country. The reason traditional approaches to the problem of poverty and race have not worked is not because of the reactions of poor and working-class white people, but because of the reactions of whites much like the lady at the lunch counter, people who have what they call a set of "beliefs," but cannot muster the real energy to act upon those beliefs.

Situations like these that I see again and again among white people and white Christians make me realize how much we have diluted the word *belief*. To me, the lady at the lunch counter represents so many people who "believe" in a cause and who know it's right but who want to stay anonymous. In doing that, they miss an opportunity to write God's history. They take their places on the outside, next to the ninety policemen, looking in through the windows, watching somebody else take the abuse that they would have received had they acted on their "beliefs."

I think the lady's reaction in the incident at the lunch counter is important because it represents the masses of people, even the "good people with conscience" in this country, who will say they believe in the symbolic forms of equality, but hedge when it comes down to paying the price for real equality. They back away when it comes down to a black person moving in next door, or a black person competing for the same job and then getting it because the company has never hired black people before and now they have a quota to hire black people. I'm not going to say that all of the equal opportunity programs are good or use the proper methods. But what I am saying is that unless equality is real in terms of economics, it will never have an impact on the communities where I know victims live.

Then what is equality? To me, *equality comes from God and expresses his supernatural love for people. Equality begins with the physical creation,* where God has woven into nature certain unquestionable facts and inescapable realities that make us all equal. His plan of creation means that all people are born into this world, all people need food, shelter, clothing, air, love, meaning—and all people will die. There is a certain haunting equality about that that is sure.

Yet, it was God's intended desire to provide for all of his children with equal abundance. That was the blessing he gave man from the start in the garden (Gen. 1:28–31). So love was the motivating force behind the equality that is visible throughout his creation.

Our equality in creation has deep social implications. Job's relationship with his servants, for instance, sprang out of the fact that God created all people equal (Job 31:13). Job wants his character to reflect the same impartiality and equality that God wove into creation.

The equality in creation is based on the equality that is a part of the Father's character, and that equality reaches with divine implications into society: "For the Lord your God is God of gods and Lord of lords, the great, the mighty, and the terrible God, who is not partial and takes no bribe. He executes justice for the fatherless and the widow, and loves the sojourner, giving him food and clothing" (Deut. 10:17, 18). In the New Testament, also, we are told repeatedly that we are to be like God, who is no respecter of persons and shows no partiality (Gal. 2:6; 1 Cor. 1:26; James 2:1–9).

But God doesn't limit his love for equality to the physical creation alone. *Equality extends also throughout the spiritual creation* and his redemptive activities on earth as well. Perhaps the greatest equalizer is the judgment which faces all people at the end of the age. Someone once said to me, "All the ground is level at the foot of the cross." What a great truth, that Jesus died for the sins of all mankind, and that everyone has equal access to the forgiveness available at the cross.

But there are also heavy social implications to the equality expressed in God's spiritual activity in creation. Perhaps the heaviest is Christ's identification with the poor to the point of equating himself with the poor person. He calls the poor person his brother: "Whatever you did for the humblest of my brothers you did for me" (Matt. 25:40, Phillips).

But now for the punch line in God's plan—*God meant for equality to be expressed in terms of economics.* This also begins with creation. All wealth traces its heritage back to the land, to the earth. Without the resources of the earth, there would be no economics. And God is owner of the earth: "The earth is the Lord's and the fulness thereof" (Ps. 24:1). This theme is echoed throughout the Old Testament and into the New. Paul says, "from [God] and through him and to him are all things" (Rom. 11:36; see also Exod. 9:29; 19:5; Deut. 10:14; 1 Chron. 29:11; Job 41:11; Dan. 4:25; 1 Cor. 8:6). It has been God's intention to let human beings have dominion over the earth, to give them stewardship over his creation. God went so far as to set up some ground rules for this stewardship which he gave to his people who were to model the way God wanted things done on earth. Those ground rules were based on equality and yet promised that "there will be no poor among you . . . if only you will obey the voice of the Lord your God, being careful to do all this commandment which I command you this day" (Deut. 15:4–5).

What happened to the equality that God intended was that human beings sinned, and in separating themselves from God, cut themselves off from their fellow human beings. This alienation between people created barriers that took on economic dimensions. God's equality is distorted by sin and results in economic injustice and oppression.

This was the downfall of Nebuchadnezzar, ruler of Babylon, for which he was punished with temporary insanity (Dan. 4:27). It wasn't until Nebuchadnezzar could understand God's ownership of the earth and recapture a sense of equality, justice and humility that he was restored to his right mind (Dan. 4:25).

The same seems to be true about Sodom and the terrible judgment God inflicted there (Ezek. 16:49). The sinfulness of human beings results in some groups of people being fantastically rich, while others remain desperately poor and oppressed (Ps. 10; Mal. 3:5; Isa. 3:14; Luke 16:10, 20; James 2:5, 7; Amos 5:11, 12).

What is God's response to the pollution and distortion of the equality which he intended? It is first, a burning love for the poor and the oppressed, the victims of man's inhumanity to his neighbors.

In fact, God's justice is biased in their favor. Instead of the judge, he is pictured as Public Defender, pleading the cause of the poor, defending the weak, helping the helpless (Prov. 22:22; Pss. 12:5; 10:17, 18).

Second, God mobilizes his forces calling those who serve him to stand for equality. He promises blessings for those who take up the defense of the poor (Prov. 14:21; Ps. 41:1). In fact, he seems to offer a profit-sharing plan for those interested: The same God who is owner of the heavens and the earth and all therein, who asks ominously, "Who has given to me that I should repay him?" also upholds the promise that "He who is kind to the poor lends to the Lord, and he will repay him for his deed" (Job 41:11; Prov. 19:17).

The means through which God desires men to create equality is right economics. This is first pictured for us in the development of the nation of Israel. God knew that the sinful nature of human beings would eventually cause the economic order to slip into an unjust distribution of wealth. He therefore instituted a structure that would create a more just and equal distribution of wealth every fifty years. The "Year of Jubilee" called for the return of land that had been forfeited because of the owner's poverty and for the freedom of those who had had to sell themselves because of their poverty (Lev. 25:28, 39–43).[2]

God's concern for equality in a broken society was also expressed through commandments like "open wide your hand to your brother, to the needy and to the poor, in the land" (Deut. 15:11). "Particularly emphasized is the responsibility to those who have no regular means of support, such as widows and orphans (Exod. 22:22; Deut. 24:19; 26:12; Zech. 7:10). But systematic practices exist to help all the poor" (see Exod. 22:25; Lev. 19:9–10; 23:22; 25:35; Deut. 15:7–10).[3]

But the same concern for an economics of equality pictured for us in the Old Testament is also a mandate for the people of God in the New Testament. Jesus' inaugural message (Luke 4:18–21), which set the tone for his whole ministry, clearly echoes the heavily economic tones of Leviticus 25 and the "Year of Jubilee." But we can rejoice that Jesus goes further to proclaim a redemptive release from all forms of oppression—spiritual, psychological, and physical. Nevertheless, Christ's message is explicitly economic and gives us a

---

[2] Richard K. Taylor, *Economics and the Gospel* (Philadelphia: United Church Press, 1973), p. 19.

[3] Ibid., p. 15.

great maxim: Like the Jubilee, the type of human development needed by the world's poor must be based on equality and have economic backbone.

It's great how God is so practical, how he knows that the real flesh of the task of human development is economics. Again, in Leviticus 19:18, where God first commands us to love our neighbor as ourselves, the imperative comes after some very specific commands to give to the poor economically—by leaving gleanings in the fields and grapes on the vine after the harvest, by not oppressing or robbing our neighbor, by not withholding the wages of a hired servant.

And how great a parallel in Luke 10:27! Right after that shifty lawyer gets done reciting the second of the two great commandments, "Love your neighbor as yourself," he asks the loaded question, "Who is my neighbor?" Jesus answers with the parable of the Good Samaritan, a prime example of love and the equality of brotherhood fleshed out economically—and expensively.

Paul captures the whole meaning of the economics of equality as the motivation behind the church's responsibility to help poor brothers and sisters when he writes, "I do not mean that others should be eased and you burdened, but that as a matter of equality your abundance at the present time should supply their want, so their abundance may supply your want, that there may be equality" (2 Cor. 8:13–14).

In this context the cross, where Christ so lavishly and richly poured himself out for us as an offering, also takes on economic teeth (2 Cor. 8:9).

The Apostle John also drives this point home for us: "By this we know love, that he laid down his life for us; and we ought to lay down our lives for the brethren. But if any one has the world's goods and sees his brother in need, yet closes his heart against him, how does God's love abide in him?" (1 John 3:16, 17).

So, how does the economics of equality relate to the local poor or black community? *First, equality itself must be fully understood in neighborhood ministry.* When an evangelist comes to a community and speaks down to the people, expressing a sort of spiritual superiority rather than a common brokenness before God, he will not be effective. When a person takes part in social action in the community but believes that he is somehow better or that the level of development he has earned puts him above the people in the community, the results are paternalism and damage to the people served. When a group comes to a community with the hope of developing it economically but without a plan for including the people in the community in that economic development through their leadership and advice, the result will be welfare which will do more harm than good. So human development must be based on equality.

Second, equality must be economic to have an impact on the poor community. That's because the way our system works is primarily economic. Many people believe that our system is primarily a political system and if you can just elect the right person then it will change the way things run. But this is not true. Our system is first and primarily an economic system. This works itself out in a number of ways in the black community.

If you came to Mendenhall today you would come down Old Highway 49. To get into the black community you would turn right off Old 49 and go over a set of railroad tracks that separate the black and white communities. Up on the hill you have beautiful homes, you have the businesses of the community, you have the county courthouse. Down below the tracks you have a honky-tonk, you have a couple of churches, and you have mostly dilapidated shacks covered with tar paper siding with rickety porches.

Now what happens to the average black person who goes across the tracks to work at their job? Let's take Arthur Lampton who has just got a job at the plant in Simpson County which makes fluorescent fixtures. He gets in his car in the morning and drives across the tracks and goes down to the plant. It happens to be a Friday so he picks up his check at the plant at the end of the day and returns home.

Before coming home he drops by the bank and pays off a part of the note he has on his car. Then he walks across the street, having cashed his check, and buys some groceries. He walks down the street to the drugstore to pick up a prescription. He was waiting to get his check before he could buy the prescription. Now he walks across the street from the drugstore to the dollar store, where he has a bicycle on layaway for his son. He pays his weekly amount down on layaway, leaves the store, and gets into his car to go home. He remembers that tonight he must go by and pay his rent and utilities to his landlord. He drives across the tracks, and the only money he has left in his pocket is enough for one more run to the store, and a little bit to spend at the honky-tonk that night or, if he goes to church, a little bit to put in the offering plate.

What this means is that virtually none of the money Arthur Lamp-

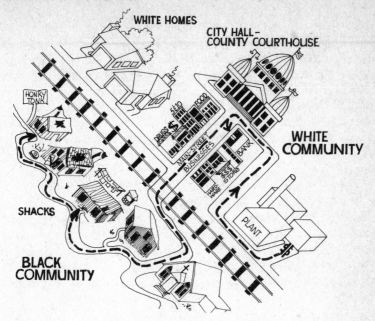

ton earned during the week in the white community is brought down to circulate in the black community, but rather is left back up in the white community, the only segment of society with the enterprises and the economic institutions designed to capture and recirculate money. And this is the same in virtually every black community in America.

Like the blood in our bodies, it is the circulation of money that is crucial, because it determines whether a community is rich or poor, healthy or anemic. You take a community like Harlem. I am told that in Harlem, with over one million people, there is quite a bit of money. But the problem is that the average dollar circulates less than five times in that community before it leaves and goes to the shops or the businesses or the savings institutions of the white community in different parts of New York. This is contrasted with communities like Manhattan in which I understand an average dollar circulates over twenty-five times.

Then finally we have to look at history to really see the role of economics in the civil rights movement in Mississippi. In *Mississippi: The Closed Society* (p. 280), James Silver carefully details how economics finally broke the back of the radical White Citizens' Council. Before 1964, the Council had a firm grip on the policies of the state. But it was finally the "business power structure of Mississippi [which], fearful of the disastrous economic impact of the state's image, spurred by the Philadelphia murders and the passage of the Civil Rights Act, as well as by the impending school desegregation, exerted its strength for law and order in compliance with the national will." The Mississippi business community was being threatened with bankruptcy as a result of the massive civil rights activity in the closed society. When the hold of the Citizens' Council was finally broken, Silver says the "impetus had come from men whose security and prestige were assured, whose motivation was neither spiritual nor intellectual but largely economic. It was mainly a matter of property rather than honor and justice." Isn't it sad that in the history of Mississippi, the business community, paradoxically, has had more impact on racial issues and the pursuit of justice than any other institution in the state including the church?

So economics is at the heart of the way our system and country and our state function. Any search for equality therefore must be wedded to the pursuit of sound economics in the community.

And this is the point of failure for most programs that have been tried in the black community. They have failed to apply sound economic principles to the problems. The result is either noninvolvement or cheap involvement.

We have already talked about the noninvolvement of the white evangelical church and how it has failed in both preaching and doing the gospel in the black community. This has a parallel failure in society as a whole that could be called the failure of conservatives. Those who will not involve themselves usually end in hating or blaming the victim for his own distress, demanding that he help himself, even though he doesn't have the resources.

But to me, even more dangerous are those cheap forms of involvement that don't have any impact and in fact damage people in the black community. We have seen the failure of one program after another as we have worked in the community. In the poverty programs and other programs of cheap involvement, we have what I would call the failure of liberalism.

For instance, the commodity program of food distribution failed because black people had never eaten the types of food given them and so fed it to their hogs. The food stamp program—a program that thousands of poor people can't afford to begin with—has failed because it ends up benefiting the white store owner rather than producing lasting results in the black community. One reason other poverty programs failed was that they would never allow for community ownership. If you started a black self-help program with government money, you could rent buildings and you could rent furniture; you could lease cars, but you could not own anything. And it was supposed to break the cycle of poverty. But ownership is the way to break the cycle of poverty.

These forms of cheap involvement are dangerous because they also threaten the real development that is taking place in the black community. What I mean by that is best illustrated by the cooperative movement in Mississippi. We had been struggling, trying to create cooperatives in Mississippi, and all at once this bulletin came down from the Office of Economic Opportunity (OEO) in Washington saying that they were going to have a cooperative day. After that, the poverty program began to move into organizing cooperatives all over the country, highly subsidizing people organizing cooperatives and people working in them. But then, when the Nixon administration came along and killed the Office of Economic Opportunity, these cooperatives began to die. And now people are saying that cooperatives won't work, when it was really the poverty program that wouldn't work.

After seeing one failure after another, I began to understand what our present-day political system is really like. Martin Luther King, Jr., had begun to lay hold of it when he said: "I've become gravely disappointed with the white liberal [he called them moderates]. . . . The Negro's great stumbling block in his stride toward freedom is not the White Citizens Council-er or the Ku Klux Klan-er, but the white liberal who is more devoted to 'order' than to justice." [4]

Somebody once drew a six-word diagram for me that helped bring this liberal-conservative distinction into focus. To the left of a vertical line were three words—*liberal, reactionary,* and *system*. To the right of the line were the other three—*conservative, radical,* and *values*. A liberal person, one who wants to give a little money and a few resources to help those who are in need, is doing that because his first love is the system—just the way it is. He wants to maintain the system and he knows that if those needs get out of hand, the system will fall. So he gives just enough in charity to keep the needs under control. But if his personal survival is ever threatened, he will

[4] *Why We Can't Wait* (New York: Harper & Row, 1963), p. 87.

turn into a reactionary or rather the most ardent and all-out defender of the system at any cost.

But the conservative, rather than making all of his decisions on the basis of what is good for the system, makes his decisions on the basis of values. You can move a person like that. If you can just give that person the ability to look at the implications of his values deeply enough, then he will become a radical, someone who will deal with the roots of the problem. He will become radically interested in the deep issues of the community, because his mind is not on the system and maintaining it but is in a set of values that is separate and apart from the system.

To me, this points up the great tragedy and yet the great hope I see for Christians today. The tragedy is that the severe racial damage that has taken place in white and black people alike has perpetuated both the inequality and the inability of people to come up with economic answers to that inequality. The result has been a liberal approach to the problems of the poor.

This is a whole other brand of racism that is fundamentally different from the redneck racism that got the widest exposure during the civil rights movement. This brand of racism begins with a mother saying to her child, "We are all the same, no matter what color skin we are." This wouldn't be a problem if she didn't really mean, "We are all white." The overriding assumption is that black people can fit into white molds and that their measure of success should be white standards. The system is really O.K.—we just need a few minor adjustments.

This attitude has infected the Christian's witness—both black and white—to the black and poor communities of this country and the world. For many white Christians, strategies for involvement in the community are based on a volunteer or charity mentality. Our white society's concept of charity is one of the main stumbling blocks to real community development. This is because in white society, charity can blind people to reality and substitute cheap action for expensive action. And when I say this to my white brothers and sisters they get very uncomfortable. But charity blinds us and keeps us from seeing that our whole system works methodically against the development of certain people—economically, educationally, spiritually, and socially. The white person who is a part of that system and benefits from it uses charity in order to cleanse his or her conscience and in order to have a means for not dealing with the big issues.

Church charity and government welfare both failed because neither understood the depth of need among the poor. Both rely on outside personnel, outside capital, without any heavy emphasis on training local people, and therefore will never reach the point of real community development. Real community development begins with an identification with the poor. It is difficult to identify with the poor and be a part of and benefit from the system at the same time.

I have seen this mentality work in volunteers who look back on their one, two, or three years of service, and say that they have already given such and such for so many years and have paid their dues. This attitude can be devastating to a community. People I'm with demand a trust relationship before they will commit themselves to me, my program, or my God. Local projects demand steadfast support in order to grow and develop. But white Christians have the luxury of "short-term" commitment, and the most deadly thing about this mentality is that it is spreading to many black people, who have experienced the mobility of the middle class for the first time, and make a big thing of dedicating maybe two years of their lives to some "charitable" work.

Another way in which this unequal white mentality affects Christian strategy for community development is through a funny sort of economic negligence, a blindness to the economics of the gospel. A person free to pop into a community for a little while and then pop out, or one who decides to financially support a project, can still very easily maintain his guts or her lifestyle back in the system and never have to deal with the basic problem of where the money comes from to do the Lord's will. I know a young lady, for instance, who got very upset with Voice of Calvary's plan to develop a Christian investment bank for black rural development. She couldn't see the development of a bank as a part of the gospel message. Reacting to the idea out of her own struggles with materialism, she had the luxury of taking a very "moralistic" position on money. But when it came time for her and her husband to build a house, they borrowed over $7,000 from her parents.

White Christians cannot afford to allow their culture (or their reactions to it) to blind them to economic reality. And the reality is that black children just do not have Mommy and Daddy with $7,000 right at hand. Yet we intend to call black young people to return to their communities out in the rurals and in the cities. To do this we must develop plans to allow them to develop their own indigenous financial support systems. In the end, to talk about human development without economic development is hypocrisy.

But racial damage has also affected the witness of black Christians to their own communities. Many black Christians are limited by a mentality that is not able to get beyond the point where "my problems are just how to survive." And survival has become a "game-show lifestyle." I have seen too many of my black brothers and sisters earning $12,000 a year but still "trying to make it." Much of the slavery we face now is within, where we as oppressed people have accepted our oppressor's value system rather than seeing the desperate psychological slavery in which many blacks live. Many of us still look to "things" as the answer to our problems. And the result is that the world "makes merchandise" of us (2 Pet. 2:1–3, kjv). We see this happening today among black people who have consumption on the brain. And it is fostered in many of our churches where the minister promotes a Cadillac-lifestyle and collects big offerings that take more resources out of the community.

I find it very difficult to criticize the black church. I thank God for the black church, that through it he was able to maintain the sanity and meet the deep emotional needs of a people under oppression. The church helped people survive. But we must move beyond survival.

The tragedy is that so many blacks have bought the American dream, have not only bought it, but bought it with money borrowed from the white man's bank at 12–18 percent interest. This is not development. And this purchase of the American dream with all of its consumerism and competition and survival mentality has stolen our minds and our resources away from the battle line. The American dream is keeping us from developing our own local leadership and our own economic base from which we can really begin to preach the gospel in our communities.

What has happened is that we've got the American dream deep within our hearts. Then we look out and see the terrible situation we as black people have been in and we say, "That's wrong!" Then after we've said it loud enough and long enough, the white liberal people come along with their programs designed to appease us. And instead of looking deep enough to see that what they are giving us isn't anything, with that greed in our hearts we look out and say, "We deserve that." The result is that we've been tricked into damaging ourselves by accepting this welfare mentality and by exploiting and ripping off the hand-out programs created by American liberalism. It is a trap because it traps our minds and our hearts.

The way it worked during the civil rights movement was when the young civil rights workers would go home to their families and to the foundations that were in their communities in the North. They would ask for money to do programs in the black community. And it was like turning on big spigots spilling out money into the black community. Those workers, then, would come back and run the programs, and black people became retarded and crippled throughout the South and in the small communities. They had never seen anything like that kind of money before. So it retarded us because it caused us to be even more dependent on white people, even though they were well-meaning, liberal white people. And that dependence is still at the heart of our poverty today.

It was against this background that black power had to develop. People like Stokely Carmichael and Rap Brown began to see the failure of liberalism and began to demand money instead of asking or begging—demanding it with no strings attached. This is a good principle. Although the spirit behind it was in no way aimed at reconciliation, these demands gave perspective to the need for equality to be economic.

Yet in spite of the tragic state of our Christian witness to the black and poor communities, the nature of political reality also gives me a great hope for Christians today. Just as the racial damage amongst us has resulted in a liberal and harmful approach to poor communities, I believe the basic values available to us in our faith can lead us to a radical commitment to the poor.

So I believe that evangelical Christians, both black and white, hold the most hope for real effective involvement with the poor black community. This has to do with my evaluation of our present-day political attitudes. I have no hope that the world will find a value system anywhere within the strategies which it has already formulated. But I am convinced that evangelical Christians, although heavily retarded during the last decades of withdrawal from social involvement, may be the only ones able to provide the technology and leadership in the development of strategy for community development.

I believe that in order to make the necessary breaks with the present system and its mind-set, a person will have to experience a deep repentance, a thoroughgoing transformation of his mind through the power of God, and an openness to biblical strategies of human development. This especially means a deep understanding of equality and the economic implication of equality. And I believe that these are found only in the context of a life committed to Jesus Christ, his body of believers, and his inspired Scriptures.

So what we have dealt with are the deep instances of racial damage in both white and black people that have kept Christian programs from being effective and have kept movements toward human and community development from being able to pursue an equality that had any sort of economic meaning.

Equality then is the issue. But as I looked out at the system of justice in Mississippi, at the end of the Sixties, the system that was supposed to maintain equality, I saw the impossibility of its breaking with the Southern tradition and the cultural values which had kept black people enslaved for generations. In fact I saw that the justice system was being wielded more and more as a tool to maintain the oppression of black people.

But my deepest sense of sadness came when I looked at the church, that institution that was to produce God's equality on earth.

I had developed a friendship with a white minister of the First Baptist Church in Mendenhall. He came to know that I understood theology, that I understood the basic truths of the gospel and that Jesus Christ was living in me. As we developed a relationship, I began to challenge him with the convictions that I had about changing our community. And he became deeply convicted, to the point that he shared it with the people of his congregation. The rejection that he felt from his people, the ostracism that he received from his congregation as a result of his new convictions caused him to go into a deep despair.

I remember one day I was meeting with him and when I left his office he was in tears. A few weeks later he committed suicide.

This same thing happened with a minister up in the Delta that I had become friends with. When the civil rights movement came to his town, he too had taken a stand, fallen into despair at the intransigence of his congregation, and then committed suicide.

These friendships showed me that culture and racism were stronger than faith among white people in Mississippi.

And so I was in a gap. It wasn't just the difficulty of raising up black leaders. No, the gap was formed by the fact that on one hand the system of justice threatened us. On the other hand the church threatened us. It was a gap where on one side there were the liberal people who wanted to minister to the bodies and the stomachs of men and women in the community but had no concern for their souls. And on the other side were the people who had a concern for the souls of men and women in the community but cared nothing about their bodies and their physical welfare. On one side there was a damaging cheap involvement; on the other a pitiful noninvolvement. I couldn't see a way out of that gap. In seeking after equality and after justice, God was about ready to take us through that gap. If we had known beforehand what was ahead, we might have turned back.

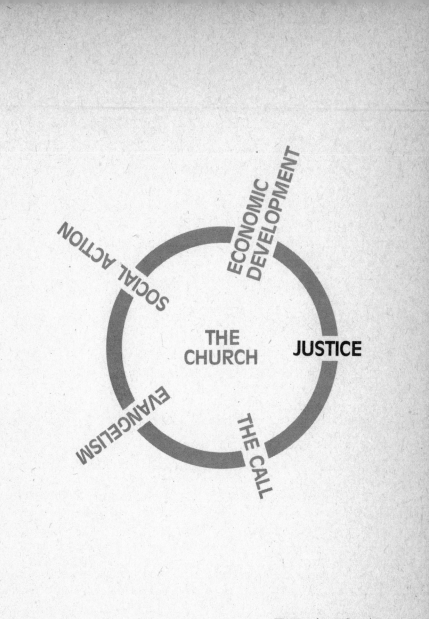

ECONOMIC DEVELOPMENT

SOCIAL ACTION

THE
CHURCH

JUSTICE

EVANGELISM

THE CALL

Part Five

16.

Locked In

It began behind bars in the Mendenhall jailhouse—I'm talking about the worst two years of my life. Seventeen of us, including Doug Huemmer and myself, had left VOC for the courthouse to check on Garland Wilkes and then over to the jail to check on Roy Berry. Some had stayed at the cars. So now here we were, almost a dozen in all—mostly kids including my own Spencer, Joanie, Phillip, and Derek—locked up in jail for trying to see if our friend Roy Berry was getting beaten.

As I think back on it, we were "locked in" not just by the bars; we were almost destined to wind up in jail. It had really started somewhere a long time before, when we had first decided to come back to Mississippi—or maybe even back further when both Vera Mae and I had decided to give our lives to Christ. But it seemed like we were locked in to a set of beliefs, and then to a calling that we couldn't escape if we had wanted to, which led like a chain reaction to us being in jail now.

Dominoes used to be one of the favorite games among the young men in the California prison camps. I always liked the way you could set all the dominoes up in a row and push over one, causing the rest to fall one after another with a clickety-clack. That's how our life had been, except the dominoes were stages in God's dealing with us, one falling right into another. First there was *the call* to live with a people. Then God had called us to share his gospel through *evangelism*—that was the next stage. He had us learn from and depend on the people, so our evangelism took us into their lives and face to face with their needs. Next was *social action*—trying to fill some of the needs we found and also communicate to the deep spiritual needs behind the physical demands of poverty or sickness. Then there was *community economic development*—because as our social action deepened, it caused us to have to deal with the questions and causes behind the symptoms of poverty.

And finally, like the last domino, our witnessing and our concern and our programs led us into a confrontation with the system perpetuating many of the problems—the issue was *justice*.

Things moved very swiftly that Tuesday night, two days before

Christmas, 1969. First there was the question of the kids. All of us
had decided that if one got locked up, we'd all get locked up. But,
how in the world could they lock up minors? Besides my kids, there
was Georgia Quinn—she must have been about eleven years old—
and Carolyn Albritton—she is now married to Artis Fletcher, the
pastor of our church in Mendenhall—and then there was Susie
Williams, Earnest Jones, and some others.

Well, the jailer soon realized his blunder. He tried to get the kids
to leave. They wouldn't. The kids were asking sensible questions
like, "Why are we locked in here?" and "When do I get to make the
one phone call that I'm entitled to?"

Pretty soon parents were coming and getting into the act. Carolyn's
daddy came and you could tell by his face that he was terrified. Why
not? Everybody else was. Carolyn yelled out, "Do something, Daddy;
do something!" But it would take much more than a girl's appeal to
her daddy to deal with this mess.

Only one person left on his own and that was Earnest Jones who
told the group he had to be at work. After we discussed it, the other
kids gave him the O.K. But everyone else just stayed.

It was a fantastically high-pitched emotional time for me. When
the officials asked again and again for the kids to leave Doug and
me in jail, the kids would refuse, making me feel like here I was
being protected or defended by a bunch of courageous children. The
kids were crying out the windows to the people gathering outside
the jailhouse. Vera Mae had left the rehearsal of the church's Christmas program. She had called Brothers Jesse and Isaac Newsome, and
they had come with her to the jail. Now she and Joanie were carrying
on tearful conversations across the bars in the window.

All of this was having its effect inside of me. It seems like things
always hit me hardest in the stomach, and my stomach was upside
down. It was at this point that I sort of first made the decision.

I decided to stay in jail and not post bond right away, and to call
for a boycott of the stores uptown. Under the pressure of the moment,
I came to a realization. I figured that things had reached the place
in our town, and other small communities just like Mendenhall all
over Mississippi, where in the end someone from each of these communities would have to be willing to give up his or her life in order
to stop the machinery of injustice from just continually grinding
people up. There in jail, I decided that I was willing to be one of
those persons.

As I remember back, again it was like I was locked in. It was one of those crazy decisions that you never would have made before, but in those critical moments, something happens. People sometimes want to make you a hero. But that's not it at all—we were absolutely terrified.

It had never come together before like this—I mean the threats of the system and the needs of the people crashing together, head-on. We had had threats before. My wife would receive calls at night: "If you want to live, you'd better get outta town." "You don't want to be a widow, do you?" Things like that. Just the July before, Doug Huemmer had been stopped on the highway by Officer Frank Thames of the Mississippi Highway Patrol. "He lectured me about how he wasn't going to stand for me to do any civil rights work in Mendenhall," Doug told us later. "If I did anything, he said he was going to harm me." [1]

And we had expressed our needs before. We as the Civic League had asked for things like black employees at the post office, FHA office, bank, and other public offices. We demanded black jailers and court reporters. We demanded the desegregation of all recreation facilities—there were none in the black community. We demanded that all black employees be paid minimum wage and that back-door cafes be closed. We demanded that the streets in the black community be paved. We demanded that police brutality and the killing of black people be stopped—including harassment, shakedowns, beatings, threats, insults, abusive language, illegal searches, and illegal arrests. But we had never been heard. Nobody ever paid the needs or the demands much attention.

But now, the threatening forces of injustice and the demands and needs of the black community had come head to head in this jailhouse—and they welded each other solid in my mind. At that point I went to the window of the jail. I was on the second floor. It was black dark outside, and I could only hear the voices down below, I couldn't see the faces. I talked about just three things—first, what the needs in the black community were and how they were not even considered important by the folks uptown; second, that I was willing to lay my life down to stop the white folks from just making a monkey out of justice; and third, that I couldn't do it alone, but that if everybody would ignore the Christmas rush—even leave the bicycles

---

[1] Quoted from Judge John R. Brown's opinion in Perkins v. State of Mississippi, 455 Federal Reporter, 2d series, pp. 16–17.

and toys and clothes they had on layaway in the stores and on the shelves—then we might be able to see some progress. That would be our rallying point. But only if we worked together.

Like I said, it was crazy. There was, at the end, quite a crowd of black people outside the window.

Meanwhile, they had tried everything to get those kids out. They decided, finally, to take Doug and me to another cell in another part of the building, sort of a divide and conquer strategy. But the kids still wouldn't leave.

Girls were slapped and pinched. We heard screaming and all sorts of noise. Finally, each of the young people was taken one at a time, kicking and screaming, out of the jailhouse.

I stayed in jail that night along with Doug. The next day I talked with my lawyer from the Lawyer's Committee for Civil Rights Under Law. We firmed up the strategy: "Wait until tonight, after all the stores are closed," he said. "Then make bond." It was Christmas Eve. Later that week he took down the demands that we had come up with and organized them and put the legal language to them that would keep us from being sued.[2] These demands, along with the selective buying campaign, were designed to be the educational process necessary to bring the kind of attention to the problem and to allow the community at large to get a good view of the kind of oppression that was taking place.

Meanwhile, my wife led the campaign with Doug and Curry Brown, one of the original members of the Fishermen back in California. (Curry had come to help us in our youth work.) Like I said before, Vera Mae is an organizer. And I would venture to say that Christmas Eve, 1969, was the worst sales record of any of the stores on Main Street Mendenhall. See, in a small town like Mendenhall, most of the stores are on one street. In our case it is only two blocks long, running from Old 49 up to the steps of the courthouse. Because of their small size, the stores usually charge fairly high prices. Being only thirty or so miles from Jackson, a lot of white people shop up at J.C. Penney's or Sears or the big chain stores in the city where they can get better buys. This means that the shops in most rural Mississippi towns depend pretty heavily on black and poor white customers.

These were the folks that Vera Mae talked to. The next morning

---

[2] See Appendix.

she placed different people—almost like street captains—at different corners to stop the cars as they came in off the road, loaded up with black shoppers trying to do their last-minute Christmas shopping. They'd say, "Don't even kill your engines; don't even get out." Almost everyone went and shopped in neighboring Magee or in Jackson.

I got a report from Vera Mae as soon as I got out of jail. I had to remind myself that this was the same woman that didn't want to come back to Mississippi nine years earlier.

We continued the marches every week through January and February. We would march on Saturday as a reminder not to buy during the week. Sometimes we'd just march and sing up to the county courthouse, around it and back—the whole thing lasting about an hour or so. We'd always meet at the co-op store and have a little rally, sort of get everyone's courage up. And we'd pray.

On February 7, 1970—it must have been our eighth march—we had a lot of students from Tougaloo College in Jackson with us. After the march was over, Doug Huemmer was driving one of two vans back to Jackson filled with students. Just as he crossed over from Simpson into Rankin County, a highway patrolman pulled him over for "reckless driving." The other van was not stopped, but the driver, Louise Fox, soon pulled over to call and tell us about the incident.

For me, that call began twenty-four hours of terror, most accurately described in an opinion written by John R. Brown, Chief Judge of the United States Fifth Circuit Court of Appeals, in the trial which was soon to be called Perkins v. State of Mississippi. Judge Brown recaps what happened as follows:

A vehicle carrying 18 blacks and 2 whites is stopped by a Mississippi Highway Patrolman a few hours after all of its occupants have participated in a peaceful march protesting racial discrimination in a nearby town. The Highway Patrol has kept the march under rigorous surveillance, and one of the vehicle's passengers notices a patrol car following them out of town.

After placing the driver of the vehicle [Doug Huemmer] in the patrol car, the officer asks him whether he and his passengers were participants in the demonstration. Upon receiving an affirmative answer, the patrolman threatens his subject, refers to the passengers as "niggers," and then radios for assistance. . . .

A few minutes later between four and six patrol cars pull up, and the officers get out with drawn guns. Rather than ticketing the driver for a minor traffic offense, they arrest him and his passengers, handcuff them, and take them to jail [in Brandon]. The driver claims that on the way he is beaten by a Highway Patrolman [Frank Thames] who has previously made threats to do precisely that, or worse, if he did not give up his civil rights activities.

Two of the Negro leaders of the protest march and a third black man [Reverend John Perkins, Reverend Curry Brown, and Mr. Joe Paul Buckley] hearing of the arrests, go to the jail for the purpose of posting bond for those arrested. After parking in front of the jail and getting out of their car they are immediately arrested by 12 officers and taken inside. One of them [Curry Brown] is beaten on the way.

Once inside the jail two of the three prisoners [John Perkins and Curry Brown] and the driver arrested earlier are beaten with blackjacks, kicked, punched and verbally abused. During these proceedings the county sheriff forces the leader of the afternoon demonstration [John Perkins] to read the demands made by his group, after telling him that he is a "smart nigger" and that his presence in the county constitutes "a whole new ballgame." The sheriff's son, who earlier participated in the Highway Patrol surveillance of the demonstration, is in the jail at the time, as are approximately 15 other law enforcement officers.

Subsequently two of the three organizers of the civil rights march [Doug Huemmer and Curry Brown] have their heads shaved, and the sheriff himself pours moonshine whiskey over one of them. The prisoners are then kept in jail overnight and most are released the following day, although one [Curry Brown]—whose head has been split open with a blackjack—remains in jail all day Sunday and is finally released on Monday after posting the $5,000 bond demanded by the sheriff.[3]

The Saturday following our release from jail, we had another march. It was Valentine's Day, 1970.

The march was crucial because it was the first time we "won," it was the first time the iron-rigid intolerance of the white power structure was broken. You see, an ordinance had been made stating that marchers couldn't come from outside a thirty-mile radius. On top of that, city hall refused to give us a parade permit. The highway patrol was to roadblock the march within about two blocks after it started. They were determined to contain us, to snuff us.

---

[3] Quoted from Judge John R. Brown's opinion in Perkins v. State of Mississippi, 455 Federal Reporter, 2d Series, pp. 49–50.

Vera Mae got a phone call from a lady working uptown. "Sister Perkins, you can't march today. There's about one hundred National Guard and highway patrol up here at the armory, and they all got guns. You tell Rev. Perkins not to go out there. They gonna kill him."

But we had to march. After our beating in jail the Saturday before, we were all bruised up, our faces still swollen and lumpy. I had spent the week recovering in Jackson, where my doctor had had to drain a cup of cold blood from my head. But if we didn't march, it would look like we had lost. So we were determined to march, even if it meant physical abuse or death.

The assistant attorney-general for the State of Mississippi was there, and he was worried. Our lawyers told him that we were going to march at any cost, and that to try to contain the march would probably mean more violence and bloodshed on the hands of the Mississippi Highway Patrol. Mississippi couldn't afford much more of that in the 1970s, so they struck a compromise—they moved their roadblock all the way back to the railroad track. They would allow us to march, but only in the black community.

Now, hardly ever did a white group compromise with blacks. So, it had to work in our favor. Anyway, we were not so much interested in visibility in the white community anymore. We were interested in unifying the black community as much as possible and in giving a sense of hope, a sense of freedom, a sense that justice was worth the abuse.

We met at the same place as all the other marches, the cement brick building with the sign on it that said, "Simpson County Co-op Store." People came who had never come before. Many believed that this would be the last march, not just for Mendenhall, but possibly the last march for all Mississippi. There was little chance that the tired workhorse of civil rights could be whipped into plodding much further into the Seventies, but for those at the store this was the peak.

People began singing:

> "My Mama, she done tole me;
> She tole me on her dyin' bed—
> She tole me, 'Son, you'd better get your freedom,
> Or I'd rather see you dead.' "

I linked arms with Curry Brown and Doug Huemmer and began walking, followed by Vera Mae, Nathaniel Rubin and Jesse Newsome, leading the crowd out of its tight-formed circle. Like a rope uncoiling the marchers left the co-op, wound down Center Street in front of our white house and the Bible Institute building, turned right on Circle Street and followed it around to Dixie Street. We marched down Dixie Street, spilling over both sides of the street, past the tin store-front that had been the Fishermen's Mission and the tarpaper shacks that lined both sides of the street.

As we marched, all the people knew the plans of not allowing us past the end of the street. They had seen the highway patrol and the sheriffs armed with shotguns and riot guns. And so they knew (or at least they thought they knew) that we were marching to our deaths.

That was the power behind the march. That was what sent women screaming into their houses when they saw us coming down the street—they were afraid of what was going to happen to us. Yet, for some strange, instinctive reason, masses of people joined the march. Never underestimate how much people love and want their freedom. We picked up momentum. Even with the ordinance we ended up with the biggest crowd ever—between five and six hundred people!

We marched up to the place where they were going to stop us and kept on going. It looked like we had won, and the highway patrol had retreated.

When we finally got up to the tracks all seemed eerie and unnatural as a squadron of sheriffs, highway patrolmen, and National Guard armed with shotguns and tear-gas rifles blocked our progress. Our group wound itself up in a knot right there in front of them.

Again the people started to sing.

"If I had a hammer, I'd hammer in the mornin',
I'd hammer in the evenin' all over this land,
I'd hammer out Justice,
I'd hammer out Freedom,
I'd hammer out Love—between my brothers and my sisters
All over this land."

Then, facing the crowd of blacks and whites, I went over our demands again. I ended by saying something like this:

"What it comes down to is that we demand our freedom. We demand the power to determine the destiny of our community. Black people will not be free until we are able to determine our own destiny. Let's all join together. Let's pray for these men standing here protecting something that is destroying them and us too. Let's pray . . . "

After prayer, the crowd dispersed—a quiet threat that had over-powered the other threats of the day.

Only a few historic black people had ever been crushed and bounced back to face the oppressor again. Yet we had not been killed. We had not been locked up in jail forever. We had not left town. We were back on the streets. We had broken through to victory.

We marched one weekend after that on February 21, 1970. And that was the last march. Our lawyers had finally gotten to the Fifth Circuit Court of Appeals. The judge there had sent down a protection order calling the highway patrol and police officials to protect us. It marked another victory.

On March 16, 1970, my trial began on the charges stemming from the Mendenhall jail episode where the boycott began. The charges against me were "disturbing the peace" and "contributing to the delinquency of a minor." We knew we were going to lose the case in the local court, so my lawyers were trying to amass enough mistakes by the prosecution to get the trial appealed.

Sure enough, I was convicted and sentenced to a $400 fine and four months in jail. But after our appealing the case, the Mississippi Supreme Court saw the shaky nature of the case—shaky even by Mississippi standards—and threw it back down to the lower court for retrial. We finally ended in a compromise.

By summer of 1970 I was tired, supertired. My mind was tired. My spirit was tired. My body was tired. I was glad that this was Dolphus's first summer program. There was nobody volunteering from outside to speak of except Louise Fox, Christine Erb and Doug Huemmer. It was a good program, putting on vacation Bible schools in neighboring churches, continuing the feeding and tutoring pro-grams. So we had the spiritual and the social together and it went great.

One afternoon I was out at the ball field with the kids when I felt some pains in my chest. I went back to my little office and collapsed on the bed. Within a few days I was in the hospital—up in Mound Bayou where I was helping to organize some co-ops. After taking some tests they found out that I had had a mild heart attack. My ulcers flared up again—the first time since 1957. In all I was in the hospital about a month that summer. I had to miss Dolphus and

Rosie's wedding because of it. I guess the pressure of the struggle was beginning to show itself.

I began taking invitations to speak again, and started traveling to different parts of the country. Our first real summer volunteer program grew out of my speaking. While I was in California visiting my good friend, John MacArthur, Jr., we made arrangements for a group of young people from his church to come and work in Mendenhall during the summer of 1971. I made the same arrangement with a group of black students when I was speaking at the University of Michigan in Ann Arbor, Michigan, in January of 1971. "This summer," I thought, "will be great. We have black students coming from a major university and white students coming from a good, fundamental church. What a combination: black and white, socially oriented and spiritually oriented, all with skills and energy!"

As I was getting on the plane back from Michigan, however, my stomach cramped up, I doubled over in pain. The next morning I was in the hospital, where eventually I had to have two-thirds of my stomach removed. I went from about 170 to 140 pounds. It was my ulcers.

All of this was an aftermath of what had begun in a jail cell with a bunch of kids, had led to the streets of Mendenhall, and had almost ended in another jail cell in Brandon. To keep going, to keep my motivation up, I had buried a lot of the bitterness and hatred deep inside. It became obvious after this major operation that the Lord was taking me through a spiritual crisis deeper than I had ever before experienced. It was a crisis in forgiveness.

That spring we decided to move our home to Jackson, to get a little distance between us and the tension of Simpson County. But that summer we lived in a trailer in Mendenhall so we could help oversee the summer program.

That summer program was the biggest failure in Voice of Calvary history. Instead of a model of how blacks and whites could work together, it was more like a state of siege. The whites were not at all prepared for the climate. They didn't have the awareness, the sensitivity to the issues of race and justice. So for them it was like diving into a peaceful pond only to discover that it was just some old rainwater covering up some cracked pieces of scrap iron and broken glass. It hurt them.

Then the twenty-five or thirty black kids who came down were out to set the world on fire. They worked in different projects. Three stayed in Mendenhall—the rest went to Jackson. Most of them had missed the action of the civil rights movement and so they wanted to make up for it now. About half of them ended up sympathizing with the new nation, the Republic of New Africa, which had its head-quarters raided that summer in a shootout in which a Jackson police-man was killed.

These kids were always threatening to beat up the white kids. They were sharp, though, most of them studying to be doctors or lawyers or engineers. My wife found herself defending the white kids a lot. And that made the black kids call her an "Uncle Tom." That hurt us.

We just existed through that summer. The biggest blessing was when it ended. Here were fragments of what we believed in coming together—the preaching of the gospel, the social action that met people's needs, blacks and whites working together. But they were coming together without any mediation. There was nothing to glue them together. The poles were just too far apart. It seemed there could be no reconciliation.

17.

People under Pressure

To stand up in an unjust society and call for justice means that I am willing to subject myself to a lot of pressure. When a person stands up on the side of the oppressed and justice he decides to trade comfort for concern, apathy for action, violence for nonviolence, hate for love. In this chapter you will hear from people who have stood under pressure.

First is Mr. Nathaniel Rubin, who is sixty-five years old and still active in the Simpson County Civic League which he helped form. Mr. Rubin has been a farmer and hauled pulp wood for many years in Simpson County.

I have always desired to see some changes in the survival of life among people, ever since I can remember. My grandfather was a sharecropper. But my stepfather, who was just like my father, never sharecropped in my lifetime. He always did what we call public work. He had been in the sharecropping for awhile but he never would bow to it. I sort of picked up some of his inheritance because I also resented sharecropping.

Two things got me involved in the movement. One was the harassment in the 1930s of black teenagers who were not allowed to walk on the sidewalks of Mendenhall. The general ill-treatment of black people made me commit myself to the civil rights movement years later.

The other thing that involved me was World War II. Soldiers returning from the battlefields could not go into a waiting room 'cause they wasn't integrated like they had been up North or overseas. I was an eyewitness in Jackson to see policemen using night sticks on soldiers coming back home because they walked through the white waiting rooms. This also tilted me toward the civil rights movement.

Then later on came the Freedom Riders on the buses and then students working during the summer. Then the voter rights bill was enacted in Congress and people came in full-time in our area to begin to register voters and that's when we became fully involved.

Later several things happened which we thought was wrong. There was some false arrests and some beatings. A young man was thrown into jail after being accused falsely of phoning a white girl. Rev. Perkins went up there with a committee to see that it was worked out—either get him out of jail or pay the fine. They was all thrown in jail.

This united us in concern and we started fully in cooperation. At Voice of Calvary we had access to the equipment like mimeograph machines and typewriters and—when we was kicked out of the other churches—a place to meet. Here the Civic League was born, one of the oldest community action programs. At one time we had near nine hundred active members. We created great things. There was the boycott. And the co-op store was born. Voice of Calvary was a program effort to help peoples.

From these things have come some tokens of betterness—streets paved, street lights, not all the time harassment in the black neighborhood. It has generated some better houses. We ourselves as a group have also put in some co-op houses that have meant better living.

Herbert Jones grew up in Simpson County and has been a member of our staff since he left the army, came to know the Lord, and joined us thirteen years ago.

I just love to share what God has done for me. I grew up on a farm in rural Mississippi. Like many black folks, I have a very religious background—I went to church every Sunday. But as I grew older, and especially when I got into the service, I knew that the church and religion wasn't able to speak to my needs. Sometimes I had doubts whether even the preacher knew what it meant to be saved. I just didn't see that religion had any impact on people and the way they lived during the week.

After I got out of the service, I was pumping gas for a man in Mendenhall. This was thirteen years ago. It was just a job. There was no future in it. I had no idea, no vision for what I would do in the future.

Then, one day, Mrs. Perkins pulled up to my pump. She introduced herself and asked, "Are you a Christian?" I said, "Yeah, sure, I'm a Christian." I really thought I was. She invited me down to the Youth for Christ meeting in Mendenhall that she and Rev. Perkins had formed.

I didn't go the first week, but the second I went down to the rented tin storefront they called the Fishermen's Mission and that was the first time in my life I heard the gospel preached.

I listened to the invitation to receive Christ and allow him to live his life through me. But I didn't go forward. I was under conviction and tempted to leave. Finally the meeting ended. I got into my car, feeling like I was going to bust inside. I drove like crazy to get home, hoping I wouldn't get in a wreck or get killed before I had a chance to get right with God. When I got home I got down beside my bed and asked Christ to come into my life.

Since then I've driven the buses to pick up kids for the Bible studies and also worked in construction. Now I head up the construction crew at VOC in Jackson.

When the civil rights movement hit Mendenhall, I saw how I could be a witness for Jesus Christ and his love for me. As a Christian I thought civil rights were important because I believe that God loves all men as much as he loves me . . . that all men are created equal. I think Christ was concerned about people being equal and free. He didn't mean for me to be no more than the next man.

So I helped register voters like crazy. Now, besides carrying children, I was taking adults to the registrar. Then one night I went into a coffeehouse for a cup of coffee and a steak and instead of going around to the back of the kitchen, I sat down in the front. On my way home I was stopped and a policeman took me to jail. I had to spend just one night in jail, but I was scared. I can remember praying and reading the little Bible I carried with me and thinking about the Apostle Paul. This was a real time of thanking God for me. I didn't have to be militant or angry. I was a son of God.

Carolyn Albritton was one of the first young ladies from the community to commit herself to the Voice of Calvary. In 1968 during the summer she worked as my secretary. She, like most of our people, had a strong religious background yet a deep commitment to Jesus Christ. When the civil rights movement came to Simpson County this created a lot of pressure inside her with her traditional background. Then there was the pressure she felt when she was locked up in jail with the rest of us two days before Christmas. Finally there was the pressure from fellow Christians at the Christian school she was attending who couldn't understand how Christians could be involved in a witness for justice.

In 1971 Carolyn married Artis Fletcher and now serves with him in Mendenhall.

Ever since I can remember I was going to church. But it was in high school that I first heard Brother Perkins and his flannelgraph stories. I had been saved before then but the new understanding from the presentations at school and the Bible studies I began attending at Voice of Calvary reassured me of my salvation. This was the first training and growth I had in my Christian life.

After I graduated from high school Rev. Perkins asked me to be his secretary and I have been working here on and off since 1968, when I graduated.

I would say the thing that meant most to me in the first years of my relationship with Voice of Calvary was the teaching from the Word of God. Nobody else was teaching what they were in terms of living our lives and giving our whole selves to God. I'd never heard it from any other church or minister. In fact, after coming to a few of the studies, I began to wonder whether Voice of Calvary was really sound or not, compared to what I knew from other churches. But as I got around outside of Mississippi, I began to discover other people who were teaching the Word of God, that Jesus is Lord of our lives. So early on I felt the pressure of being different. Plus my family wanted me to be committed to my home church instead of Voice of Calvary. It was a painful and confusing time sometimes. But I had to make a decision and I chose to stay with VOC.

In the fall of 1968 I began to attend a Christian college in California. I was an English Literature major and a Bible minor. There were no Christian colleges in Mississippi that I could go to.

Being one of the only blacks there I had to make some adjustments. I was always striving to study hard, to do my best in whatever I did because it would make me look bad as well as other black people if I didn't. I was always conscious of this pressure.

I remember when one of the men there showed a film explaining the seven major points of communism and then using Dr. Martin Luther King as an illustration, using everything that he had done to show that he was a communist. All the black students decided to just leave. But by the end of the film some of the whites wanted to know why we left. We tried to explain but it was hard to really communicate to them how we felt. After seeing that film they just could not understand how we could think that Dr. King was not a communist.

By 1968 VOC was pretty heavily involved in voter registration and the civil rights movement. I had determined that I would do whatever I could too. I knew what it was all about. I had worked for a cleaners in Jackson, for instance, in the summer of 1967. One Saturday there was nobody there but the boss, who was a white man, and me. The black males and females had one bathroom out in back. The whites had two bathrooms on the inside.

But somebody had taken the key to the black bathroom and there was no way I could use it. So I asked the boss if I could use the ladies bathroom on the inside. He said, "No." I had worked there all summer and he still said no. So I had to walk down the street until I could find a bathroom I could use.

Things like this gave me determination to do whatever I could to help the cause of black people. I thought that this was a part of my duty as a Christian. Whenever there was a march I participated, although I was always afraid with all the police, guns, and dogs.

I was here on Christmas vacation from school when the marches started in Mendenhall. I was one of the group who went up to check on Roy Ray Berry, my cousin. We were all locked up in jail. I remember singing freedom songs in the cell when they teargassed us. We had to drag the boy closest to the entrance back because he passed out. I was scared. But this just gave me more determination that I would do whatever I could for the cause of civil rights.

When we got back to school we would get reports of other marches led by Brother Perkins. And people at school would come to us asking, "What is this all about, why is he marching?" One of the main questions was, "Why doesn't he as a Christian just stick to preaching the Word and get out of civil rights?" We were constantly confronted with this. We tried to explain that preaching the gospel involves our total life, that we can't separate our bodies from our souls while we live here on this earth. It was a struggle trying to get people to understand that he was called to meet the total needs of people.

This caused isolation. A few people tried to understand. Others didn't try. Others were antagonistic. My English professor knew a little about civil rights and he tried to help our class become a little more open-minded by letting his class discuss what was going on in Mississippi. After I or someone else would share what was happening, some of the students would say, "You're a liar. I don't believe it. Nobody gets beaten in Mississippi, nobody gets beaten in America. This is America. This doesn't happen here. This is a free country—people can say what they want to say."

The whole class would end these discussions in an uproar because people just couldn't believe that this could happen in America. This happened more than once. And the classes became so antagonistic and attitudes became so bad that our teacher would have to end the class.

At the same time there were the few who did see what was happening and they'd say, "Let's get together and pray." So during this time that Brother Perkins was in jail we had prayer groups every night praying specifically for him and for his life.

Dolphus Weary, as he has looked at the situation for over twenty-five years, sees the progress that comes from people willing to put up with the pressure and sees the pressure of future needs that still demand attention.

What you had in the Sixties was a solid minority that stood strong with Voice of Calvary during the struggle for civil rights. Those were people who saw their humanity as being more than their livelihood and more than their jobs.

When you come in with a struggle like that, you are going to uproot the whole system. People began to get fearful. First, the boss man would threaten them on their job. Many people have come to me and said that because of their association with VOC somebody wouldn't hire them. That's the type of oppression we still face. We are talking about now, in the Seventies.

So a lot of people shy away from Voice of Calvary because VOC stood strong in civil rights. They want to reap the benefits of more jobs and things like our gym on a sly, sneaky level, but don't want to stand themselves.

From an historical perspective, I see that that was the only way that we could have gone. First, because we've got to live here with the abuses. Second, because we believe that Jesus wants people to be free to be whole human beings, men and women. Christianity is freedom. I think about the people who left their homelands to found America seeking religious freedom. In the civil rights movement, too, blacks have had to seek a true and meaningful freedom.

I have seen progress because I've been here. I've seen it in relationships. This is my most striking statement: After graduating from junior college at age twenty, going to school in California was the first time in my life that I had talked face to face with a white person in my peer group. Now it is commonplace—in schools, restaurants, hotels. I can feel the gradual progress.

It's because somebody took a stand. Not because people sat back and said, "The Lord is going to take care of this." Instead people went out and said, "I trust the Lord to use me to help make a difference in this situation."

There's still a long way to go. Just a few months ago in Mendenhall there was an incident between a white store owner who still believes black folks are nothing and a young black lady at the bank. The merchant came into the bank and broke in line before the lady. While he was in front of her he pushed her and cursed her and ended up hitting her so hard that he almost broke her neck. She has had to wear a brace on her neck for two months because of that lick. One of her teeth was knocked out and the inside of her mouth was gashed. As a result the lady missed about four months of work, not to mention the doctor bills.

It was discovered that the man had done several other things to black people. Yet the authorities fined him $25.00. If he had been a black man we'd still be trying to dig him out of prison. What we are doing is asking people to not buy at the man's store. This communicates. Somehow equality is sometimes best communicated in economic terms.

Old man Michell Hayes made a profound statement the other day. He said, "A person shouldn't have to beg and pay at the same time." If my money is as good as anyone else's, then I am just as much a person.

Dozens of people, black and white, might be behind bars today for such offenses as sitting at a lunch counter or walking in a group up Main Street in some town had it not been for the tireless efforts of this nation's civil rights lawyers. These men and women sacrificed high paying positions, prestige, and comfort in order to make this country's legal system work for people suffering under the injustice of racial discrimination.

Attorney Frank Parker is one of the many fine lawyers who represented me in the courtrooms of Mississippi. His background as a graduate of Harvard Law School, two and a half years of work on the U.S. Commission on Civil Rights, and experience as a white in the South with the original group of law students that came South to work in the movement give him a historical perspective that is unique. Since 1968 he has served those of us in need of legal assistance in Mississippi.

I met Rev. Perkins as a result of my representation of him initially in the case where he and the Tougaloo students were arrested.

The procedural background of the case went like this: We initially removed all the charges from state courts in which the charges were launched against Rev. Perkins and the others to federal district courts for dismissal. At the same time we also filed a lawsuit asking the federal district court to enjoin those prosecutions and to issue an injunction against the prosecutions.

We lost the case to the extent that we were unsuccessful in our removal action. The Fifth Circuit Court of Appeals held that the claims we presented were not subject to removal from state court to federal. But as a result of our exposure of the police brutality to the defendants and the harassing nature of the arrest, the prosecutions and the fact that we filed for damages against the police officers, the state eventually agreed to drop all the charges in exchange for us dropping all our damages. So eventually the whole thing was compromised on favorable terms to us.

The case itself has a great deal of historical significance. First of all, it shows that the pattern of harassing, arresting and brutalizing of civil rights demonstrators on the part of the highway patrol that was very evident and which the country saw every day in the 1960s continued into the Seventies. This clearly showed that the highway patrol and local police and sheriff's department and local authorities still were not willing to accept the right of black people in Mississippi to demonstrate, which was a denial of their rights.

The case shows that civil rights progress is not based on a continuum. In other words, people tend to look at these things in terms of a historic pattern. You have to understand, however, that there were many areas which the movement passed or left untouched. There are places today in Mississippi where the local officials still refuse to accept civil rights and the constitutional law. In many of these areas, if people took to the streets to demonstrate and protest today, they would still be arrested and beaten up by the police.

Beating of black people by police, sheriffs, and highway patrol occurs every day in Mississippi. Sometimes it makes the news, sometimes not. If we devoted our attention to each instance we wouldn't have time for anything else. So what we have to do is take only the cases which involve groups of people being harassed on a systematic basis.

The civil rights movement as it was known in the 1960s in Mississippi has pretty much died out in terms of taking to the streets or mass movements in which large numbers of people are involved on a day-to-day basis. We have very few full-time civil rights workers here in Mississippi anymore. The movement has changed its emphasis and strategy and tactics from mass demonstrations and direct action into a movement for political, social, and economic equality. This is indicated by the large numbers of black people running for political office for the first time and by movements for economic independence and equality such as the cooperative movement. These forms of action are not visible, they are not front-page news, but they are still extensions of the civil rights movement of the 1960s.

Many activists have left the state. Some refer to these people as having "burnt out." There are a variety of explanations for this. First there are the structural reasons. Looking specifically at the civil rights legal organizations, for example, the systematic sense of support, the national support for such organizations has declined considerably. In some areas it has dried up. Foundations and organizations who in the past have provided funding are no longer willing to fund the kinds of litigations still going on in Mississippi. Without funding, people must leave.

There are also personal reasons. My understanding of that dynamic comes from my own experiences in this office for the past eight or so years. The primary reason that lawyers leave is because their wives and/or families are uncomfortable here. Most leave a very comfortable social existence in the North as prominent social figures in the community, and they come down into a hostile environment, because most civil rights lawyers who come here live in white communities. The white communities have been extremely hostile to them to the point where I have known lawyers whose wives have said, "If you don't get out of Mississippi I am going to leave you and take the children." So they left.

I have not lived in the white community. I have not had any problems with my wife and family living down here, so I haven't experienced the same kind of problems many other lawyers have faced.

Has Mississippi changed? Well, you have to distinguish between middle-class goals and values and the values and goals that make for real progress.

In terms of middle-class goals—for example, staying in hotels, eating in restaurants, registering to vote—many barriers have disappeared. But in terms of any structural changes very little progress has taken place and in many areas we have gone back.

Take for instance the gap between black people and white people in per capita family income. The gap has widened since the Sixties. More than half (59 percent) of black families are still living in poverty. Then, though some black political candidates have been elected, the number is so few that it is hard to see it as progress.

Until fundamental changes are made in the economic structure of Mississippi I am not optimistic. It seems that white people in the state and over the country at large have conditioned themselves to a situation of economic imbalance where blacks will remain at the bottom of the structure.

What about the church? The white church institutions in Mississippi have been the last bastion to racism and discrimination. The churches in the state continue to exclude black people from church activities for the most part. The churches in Mississippi were among the first institutions which responded to public school desegregation by establishing racially segregated private schools as an alternative to public schools in the churches themselves, and have spoken out against any kind of civil rights progress that has taken place. So if somehow all the church and church institutions had been wiped out in Mississippi, we would be much further along in terms of progress than we are at the present time.

In the black church there was a split between the churches that provided leadership, resources, and buildings for the movement, and the churches that felt they could work within the white power structure. The second group's activity was regressive, it did not help and in fact set us back. I myself have heard even here in Jackson black ministers denounce civil rights activity on the theory that if you have salvation you can go to heaven and you don't need civil rights.

In terms of plain economics, churches spend millions of dollars sending missionaries to Africa and other countries in Asia to eliminate poverty and disease. Yet here in Mississippi, doctors have done surveys that show that we have the same conditions.

If churches in Mississippi and across the country could be challenged to eliminate illiteracy, disease, and poverty in Mississippi, change would be automatic.

18.

Mordecai at the Gate

"Reverend Perkins is Mordecai at the Gate. His allegations and proof demand that we let him in." So wrote Judge John R. Brown in his opinion written for the Brandon case (Perkins v. State of Mississippi).[1]

If what Judge Brown wrote is true, it is because he saw in our case some of the same issues and dynamics surrounding a quest for justice as were operating in the time of Esther and Mordecai.

The Book of Esther gives us a moving picture of two individuals and their struggle to get the justice that will save their people. To recap the story, the Jews were living in Persia, not quite in captivity but as an inferior race. The king was Xerxes (Ahasuerus as the King James calls him). Suddenly, because of the pride-fed hatred-turned-racism of Haman, the prime minister of the land, the whole Jewish population of the empire was in danger of annihilation (Esther 3:5, 6).

Now the queen of the realm was Esther, the adopted daughter of Mordecai, a Jew. When Mordecai heard of Haman's plan, he went to stand at the gate of the palace.

It was through the love relationship between Esther and Mordecai that his deep concern was communicated to her. Mordecai asked her to go to the king and plead for her people (4:8). But at first Esther was reluctant. To go before the king in his inner chamber without being called was an offense punishable by death. The king had just dismissed one queen for not coming when he called. What might he do if Esther were to break this strictly enforced rule?

But Mordecai challenged his daughter: "Think not that in the king's palace you will escape any more than all the other Jews. For if you keep silence at such a time as this, relief and deliverance will rise for the Jews from another quarter, but you and your father's house will perish. And who knows whether you have not come to the kingdom for such a time as this?" (4:13–15).

Mordecai's words hit home, because Esther's courageous come-

---

[1] Perkins v. State of Mississippi, 455 Federal Reporter, 2d Series, p. 12.

back echoes the depth of her father's own concern: "Then I will go
to the king, though it is against the law; and if I perish, I perish"
(4:16).

God has not changed, nor has his love for justice. Man has not
changed much either, nor has his ability to create injustice. So I can
really relate our struggle in Mississippi with that of Esther and
Mordecai.

In the first place, there is always *the reality of injustice*. Injustice
is when power creates victims. Haman was about to take his personal power and wrap it around his selfish ambitions and create
thousands of victims—dead Jews. The same thing was happening in
Mississippi. Power was creating victims. The result we called injustice.

The unfair arrests, the beatings, the other oppressions were ob-
viously unjust. But to see injustice infect the state's whole system,
including the legal system, was the heaviest thing. In his study of our
case, Judge Brown documented this legalizing of injustice a number
of times.

Commenting on our case, Judge Brown sums up the charges by
saying:

> And yet, thus far, we have not even directly considered the
> most crucial fact of all: the undisputed and indisputable lack of
> any evidence whatever to support the criminal charges against the
> defendants. If there were some evidence—*any* evidence—tending
> to show that any of the petitioners committed a criminal offense,
> it might at least have some bearing on the otherwise uncontested
> inferences to be drawn from the circumstances previously de-
> scribed. We need not try the defendants here in order to consider
> the point. The question is not whether they are innocent or guilty.
> It is simply whether there are *any* facts in this record, no matter
> how tenuous or remote, suggesting that the criminal charges have
> been brought in good faith for the justifiable purpose of enforcing
> Mississippi law.
>
> There is no such evidence. At the hearing in the District Court
> the petitioners presented overwhelming proof that all of the charges
> pending against them are totally without foundation. Rather than
> attempting to counter this massive barrage of testimony, the State
> of Mississippi stood virtually mute. Under such circumstances
> silence by itself constitutes evidence of the most convincing
> character.

But beyond our case, Judge Brown points out that even the "advocacy of social equality between the white and black races" was "a criminal offense in Mississippi" punishable with up to "five hundred dollars or imprisonment not exceeding six months or both." Also, "on the dates of the events in question, all Mississippi law enforcement officers were under a statutory duty imposed by the State Legislature to 'lawfully' prohibit any attempt to cause 'mixing or integration of the white and Negro races in public schools, public parks, public waiting rooms, public places of amusement, recreation or assembly' in the State." [2] Yet these were some of the issues that took us into the streets. It put us in the position of Esther, who also felt she had to make her appeal, even "though it was against the law" (4:16).

What we faced was a system without a basis for justice, what Judge Brown called "Mississippi's 'steel-hard inflexible, undeviating official policy of segregation.' " [3] And this was just a part of a system that included a good bit of the rest of the country. As Judge Brown put it: "It is no mere coincidence that Negroes have figured prominently in many of those cases in which the Supreme Court has reversed State convictions grounded on evidence so insufficient as to constitute a denial of due process of law." [4] That's almost airtight—a way of life forces a race of people into a box of systematic destruction with a legal structure perpetuating the inequality by putting the lid on most challenges that might come from the people in the box.

To face a system like that there must be a *thirst for justice*. "Blessed are those who hunger and thirst for righteousness, for they shall be satisfied," promised Jesus (Matt. 5:6). And there was to be enough justice to satisfy everybody's thirst. "Let justice roll down like waters and righteousness like an everflowing stream," commands God through Amos (5:24).

Mordecai's message gives Esther a thirst for justice. In fact, we can see him here like God and Esther as the people of God. God is calling his people to move and to commit themselves to justice. It's the same call we hear throughout Scripture. God wants his people to burn with a love for justice (Deut. 16:20; Ps. 37:28; Isa. 61:08; Micah 6:8; Matt. 23:23).

Mordecai's message has three pleas that catch Esther's ear. "Think not," he begins, "that in the king's palace you will escape any more

---

[2] Ibid., p. 48.   [3] Ibid., p. 49.   [4] Ibid., p. 46.

than all the other Jews." *Not until we are all free will any of us be free.* I remember when the black representatives for the Democratic Party went to Atlantic City in 1964 to try to unseat the all-white Mississippi delegation. The black delegation of about ten was offered two seats. Fannie Lou Hamer, from Rulesville, Mississippi, got up and said something like, "Either we all sit or none sit. We are all tired."

To me, this is where patriotism and love of country come from. I see it in the great documents of our country: "with liberty and justice for all"; all men are created equal and endowed with . . . rights and among these are life, liberty, and the pursuit of happiness."

But it was during the civil rights movement that I began to see that the Declaration of Independence and the other great documents of our country were not real even for white Christians. I saw two white minister friends of mine get an awareness of the injustice in the black community, get a zeal for sharing that with their congregations, and then get rejection which led to despair and suicide. I could see that these men and many more like them didn't have real life, because they could not apply their real life to people around them. They could not seek liberty for the black people around them, yet they themselves could not have happiness once they understood their responsibility. So they were not free. This was Mordecai's plea: "Either we all are free or none are free. Whatever you do, Esther, don't let your privileged position now hide that fact from your eyes."

Then came the second plea. "For if you keep silence at such a time as this," said her father, "relief and deliverance will rise for the Jews from another quarter, but you and your father's house will perish." *Silence is injustice.* The picture here is that God is at work to produce justice in this world—in this case to protect his people. We can either have the privilege of participating with him in revealing his justice and freeing people up, or we can be silent. Silence is more than a lost opportunity. It means becoming a part of the system of injustice, a part of that movement in history which is diametrically opposed to what God is doing. Ultimately my silence is destructive, part of the system of death in the world.

This might be the position that the white evangelical church has gotten itself into in the past decades. Its silence regarding the issues of justice may have been cause for God to raise up a primarily secular movement, the civil rights movement, to deal with his heart's concern here on earth. "Deliverance will rise . . . from another quarter," says Mordecai.

As in the days of Amos to lose the thirst for justice can lead to a drought of God's word (Amos 5:21–24; 8:11–12). Does that explain the emptiness in so many of the churches and the pulpits of our country?

Esther hears the implications of Mordecai's words and listens even more closely.

Mordecai's last plea is positive. "Who knows," he questions, "whether you have not come to the kingdom for such a time as this?" What he is saying is, "You, Esther, might be the special agent chosen by God to do his will." *God uses people to demand his justice on earth.* To me there is nothing more fantastic but mysterious than the fact that God uses people to accomplish his purposes: what a great privilege of being with God in his work!

Mordecai's message—that none are free unless all are free, that silence is injustice, and that God uses people to call for justice— creates in Esther that thirst for justice that causes her to be willing to risk her life and position for her people in their time of need.

I had my Mordecais, those people who could call me to account and inspire me with their thirst for justice. But after inspiration, there is the cost. *Justice has a high price.*

Extremism is the first price paid for justice. It is the risk of taking a stand, of losing friends or making enemies. One of my favorite quotes comes from Senator Barry Goldwater: "Extremism in the cause of Liberty is no vice." To take a real stand for justice is extremist. God through Isaiah was extremist when he said, "Cease to do evil, learn to do good; seek justice, correct oppression" (Isa. 1:17; see also Ps. 37:28; Prov. 8:13; Rom. 12:9).

The price of justice is so high that if we are not extremist it won't be paid. Fidel Castro knows this. After a Senate investigation revealed that the CIA had tried to kill him eight times, he asked this question: "Do you know why none of the eight assassins got me? Because they weren't fanatic enough! Not one of those hired killers was willing to lose his life in order to accomplish his objective. If they had been, they would have killed me."

As Christians we stand under the same indictment. We are the only ones who can deal with the real problems of oppression and racism and human need, because we are the only ones who know the secret to Christ's ministry. And the secret is this: "If any man would come after me, let him deny himself and take up his cross and follow me. For whoever will save his life will lose it; and whoever loses his life for my sake and the gospel's will save it" (Mark 8:34–35). In order to follow an extremist, we must be extremists. There must be some of us who can count the cost.

When a few of us decided to witness for justice, it became *physically dangerous*. This is another part of the high price of justice. The society in which we lived defended itself with all of the resources at its disposal. Judge Brown explains in his summary:

. . . 'this case involves a shocking and revolting episode in law enforcement.' It also provides us with still another classic example of the misuse of State criminal procedures for the sole purpose of intimidating the exercise of equal civil rights.[5]

Again, Judge Brown notes the reaction of a society threatened by people asking for justice:

. . . We must conclude that Douglas Huemmer and his 19 passengers were arrested and charged and now face prosecution in the State courts because—and only because—they had participated earlier in the day in the Mendenhall protests, activities immunized against official intimidation by the Civil Rights Act of 1968. Rev. Perkins, Rev. Brown and Buckley were similarly treated because—and only because—they had dared to exercise their Federally protected right to protest racial segregation in Simpson County. There is simply no other rational explanation to account for what happened.[6]

When the Nazis conquered Holland, I am told that they forced the Dutch factories and factory workers to produce war materials. I have heard that members of the Dutch resistance would take jobs in these factories in order to obstruct productivity and deliberately subvert the German war movement. One way of doing this was to take off their wooden shoes, called *sabots,* and throw them into the gears and the turbines of the industrial engines or machines, causing them to breakdown. That, supposedly, is where we get our word *sabotage.*

Tom Skinner uses the phrase "spiritual sabotage." We have some great examples of spiritual sabotage. Jesus himself was the best. His

---

[5] Ibid., p. 58.   [6] Ibid., p. 51.

"sabot" was himself, and by throwing himself into the machinery of sin, he caused the ultimate breakdown of Satan's whole movement of destruction.

This is the price of justice. Esther decided to pay that price. After her conscience and self-interest had been spiritually sabotaged by Mordecai's message, she threw herself into the machinery of injustice and sabotaged Haman's plan. Sometime back in the Mendenhall jail, we made the same decision.

There are some who will say that extremism is wrong, that it leads to violence or evil. I find these people are too in love with the system to challenge it. Then there are those who will say that risking your life is not important, since it won't do any good anyway. I find these people are too in love with themselves and their comfort to move.

Both extremism and the risk of witnessing for justice get results. Those results are the *fruit of justice*. The streets are paved in Mendenhall's black community today. There are quite a few nice new FHA houses because we got a black man a position in the Farmer's Home Administration. Black people are working in the highway department. Black people are receiving minimum wage. Black people can work at the plant now. Black people can vote in Mississippi today. Black people can swim at the pool and at the local lake. Black people can be reasonably sure that they will not be beaten by police and if they are, they know that they can get the necessary legal counsel. Black people can come at least to our clinic in Simpson County, the VOC Cooperative Health Center, and not have to stay in separate waiting rooms or wait while all the white people are seen. If there had been no Rosa Parks or James Merediths or Medgar Evers or Martin Luther Kings—if nobody had come and marched from the co-op—if these people would have turned to moderation and gradualism, the laws and policies and structures and culture and traditions that perpetuated our closed society and any closed society would never have been challenged.

Another great quote: "The price of freedom is eternal vigilance." There are many injustices still taking place in the state and country because of prejudice and discrimination. It has not been like under the rein of King Ahasuerus, where an edict could be written, enforcing the hard, fast rule of reform (Esther 8:10). The struggle is not over. In many places it has barely begun. But we have tasted some of the first fruits of justice.

The highlight of our movement was the Mendenhall trial—concerning our imprisonment with the kids—which was tried in our hometown shortly after the beatings and the marches. In that courtroom I saw how justice and the principles of liberation and leadership and inspiration work in people on a local level. I believe that we won at Brandon, but the results are just not all in. But the results of the Mendenhall trial were immediate and visible and uplifting. They added momentum and strength to the struggle.

First, the trial had an impact on the future young leaders of Mendenhall. This has to do with the whole idea of self-determination and motivation as it worked itself out among the kids who were a part of that young movement. Most of them were seniors in high school. The way this expressed itself was the way these kids wanted to identify with me. Because of the fact that they admired Curry and myself, their actions around the trial were like a defense for us, showing gratitude for our leadership. It was like the leadership communicated by Mordecai through Esther: all of Mordecai's concern and commitment were communicated through his love for Esther as his daughter. The same has happened between me and these kids.

What happened was that the leaders and football players organized a walkout. This was in 1970 when they were still at the all-black high school. (In the coming fall all the schools would be integrated.) But during the two days of the trial, at ten o'clock when it was time for court to open, a group of kids would quietly leave their classrooms and come on up to the courtroom to watch the trial. So the trial, in what it called these young folks to do, caused them to stand up and be men and women.

In fact, the impact on the young leaders spilled over to the next school year, the first year of total integration. That homecoming was the first time a black girl and a white girl ran against each other for queen. When the black girl won, the school administration expelled her on a trumped-up charge. In protest every black student but one went on strike. Even some of the white students sympathized with the blacks, although they never left class. It looked for awhile like the administration might yield and the girl would become queen. At one point they even compromised and said there would be two queens, one black and one white. But the black students wouldn't accept this. Finally, under the pressure, the black family transferred their daughter to another school.

Both with the young people and the adults, the issue was facing the power structure uptown. And the dynamic here is what Frantz Fanon says in his book, *The Wretched of the Earth*,[7] about the need for an oppressed person to be able to face his oppressor before he can be liberated. I believe that a person only becomes whole, a man only becomes a man and a woman a woman, when he or she is able to look their enemy or their oppressor in the face and deal with him on his own ground. That is why sports are so important to black people, because that physical competition, that real struggle with the "enemy" or the "opponent" in open competition, is freedom, it's personhood.

Justice is important because it can be that open field where the oppressed and the oppressor meet. But where justice is distorted, it can't happen, and that's why our trial in Mendenhall was so important. We became the vicarious expression of all the black people in the county standing up to face the oppressor. We became the means through which every black man or woman could stand up to the white power structure and look them in the eye and be victorious.

This was at once the sweet and pitiful side of the trial. It was sweet because it created a unity among the people. Black folks from all over the county sat in court those days. The courthouse was packed. Before this time, all the black folks had had to sit in the old, dirty balcony. With integration, people could sit anywhere. There was symbolic unity in the fact that this was the first time in history a black woman lawyer, our attorney Constance Slaughter, had ever tried a case in Simpson County. So the blacks came out in a sweet unity to identify with me.

Mordecai saw his people identify with him too, not out of some charismatic feeling, but because of the fact that he had represented them in the struggle for justice. "He was great among the Jews and popular with the multitude of his brethren," the Bible says of Mordecai, "for he sought the welfare of his people and spoke peace to all his people" (10:3).

But in our case the pitiful side of justice and the trial was that the people thought that their coming out and identifying with us would make certain that justice would come. And when the white people went on and did what they had to do before all of our people, it startled the blacks, and made injustice look that much worse. I could

---

[7] Trans. Constance Farrington (New York: Grove Press, 1965).

see as the trial went on that the black folks were more than horrified. There was a great sense of pity and sadness. They could not see how I could endure under that.

I wasn't enduring so well, either. The lawyers had already told me that we were going to lose the case, and what we were doing was putting up a stand in order to get something we could appeal on. But the pity that weighed on my heart came when I felt the expectation of the people, when I saw their hopes for justice crushed and depressed into a fateful despair.

But I had underestimated the love of the people. At one recess I decided to go for a little walk outside. If I had been winning, there would have been all sorts of people coming up to me and congratulating me. But when you don't win, you're alone. People don't want to make you feel worse.

So I took this ordinary walk and this old lady walked up with a little steel in her eyes—not pity but fire—and said, "Stand up, Son!"

That was an emotional moment for me. I saw in her all the respect I have for Mr. Buckley, Mrs. Fletcher, Mr. Rubin, Brother Jesse, Mr. Mitchell and all the rest of the people who had taught me, who had stood up over the years. Suddenly I realized that there were masses of black people who couldn't articulate or express the mysterious depths and yearnings they have for freedom. She was not just trying to pat me on the head and make me feel good. She was saying, "We're with you! You are going to win! You are right! You are doing what we all would like to do but can't!" She was speaking to my need, not like a mother comforting her hurt child, but like a mother who is encouraging her son to do something that she can't do herself.

I remember that final scene in the film, "The Life of Miss Jane Pittman." It was about an old black lady living in the South and getting involved in the civil rights movement. In the last scene, she was in front of the police station. She had just found out that their young black leader—who had been like a son to her—had just been killed. In front of the white policemen, she deliberately but slowly walked with the help of her cane up to the drinking fountain marked "Whites Only." She bent down and took not a sip, but a long deep drink from the fountain. Every black person watching that scene took those same slow steps, felt that same cool drink, and stood up with the same calm defiance. And so, this lady, my friend, was telling me, that every black person in Simpson County was walking with me to the fountain of justice that morning. She was telling me to drink deeply because I was drinking for them all.

Well, in the end, we won the battle we lost. We lost the battle in court, but when you lose in court in Mendenhall, people expect you to be put in jail. But we weren't in jail. Not only that, we stayed in Mendenhall, we continued to stand up and move around in the community. So even our presence became a moral victory. We had done something no nigger had ever done before, and were still free.

Then the decision was appealed to the Supreme Court. And when the Mississippi Supreme Court got hold of the case, saw that it was so rigged and tricky, and sent it back to be compromised on the local level, that was another symbolic victory. No nigger from Simpson County had ever appealed anything, we'd always been intimidated at the local level and never had the committed attorneys like Connie Slaughter, James Abram, Larry Ross, and Frank Parker and the others to fight for us. So it was a historical precedent that broke the hold of intimidation.

So for me—through the unity and the rising leadership, through the identification and the love of the people—I felt emerging the same victory that Mordecai and Esther must have felt when Haman was deposed.

It was still all symbolic victory. But then out of that movement and after the failure of our 1971 summer program we began our physical community development. We built our gym in 1972. We built our clinic in 1973. In 1974, our clinic which was in the low-lying area of the black community was flooded. Then in 1975, we opened a new one—in a building formerly owned by a white doctor, a clinic built right across the street from the county courthouse!

It is no accident that black people now receive some of the finest health care in Mississippi across the street from the silver rotunda around which we marched and where we were tried. It is no coincidence that a struggling black ministry finally cracked the white economic structure, so embedded with hostility. It is no happenstance that the back door is locked, the old black-only waiting room is turned into a childcare room, and the front door swings open for all people, black and white. These are the natural results of a living God's strategy for justice, a justice that goes beyond symbol to real power; a justice that confronts the obvious, visible injustices like separate drinking fountains and police brutality, as well as the structural, the covert, the hidden values and policies of systems that go on creating victims.

These were the blessings of justice. But there was another side too, a destructive side. The very justice that I loved could tear me up. We were right, the whites were wrong, not just wrong but evil, not just evil but damned. There was the absolute physical violence of the sheriff and highway patrolmen. And then there was the quiet, sophisticated violence of the judges who had to deliberately apply their reasoning minds to the maintenance of oppression. Justice was important, but it stopped short, it left me too close to justifying my bitterness, too close to hatred.

19.

Why
I Can't
Hate
Anymore

During my night in the jail at Brandon, God began something new in my life. In the midst of the crowded, noisy jailhouse, between the stomping and the blackjacking that we received; between the moments when one of the patrolmen put his pistol to my head and pulled the trigger— "CLICK"—and when another later took a fork and bent the two middle prongs down and pushed the other two up my nose until blood came out—between the reality and the insanity, between the consciousness and the unconsciousness that would sweep across my dizzy mind, between my terror and my unwillingness to break down, between my pain and my fear, in those little snatches of thought when in some miraculous way I could at once be the spectacle and the spectator, God pushed me past hatred. Just for a little while, moments at a time.

How could I hate when there was so much to pity? How could I hate people I suddenly did not recognize, who had somehow moved past the outer limits of what it means to be human? It would have been different if the men had been in control of themselves. But the realization that kept pressing in on my mind was that these men were infected, hopelessly sick, possessed by something which caused their faces to lose that ingredient that made normal features look human, but when missing left faces that could only be described in terms of the animal.

But I don't think it was just the pity I had or the deep sickness I saw alone that pushed me past hatred. It was also the fact that I was broken.

You see, even after I became a Christian I had avoided poor white folks. Because of my economic motivation and understanding, I knew that they were trapped just like I was trapped. I saw them as too stupid. I just didn't talk to poor white folks. It was almost like they were niggers. As I think of it now, I feel bad about it.

The Brandon experience just might have been a way of God bringing me to the place where he could expand his love in me and extend my calling to white people as well as black people. See, for those poor crackers to beat me up in that jail was bringing me low, it was really bringing me low. If dignified people had gotten me—if I had been pursued by the CIA or by some sophisticated criminal minds—I could have gone down in glory. But to let those fools beat me like that, well it broke me.

And I believe that it was in my own broken state that the depth of the sickness in those men struck home to me, and the fact that I was like them—totally depraved. I had evidence before me and in myself that every human being is bad—depraved. There's something built into all of us that makes us want to be superior. If the black man had the advantage, he'd be just as bad. So I can't hate the white man. It's a spiritual problem—black or white, we all need to be born again.

I'm not saying that all my bitterness was gone, wiped out. But it was a beginning. And in the court cases that followed I had to struggle more deeply with bitterness. Finding no justice in the courts, my own deep sense of justice could allow me to justify my hate for white people. The failure, the frustration, the powerlessness of my situation as a black person in the South pressed me. What it was squeezing out of me was more and more bitterness. Like a lemon—so fresh and sweet looking on the outside but hiding such a sour taste. And the bitterness just made the frustration worse. I could hear the same thing happening across the country. Some of my people were saying, "Fight back! Use violence! Arm for the Revolution!" This was the deep struggle going on within me as a Christian for over a year. It wasn't until I was laid on a hospital bed with two-thirds of my stomach removed that I could really deal with it.

I saw how my bitterness could destroy me. The Spirit of God had a hold of me and wouldn't let me sidestep his justice. And his justice said that I was just as sinful as those who beat me. But I knew that God's justice is seasoned with forgiveness. Forgiveness is what makes his justice redemptive. Forgiveness! That was the key. And somehow, God's forgiveness for me was tied up in my forgiveness of those who hurt me. In the hospital room I would reread Matthew 6 over and over, especially where Jesus says, "For if you forgive men their trespasses, your heavenly Father will also forgive you; but if you do not forgive men their trespasses, neither will your Father forgive your trespasses" (Matt. 6:14–15).

We were right. In all of our demands, in all of our demonstrations, in our programs we were right. But now God was saying, "Being right is not enough. You must also be forgiving." In order for our witness for justice to be redemptive, it had to be seasoned with forgiveness.

As I lay on my bed and thought and prayed about his forgiveness and what it meant to me, I began to apply his forgiveness to the faces of the men who had beaten me and to other white people. The scars and hurts of the past seemed to fade away. I realized that God was doing something in my life that reached all the way back into my childhood, all the way past that Saturday morning when Clyde was shot, past the day I had worked for the buffalo nickel and the dime. God was cleaning me out.

For a while I had seen my pain as the violent, convulsive end to everything I'd worked for. But now God's Spirit made me see it as the painful, bittersweet beginning to everything he was going to do in Mendenhall. We were just getting started!

Immediately I could see how, without forgiveness I had limited God's will. I remembered back when Ed Anthony and I would go to the prison camps together. Ed and I developed a unique and strong relationship. It has been friends like Ed who have kept us, who would die with us. Yet in the midst of our relationship was a struggle. Ed was a deep conservative, and in our love for each other, there was always that question whether I was conservative or liberal. The beauty was that our relationship went deep and could handle that struggle. Anyway, I began to share my growing burden with him. "Ed, I really think God is calling me to preach the gospel to my black people."

"But John," Ed would come back, "maybe God is calling you to preach the gospel to everybody." What I heard him saying was that maybe you can't free one without the other. Maybe what frees blacks frees whites too.

This was the side of God's will that he was showing me a glimpse of at Brandon. It was easier for me to "do God's will" as I was relating only to blacks. But God's will is bigger than black, just like it's bigger than white. Now God was giving me a call to both sides of American reality.

But if the understanding came at Brandon, and later on my hospital bed, that forgiveness was my only hope and that hate could destroy me, that my call to preach the gospel extended now to white people, the actuality didn't come until later through contact with people. There has been the growing volunteer program which had a new beginning in 1972 with the participation of a group of six college students from Glendale Presbyterian Church. Since then, through the Brethren Volunteer Service, Presbyterian churches in Colorado Springs, Aurora and Evanston, Illinois, and a growing number of long-term volunteers including many experienced and retired people along with college students, I have seen the roots of reconciliation reaching deeply into the hearts and lives of others as well as myself.

After we started our ministry in Jackson, Mississippi, we received a call one day in the summer of 1975 from Community Legal Services. They had heard about what we were doing and wondered if we could put up an older couple who were down and out, for about two weeks. There was no emergency housing in Jackson beyond one-night rooms at the Salvation Army. We were not at all geared for this kind of ministry. But we prayed about it and said yes. We felt the Lord telling us to turn no one away.

It turned out that the two were white, in their late 40s. One of our staff members went and helped them move their few belongings out of the rusted shell of an old bread truck abandoned on some boggy, partially reclaimed swampland. Out of their life with us, finding clothes and food and housing, has come an emergency housing and counseling ministry.

But these people and others have been the best thing for the balancing of my life that I've ever had. I think it's because God's will is designed to break you. God will continue to bring those things into the lives of his people that will break them and make them bankrupt. It happened with Abraham when he was asked to offer up Isaac. And, of course, it happened with Christ, broken for us on the cross, the perfect vessel of God's perfect will. God's will keeps me at a state of brokenness. God's will is our afterjoy, the joy of seeing growth come out of hardships. For me, this took place at Brandon. It has resulted in an ability to love even poor white racist people.

Now, this new call has really affected my preaching. In fact, I've about come to the place in my life where I can see that the only way to really be "prophetic," to really say "thus saith the Lord" is to let the two-edged sword of God's Word cut both the black and the white at the same time. This is so important because the racial damage is so deep in both the black and the white communities in this country. If I were to compare it to a disease it would have to be high blood pressure, what doctors call the "silent killer." This is because it can go undetected like hypertension and yet affects the psychological, social, and economic lives of its victims. And racism renders ineffective any attempts to create the type of Christian community development that is needed to reach the victims in the poor communities.

You see, God's new call has also affected my whole approach to community development. "One can't be free unless all are free," had practical impact when it came down to doing something creative in the community. Black leadership—the first essential ingredient for development—and technology—primarily at the disposal of white people and also absolutely essential to applying the gospel to the needs in the community—couldn't come together without real racial reconciliation. *Reconciliation* then became the most important ministry, the most relevant impact the gospel could make for reaching the poor.

But, reconciliation is so difficult because the damage is so deep. If I were to sum up all that I know and feel and have said so far in terms of the nature of racial damage in this country today, I would use two words: *guilt* and *blame*.

Guilt sums up what I believe to be the burden of racial damage among whites. Deep guilt feelings about the way black people have been treated are real and present in most white people in this country. I saw this emphasized in one psychologist's report on Patricia Hearst. He said that like most of the people in the Symbionese Liberation Army, Patty was highly educated, affluent, and looking for meaning. He also said that Patty and the other white members of the group became loyal to the black leadership in the SLA because their deep sense of racial guilt caused them to exalt the black leaders and be manipulated around their search for missing meaning.

Guilt will make us do funny things, usually unhealthy things. The way this works in most people, including white Christians, is not in terms of the creative, steadfast development in the community, but instead in terms of cheap involvement. Cheap involvement—like welfare or give-aways—is designed primarily to deal with my guilt, not the problem. What we need are Christians who can get beyond their guilt and so get beyond light charity and really get involved in the black and poor community. I personally believe that it is only the supernatural power of God's forgiveness that can deal with personal guilt and put it behind you.

But then, after that guilt is behind you, you must go on to deal with problems in the institutions in society. Once white people get freed from the guilt and oppression of racism, the reality is that they still hold the power in our society and must take responsibility for the use of it. One of the most beautiful ways that they can take responsibility for it is to move into the black community with the technology that they have as whites and put that technology behind creative black leadership.

Blame sums up what I believe to be the burden of racial damage among blacks. And biblical, supernatural forgiveness is also essential for the black man or woman dedicated to proclaiming Christ and developing the community. The sins in the black community that can most deeply paralyze can be either the idea of being an Uncle Tom or of justifying weaknesses by blaming the whites. They are two sides of the same coin, one coming out of humble dependence, the other out of resentful dependence.

As long as I can justify all of my failures by projecting them on white people as the cause of my trouble, then I can't deal with reality. I've got myself in a position where I cannot be held accountable for the job I'm doing in the community. I can't grow. I'll either become an Uncle Tom in order to get by, or I'll become a militant faultfinder. Also I can't mobilize the resources which I need to pull together the ministries that will speak through the people's felt needs to their spiritual needs.

The power of the black Christian is in his or her ability to forgive. It took me a long time to find this out. I had built up a deep bitter feeling against white people that was crippling me inside. I couldn't move creatively in the work I had to do. But somehow God, in causing me to do his will, was moving me to a point of confrontation with the oppressor in our community that would lead me to have the forgiveness for my enemy that I would need to love him.

Now for us as black people this type of freedom will give us the ability to lead in the community. And this is crucial, because we need to learn how to utilize all of the technology available for work in our communities. For instance, when the civil rights movement began to really get dedicated to economic development in the cooperatives, I saw civil rights leaders who were the most dynamic and charismatic leaders in the community. But many times they just had not been exposed to the managerial skills to pull off real economic development.

We need to take the traditional dehumanizing relationships between black and white people who have suffered racial damage and turn them inside out through forgiveness into something creative. We can do it if we put white technology behind black leadership. Whites, so accustomed to their superior religious position as sons and daughters of God, need also to become servants. Blacks, too often reminded of their inferior position as servants, need also to know the freedom of being God's children, members of his royal family. In the community these relationships can become the flesh and blood behind reconciliation.

If white people can move beyond their guilt, and black people can move beyond their blame, we can use the leadership that is rising up in the black community, and the technology in the white community dedicated to work behind that leadership, to create beautiful evangelistic, social, and economic alternatives in the poor community. We cannot afford to let our guilt turn into paternalism. And we can't afford to let our blame turn into that bitterness that lashes out at people who threaten us simply because they have more technology than us.

My hope is best described by a story I heard Mr. Buckley tell once. A man had a huge wagon full of logs down in a ditch and he had two enormous horses that were trying to pull it out. As one horse would pull, the other would fall back; and as the other horse went ahead to pull, the other one would fall back. They were never pulling together.

Then along came a man with a pair of little Spanish mules almost half the size of the horses. He watched the horses try and try, again and again. Then the man with the mules said, "Let me try to pull those logs out."

The man with the logs looked up at him and he said, "Are you crazy? Those little mules couldn't pull this wagon if it was empty."

The man with the mules looked down and said, "Unhitch them horses and I'll show you."

So the man unhitched his tired horses, and they hooked up the mules. And as Mr. Buckley says it, "Those mules just fell into their harness together, and commenced to pullin', both right at once." They were strained out to the point where they were almost on their knees. Inch by inch the wagon started moving up out of the ditch. By and by, after pulling together in the yoke, that wagon was out of the ditch.

If white and black people could yoke up together that way, some real burdens could be moved. That's my hope.

This hope—founded on forgiveness and reconciliation—demands some deep changes in values and requires us to allow God to deal with us as people in ways that are almost unheard of in our society.

White people must allow the gospel to penetrate their culture. Whites must allow the gospel to speak deeply to their broken, exploitative, superior, and unjust lifestyles and attitudes. White Christians who claim Christ as Savior must also make him Lord over such areas as spending, racial attitudes, and business dealings. Whites must see that the oppression of black people in this country runs deep throughout *both* our cultures. And anything short of a fundamental change of values—which I believe possible only through a relationship with Jesus Christ—will result in viewing the problem as "the black problem" and offering solutions like charity and welfare which have within them the same seeds of destructive exploitation and dehumanizing greed that oppress the poor in the first place.

Black people must allow the gospel to penetrate their culture. Integration, equal opportunity, welfare, charity, and all these programs fail to deal with the deep-seated values that cause the bankruptcy in our black communities. These programs only serve to conform people to this world. Only the gospel can transform people by the renewing of their minds (Rom. 12:2).

The problems we face are primarily problems of values, not structures. It is not reform we need, but revolution, a whole new thing. The old needs to be passed away and the new ushered in. We cannot afford to easily condemn the white person by judging his past or simply condone the black person by understanding his past. We must call each other to be transformed.

But this breadth of transformation, this depth of forgiveness, this quality of reconciliation is painful. Many will try to cheapen it by saying, "Let's just forgive and forget! Why open up old wounds?" But learning does not come out of forgetfulness. There are many who are like the false prophets of Jeremiah's day: "They have healed the wound of my people lightly, saying, 'Peace, peace,' when there is no peace" (Jer. 8:11).

I am told that a burn victim is constantly going through the agony of having his dressings torn off again and again in order to make sure that all of the dead and decaying tissue is completely off the body so that proper healing can take place. The racial wounds that mark this country were burned into our cultures for over three hundred years. It may take a long, sometimes painful process to remove all of the dead tissues of racial prejudice, guilt and blame so that real healing can take place.

As I lay on the hospital bed in 1971 I had no idea how this healing could take place between blacks and white. I had no sense of what it would take to get beyond guilt and blame. But I had some good models, even then. There was Dr. Harvey Sanders, the black doctor who operated on me and reminded me that there were black people absolutely committed to people and their needs. There was Dr. Joann Roberts, a white Catholic lady, who would talk to me and give me a sense of hope and who wouldn't allow me to pity myself or to hold myself back like an invalid.

Out of that pain, however, did come a sense of what God had done in my life—the transaction of forgiveness for hatred. And I understood that I could not do what needed to be done alone. The reconciliation and the transformation that were necessary would have to take place among people absolutely committed to Jesus Christ.

I began to think of our little fellowship back home. Here were people who would die with me. Here were people who had faithfully supported the evangelism, compassionately led the social outreach, who had organized themselves and their resources to develop the economics, and who had endured a witness for justice. I thought of my friends in California and in different parts of the country who had sacrificed with us. We were so few, and yet we had done some things. What were we?

Then I thought of what Jesus said to Peter: "on this rock I will build my church, and the powers of death shall not prevail against it" (Matt. 16:18). It came to me . . . we were the church.

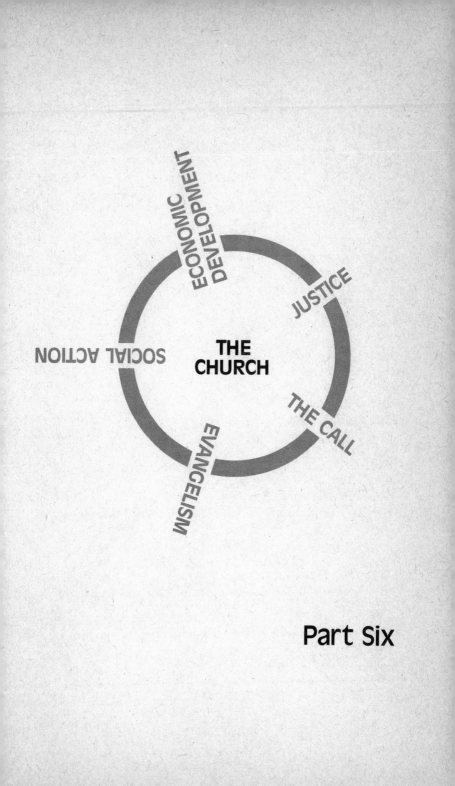

ECONOMIC DEVELOPMENT

JUSTICE

THE CHURCH

SOCIAL ACTION

THE CALL

EVANGELISM

Part Six

20.

Becoming a Body

On Friday night, April 12, 1974, I stood with Dolphus Weary on a railroad embankment watching floodwaters stream through the doors and windows of his house. We walked on down toward the railroad trestle and heard somebody shout, "The Berrys' house, it's floating this way." In awe we watched a home, lifted from its foundation, rocking like a ship, momentarily catch fire and crash into another home already broken on the trestle bridge.

The record-breaking fifteen inches of rain in less than thirty hours proved as challenging as any human threat we had faced in the past. Two nights before Easter Sunday, 1974: this was the night we had chosen for the dedication of our new X-ray machine, which neighboring churches had worked so hard to raise money for, and that churches all over the country had contributed to. And now, the X-ray was under water, along with the drugs and the files in our health center. The chapel, the tutorial school, the gym, the co-op store and housing—all were flooded.

It was difficult for me to understand the relevance of the promise "that in everything God works for good" (Rom. 8:28). You see, I had just moved my office to Jackson. My wife and I had been commissioned by the ministry in Mendenhall to start a new work in Jackson. And it was hard for me to take my hands off. With this disaster, my doubts about whether the ministry would maintain itself in Mendenhall were doubled.

But during the crisis of the flood and in its aftermath, God showed me some things that affirmed me so deeply that today they are the basis for our vision of ministry.

The first thing God showed me was that we had some people—some faithful people. Dolphus and Rosie Weary were like rocks, even though their house was almost wiped out. We had a little prayer meeting with our staff after we came back off the railroad embankment. There were Joan and Ervin Huston, a white couple from the church of the Brethren, who had come in 1972 and lived for two years right next door to the clinic, Joan as a nurse and Erv as administrator. There was Joan's sister, Mary Bucher, who served as my personal secretary. There was Vera Schertz who had come the summer before "just to volunteer for a few weeks" but ended up staying. (Vera is still with us today.) And, of course, sitting beside Dolphus was Herbert Jones.

Here in one room were blacks and whites, both hurt by the waters rushing by a few blocks away, but both absolutely committed to digging out. Here was reconciliation at work. We had come a long way since that terrible summer of 1971.

We prayed, remembering the people, many of them stunned, some wandering aimlessly through the shallow waters. The strategy that arose from that meeting was the same strategy that was used to confront the crisis of education, poverty, and health care among our rural people. As it formulated, I could see that it was the strategy of Christ himself: finding needs and filling them.

But from that meeting onward I realized something else that changed my life: they could do it without me! I felt terrible and exhilarated at the same time. I felt rejected and uplifted. They didn't need me.

I could see more than ever that the Lord was creating more than a program here in Mendenhall. He was creating his church, the Body of Christ. I saw the deep unity between black and white brothers and sisters and remembered Paul's words in Ephesians: "For he is our peace, who has made us both one, and has broken down the dividing wall of hostility . . . that he might create in himself one new man in place of the two, so making peace, and might reconcile us both to God *in one body,* thereby bringing the hostility to an end" (Eph. 2:18–19).

Then I thought about Dolphus, Rosie, Herbert, and about Artis and Carolyn Fletcher who would be returning to live that summer. I looked at their commitment and sense of responsibility and leadership. It brought to mind the thirteenth chapter of Acts where it is recorded that after just one year of ministry under Paul and Barnabas, God had raised up leaders—prophets and teachers—from the local community itself. Paul and Barnabas could be commissioned to go on and do the same thing elsewhere. Suddenly I realized that I had been commissioned none too soon. God had raised up indigenous leaders here too.

Somehow we had come full-circle: from a call to evangelism, to social action to economic development to witnessing for justice—the cycle had pulled others in and they had begun again, they too had answered the call to commit their lives to preaching and doing the gospel in Mendenhall.

And to my amazement I could see that in stumbling around the steps of that circle, in trying to be faithful to God in the situations in which we found ourselves, we had become a church. The circle described a church, a continuing process of doing each one of those things over time, each one accentuating the other.

I watched the impact that our "church" had on the rest of the town during the flood. It wasn't the impact of some charismatic individuals, but the impact of a corporate body, unified in heart and spirit, on the corporate structures of the city.

At 9:00 P.M. I waded with Dolphus and some others through the water to one of the two small neighborhood churches packed with flood victims. We went directly to other men and women in the community and spoke of getting the people together and having a meeting.

About twenty-five minutes later, we opened the meeting with a prayer for unity. And our unity began to reflect in the people as they shared their concerns and despair. Out of this unity of despair grew hope. A disaster committee was formed of community leaders. The chairman: Rev. Dolphus Weary.

Someone got up close to the end and spoke: "You know, this is one of the first times I can remember that the people of Mendenhall have got together as a community."

As I went back to Jackson that night, I was surprised to find that the actual flood was no longer dominating my thoughts. Instead there was the realization that God was doing something a little heavier.

Within twenty-four hours the Community Disaster Committee, under Dolphus's direction, had drawn up a survey form and surveyed the total damage of their town before the Red Cross could even get there. The unity crossed racial lines as the committee which represented the primarily black, low-lying section of town, called upon their mayor to represent them to the governor, providing him with the latest damage statistics available anywhere.

The clean-up and aftermath of the flood confirmed some other realities in my mind. We saw churches and individuals from all over the country respond to the Voice of Calvary's specific needs. There was $8,500 worth of damage done to the X-ray machine alone. Yet, all through that spring and into the summer we received gifts of money, equipment and volunteer labor, which all went to confirm the fact that we were a part of a larger Body of Christ that spread across the nation and around the world.

Then as I watched the original Community Disaster Committee under Dolphus's guidance begin to move into the areas of relief and clothing distribution, of replacing old mattresses and furniture, and finally leaving the issue of the flood and finding a new basis through which to deal with the growing drug problem in Mendenhall, I saw something else. I saw the importance of Christian leadership rising out of and living within a neighborhood. This small body of believers which I had left were proving to be many times more effective than the most highly skilled and trained professionals from the outside. It was because they felt the weight of the problems, they lived them. Dolphus's house was flooded too. This was an element of church that I had known in my guts before, but had never before identified.

The ultimate in blessings rising out of the flood was, of course, our moving the clinic uptown. In fact, just one year later, on Easter Sunday, 1975, we dedicated our new health center directly across the street from the county courthouse. This moved us beyond symbol into the realm of reality. Our marching around the courthouse was a symbol of an alternative to the corrupt framework of laws and traditions that perpetuated the injustice. The clinic is a creative living and moving force, healing people and relationships, overcoming the actual systems and symptoms of injustice.

So, the whole flood experience was for me a little picture of what God had done and was doing with Voice of Calvary. It was a picture of hope that I needed. The waters would recede and the clean-up would eventually be over. But there were greater disasters in the areas of evangelism and education and economics and health care that were far from over. The human disasters that the Voice of Calvary was attempting to minister to would just not evaporate or run quietly down hill into bigger rivers far away.

But what God was showing me was that our low point, our point of failure and frustration in 1970 and 1971 was really just the beginning. As I looked back I could see that from that point of crisis swelled a flood of new directions and ministries and dreams that today are being realized.

Up until 1971 we had been relying on the friendship of a few individuals and churches for our support. Calvary Church in Burbank was about our best supporter along with Arcadia Union Church, Berean Bible Church and people from the old Fishermen's group—

Mama and Papa Wilson, Jim Winston, Curry Brown who had come down to work with us—and a few others.

But in 1972, we had some real breakthroughs. Early in that year I had spoken to Glendale Presbyterian Church in Glendale, California. The people welcomed me warmly, and I'll never forget the words of the senior minister there at that time, Rev. Bruce Thielemann: "John, we're going to get behind what you're doing." Then a group of six young people came down to work in our tutoring school and construction projects as well as doing vacation Bible schools.

Artis Fletcher, who had been sent out to get his theological training in Southern California, was offered a teaching assignment at the Glendale Church on Sunday mornings. Through that relationship with adults and the willingness of the young people to learn, we came up with a situation where a whole church could begin to be sensitized to the needs in the rural black community. What you have to remember in all of this is that the church is located in an all-white community in Southern California! That was the amazing thing. Yet the Glendale Presbyterian Church began to be another model for the way white churches could be involved in the black community.

Early that summer we planned the construction of our gymnasium and vocational training building. We laid the slab and before we put the building up we held revival services every night for a week out on that vast expanse of concrete. They were led by Brother Jack Shaw, a white Southern Baptist preacher from Dallas, Texas. God was really working! We had met Jack earlier in the summer at Explo '72.

By the time we finally put up the frame and laid the cement blocks in place, the community was spellbound with the sheer visible impact of the building. Most folks couldn't understand how we could ever pull it together. It has drawn young people off the streets. Tutoring, vocational training and adult education take place in its rooms.

That summer of 1972 began a pattern for the way God would bless us richly in the future.

Since then we have had speakers—I mean great speakers—come and share with us on everything from "family relations" to "management by objectives." They have included Tom Skinner, Ted Engstrom, Sam Dalton, Richard Williams, Clarence Hilliard, Rich Berry, Ben Johnson, George Moore, and Bob Mitchell.

Since that summer our volunteer program has continued to have people come and work all through the summer. In 1973 we had another group from Glendale including H. and Terry Spees (who have been with us ever since). We had our first Christian black college volunteers that summer of '73 from the work of the Navigator's black campus ministry director Rich Berry in Tuskegee, Alabama. Other blacks have volunteered since.

We then began to receive applications from people interested in long-term service. We had young people working out their conscientious objection status from Germany. People from the Brethren Volunteer Service came for lengthy stays, and we've had volunteers from the American Friends Service Committee.

The volunteer tradition at Voice of Calvary has been a beautiful one. Many people have come back again and again for summer service, and some have come to stay.

One of the most dynamic forms of volunteer involvement has been with large groups of adults and kids who have come from churches all over the country to do some tremendous work. They include Aurora Presbyterian Church and First Presbyterian Church of Evanston in Illinois, Village Baptist Church from the Chicago area, First Presbyterian Church of Colorado Springs, Blue River Church of the Brethren in Indiana, First Church of the Brethren in Baltimore, Walnut Creek Presbyterian Church and Santa Ana's Trinity Presbyterian Church in California, Central Park Baptist Church from Richardson, Texas, and LaGrave Christian Reformed Church in Grand Rapids, Michigan.

In the years since 1971, God has flooded us with programs and outreach as well. I have mentioned most of them already—for instance, the health center. In 1974 came our biggest venture— moving our headquarters to Jackson, Mississippi's capital. But in the nearly three years since that move, God has blessed us. First, there has been the development of another core of committed Christians struggling to be the Body of Christ in this city. Reaching out from that body have been programs—little programs like Neighborhood Youth Club, using our old Child Evangelism materials to reach youngsters for Christ and then their families; and larger programs like Jackson Bible Institute, involving a curriculum of basic Bible training as well as special classes like Black Church History, Family Relations, and Evangelism training.

We now look at our Jackson ministry as a seed bed. Mendenhall was the seed. In Jackson we are trying to develop the people and the programs and the resources to a point where they can be transplanted into other towns and counties and cities all over Mississippi.

The Lord led us to the people. When we moved to Jackson, we bought a big, run-down two-story house with an old dairy barn in back of it, located about seven blocks away from Jackson State University. We have developed many strong relationships with students on campus, about a dozen of whom graduated from our program in Mendenhall. We have students working in accounting, writing, leading youth clubs, typing, and construction. I believe that the Lord is developing a "people bank," a pool of young Christians who will someday be led by the same vision for community development back out into their rural hometowns. As this happens, VOC will be like a rural home missions society.

But what about the times in which we live? At what point in the progress of racial reconciliation is VOC's strategy intercepting Mississippi?

I see many hopeful signs. Locally, there have been the Mississippi Faith at Work Conference, and the Mississippi Billy Graham Crusade. I have mentioned the developing relationship that we have with local white pastors. Just recently the first group of young people from a local white church came over and worked and sweated with us as they painted a house in the community.

I had a chance to share my testimony at a crusade in Cleveland, Mississippi—up in the Delta—conducted by Leighton Ford. The reception that my wife and I received from both black and white Christians was a testimony to the fact that the Holy Spirit's work of reconciliation is being allowed to take place in the hearts of people in Mississippi.

I see evangelical Christians, especially around groups like the Evangelicals for Social Action, beginning to reclaim the heritage of serving justice that has marked evangelicals of other generations.

In the midst of this my hope rests on what God is doing in his church. Voice of Calvary's energy and testimony comes out of the fact that it is more than an organization. God is building his Body here among us. I believe that in order to really deal with the depth of the problem in the society, we must deal with it in ourselves first. And the church is the only institution I know of that offers the basis for a discipline, a commitment, a hope, a truth that is stronger than racism and stronger than any institutional form that clothes racism.

It is this fact, based on the promise that "through the church the manifold wisdom of God might now be made known to the principalities and powers in the heavenly places" (Eph. 3:10), that gives me the greatest hope, that turns my thoughts toward planting the church in the rural community and seeing Christ walk again in his Body among the victims of our land.

21.

What Is God Doing in His Church Today?

Sometimes I feel like the man who discovered the wheel. I run around with my discovery only to find out that not only has the wheel been discovered before, but it has been chrome-plated, motorized, and marketed.

The wheel we've discovered is the church, spinning out of a call to evangelism, social action, economic development, and a witness for justice. Nothing new, just one more expression of Christ's Body here on earth.

What it has taught me, though, is that no matter where you begin with God's Word, if you follow it to its deepest, most radical implications, it will lead you to other people and finally to becoming his church. We started with evangelism. But I have seen others come to us having started with a deep concern for justice although without a deep evangelical zeal, in fact, some without a faith in God.

One young German fellow, an electrician, came to our new project in Jackson from a deep experience in the Kibbutzim, the collective farms, in Israel. He had a deep commitment to working to reconcile Germany with Israel and to pay some of the reparations due the Jewish people for their terrible afflictions at the hands of the Germans. He had a deep sense of justice. Yet this young man had little sense of a personal commitment to the God who set the standards for justice. In fact, he called himself an atheist. He would interact with us and as we would live and work together we would talk about our motivation. He began to have trouble with our fundamentalism. But from one person to another he saw something that he couldn't contest: the love of God giving people a common basis for work and reconciliation across racial and economic barriers.

By the end of the summer, Robert gave his life to Christ. His deep love for justice had led him to the Lord.

There is one verse that I always use when I give my testimony about how God's Word worked in my life: "The word of God is living and active, sharper than any two-edged sword, piercing to the division of soul and spirit, of joints and marrow, and discerning the thoughts and intentions of the heart" (Heb. 4:12). This is how it has worked in our midst. We didn't just read our Bibles—we still don't just read them—but like Paul says, God's Word through Christ "dwells" richly in us. And I sincerely believe if a person grabs hold of one small part of that Word, if he holds on to it firmly and allows it to live in him, then the Word will carry him to a deeply radical commitment to Christ that will become well-rounded in its application toward evangelism, social action, economics, and justice.

When we see this happen, what we are really seeing is the marriage of faith and works. Our faith becomes active along with our works, our faith is completed by our works (James 2:22).

There's a railroad sidetrack for the lumberyard that runs within a few hundred yards of the Voice of Calvary in Mendenhall. At the end of the day, the locomotive, with several other cars already attached to it, transfers onto this track and begins backing up towards a line of cars stacked with logs. Back, back it goes until—boom!—the impact of the train forces the couplings together. The two segments of the train are now one. But the shock and impact of their joining are felt through the whole train and are heard for over a mile around. We can have the same kind of impact out in the world when we bring faith together with works.

I am excited about being a part of what God is doing in this world to bring faith and works together. Because it seems like, as I look back, what is happening in my lifetime, and especially in the last ten years, is that God is giving us a New Testament meaning of the church. It seems like the Spirit today is giving us an understanding of the church as the Body of Christ, the replacement of Christ's physical body in a local neighborhood.

Yes, I see the Spirit of God at work today nourishing and knitting people together through joints and ligaments (Col. 2:19) into local fellowships that can effectively embody the life of Jesus in their neighborhoods. And this is contrary to the traditional teaching of the church in our age. People usually say that the Body of Christ is that universal, invisible, worldwide body of believers. And that is true. But the Apostle Paul did not spend a lot of time talking about that body.

I'm glad he didn't, because in our society, if I only believe in the "universal" Body of Christ, then I can still maintain the type of individualism that leaves me unaccountable to people's real needs and unchangeable in my own pursuit of life, liberty, and happiness. If my body is worldwide, then my theology never becomes practical enough to deal with the needs right in my own neighborhood. Instead my theology becomes heaven-centered and irrelevant to real human need.

But there are examples developing where individuals are laying hold of God's promise that Paul spoke to the hearts of local assemblies of believers: "So we . . . are one body in Christ, and individually members one of another" (Rom. 12:5). We are part of each other. Like he reminded the Corinthians in their particular struggles in their sinful Greek city, "If one member suffers, all suffer together; if one member is honored, all rejoice together" (1 Cor. 12:26). This is the beautiful but ancient experience that God is restoring to local fellowships today!

Now, I think two things are happening as we rediscover the importance of the local body, as we commit ourselves to being the replacement of Christ's body in our neighborhood and to carrying on the ministry he began some two thousand years ago.

First, I believe that God is showing us again and afresh the meaning of the gospel. This is something that has been lost in the evangelical church world. The real meaning of the gospel has been clouded up with doctrine.

You see, if you were to ask almost any evangelical in this country, "What is the gospel?" chances are they would say to you, "The gospel is the death, burial, and resurrection of Jesus Christ." And if they are really fundamental they'd add the Second Coming. Now I believe in all these things. These are the propositional facts of the gospel. But the gospel is more than that. The gospel is the manifestation of God's love in history, the making visible, the incarnation of God's love in time. The death of Jesus Christ on the cross was God's way of showing to the world, in one act at one point in history, that he loved us.

That act of love will never be repeated (Heb. 7:27). Yet God desires his love to be made manifest over time, throughout history. And this is precisely where the Body of Christ comes in. As we rediscover the local body, we also rediscover that what God wants to do is duplicate that once-in-history manifestation of his love throughout all history by putting the same life of God again on earth, so that people can see Christ.

This is what Jesus meant when he said that we are to let our light so shine before men so that they may see our good works and glorify the Father (Matt. 5:16). People will know that we believe in Christ's death, burial, resurrection and coming again because they see us living together, following him. They see him fleshed out in our midst.

The second thing that happens when we rediscover the importance of the local body of Christ is that *God* restores to the body the gifts of the Spirit. We are seeing people in local bodies dealing with each other in ways that hold each other accountable to the high calling of replacing Jesus Christ's body on earth, who are beginning to recognize the gifts of the Spirit within them. Even leadership people in these bodies are beginning to recognize the fact that it is not their responsibility to do all the leading and all the work but to equip the saints for the work of the ministry for the edifying of the Body of Christ. God is doing a new thing.

And it could only happen as we rediscover the local body. Because the gifts are seldom mentioned in terms of individuals—only in the context of the body (Rom. 12; 1 Cor. 12). These gifts are not given to glorify persons individually, but to help build the body, to cause it to function as a powerful whole (Eph. 4:11–12).

The exciting aspect of this is that as people become eyes and ears, mouths and arms, hands and feet to each other, we can see Jesus walking the earth again, able to carry on the same ministries he carried on when he was here before. Just as he said, "the Father who dwells in me does his works" (John 14:10), so now, the Son who dwells in us, Christ's new body, does his works.

The implications of rediscovering the local body are mind-boggling. First there is the impact that it has in terms of teaching, education, and change. Anybody who has worked to develop a community knows that the most powerful form of education and change is a model.

Change begins with individual action. Every great historical movement has its roots in individual's acting upon what they believe, working it down into their everyday life. But that is just the beginning of change.

There is nothing more powerful than changed individuals putting themselves together to model what they believe. I hear a lot of people talking about going into the system and changing it from within. Aside from the fact that I may sell out my beliefs for a piece of the action once I'm in, or lose sight of the battle line, or just get worn out, lonely and frustrated, I would never substitute working for change inside the system with developing a model outside. Because if I don't have a model, if I am in a position where I must wait on the system to change before I act on what I believe, then I am nothing, no different from anybody else.

But a model has power that can be communicated because it can be seen. Models break old cycles of thought and behavior. And this is where the Body of Christ is so important.

The historic individual man, Jesus Christ, was a model strong enough to break my individual cycle of sin and to give me a model for a new life. I can point person after person to him and that historic individual life and expect the same result.

But what I struggle with also are corporate sins. Things like racism and oppression, injustice and inequality that create cycles of poverty and dependence for people from which there are few escapes.

It is my conviction that God has given us the church—a corporate expression of Christ, a corporate model of his love—to break these corporate and institutional cycles and patterns that are so difficult for us to deal with alone. To me, the way to real change is through a group of people who have been "crucified with Christ," so that he can live in them to set up an alternative, the Body of Christ. And as that body takes its responsibility in that neighborhood to do the work of the gospel, it will be creating healthy, corporate models of economics, education, health care, nutrition and day care. This is the power behind Voice of Calvary—not just the power of an organization, but the power of the promise that God has put Jesus in charge of all things especially for "the church, which is his body, the fulness of him who fills all in all" (Eph. 1:22–23).

By submitting myself to a local body, I can name those to whom I've submitted myself. Accountability becomes real. I have little choice but to act on my beliefs. And I can see specific needs in my local town as well as needs throughout the world. Once I do my thing in Jerusalem, I see clearly how to do it in Samaria and "the uttermost part of the world." I therefore have objectives—to help in a school, to start a day-care center, to share Christ with this person, to start a Bible study at this lady's house, to help put a roof on this house, to begin a mini-clinic. My theology becomes very liberating rather than restricting because I see how it relates to so much more than just orthodoxy and verbal beliefs and being a church member. I can feel good sharing Christ's ministry, taking responsibility for the particular needs in the neighborhood which cry out for spiritual and physical healing. I feel better when I see how effective even a small group of people can be in performing that healing. And as local congregations come alive, they confirm by their unity of action, their love, and reconciliation, that Jesus walks in the midst of his universal Body (Rev. 1:11–16).

I can sum up all that I believe about what God wants to do with his church today by saying that there are now, for us, three faces of Jesus that we must be aware of and seeking if we want to be effective.

I first see the face of Jesus in the Scriptures. This is the Jesus of history, the one who saved me and commands my obedience, the one whose baptism I share. We meet Jesus in his Word.

As I'm buried to my old self and rise up to a new life in baptism and obedience to Christ I see the second face of Jesus. Paul says that "by one Spirit we were all baptized into one body—Jews or Greeks, slaves or free—and all were made to drink of one spirit" (1 Cor. 12:13). I see the face of Jesus as I become a part of his Body. I see how he desires reconciliation and relationship between me and all other people. We meet Jesus in the Body.

But there is a third face of Jesus. If the first gave me personal righteousness before God and the second gave me relationship with my brothers and sisters, the third calls me to make that righteousness and those relationships relevant to the needs of the victims around me. Of the three faces that are Jesus, this is perhaps the most difficult for us to look into. In the 25th chapter of Matthew, Jesus explains that although we must look into it some day, we have a choice as to when. If we choose to seek out the victims in our society and to minister to them—hungry, thirsty, unwelcomed, naked, sick, imprisoned—then we will see Jesus' face in the least of these. We meet Jesus in the victim.

But if we choose to ignore the victim, we will have to wait until the judgment to see the third face of Jesus and then risk our exposure and the chance of hearing either "Come, O blessed of my Father," in spite of our neglect, or "Depart from me, you cursed," because of it (Matt. 25:31–46).

For us who have seen the first two faces of Christ, who have been individually justified, who know the righteousness he gives us before the Father and the relationship he gives us with our brothers and sisters in the body, perhaps the third face of Jesus, the victim, is the most important. In fact, perhaps it is our response to this face of Jesus that determines whether our responses to the first two were real and legitimate.

And yet perhaps it is true that it is not that easy, once seeing those hungry eyes, the thirsty lips, the naked body. Perhaps it is very difficult to determine the right response. How? That, to me is the question facing the church today at what I believe to be one of its greatest moments in history. How do we face the victim?

A Quiet Revolution through the Church

When I am told about the growing hunger problem in the world, I am not startled because I have seen the hungry grow retarded and the retarded live a life of misery and poverty right here in Mississippi.

When I am told that the world with its growing number of victims can at any time explode into a state where possibly all of us will be victims, I am not startled because I have seen too many people already victimized by a cycle of poverty which has manufactured brokenness since as long as I can remember.

When I am told that the fabric of life and culture as we know it is threatening to unravel, I am not startled because I have seen the tattered remnants of many lives already destroyed by the faceless power of oppression.

But what does startle me is the church and the lack of response by the people whom God has called to be salt and light in a decaying world of deepening dusk.

It startles me when I look out and see that the only people equipped with the faith, the love, and the values necessary to redirect life in our society and heal some of its many victims are without a comprehensive strategy. It startles me to see Christians more intent on getting their piece of the action than on saving people from being destroyed by poor health, poverty, and an ignorance of the plan of salvation.

We need a quiet revolution!

To quote Senator Mark Hatfield, "What will be required is what has always been most difficult to accomplish without violence: a redistribution of power, and the wealth that brings power; an end to preemption of resources by the rich; and a replacement for the kind of economics which divides the world." [1]

I see with hope that God is beginning a quiet revolution in his church—rebuilding the Body of Christ with a sense of the gospel and with an understanding of the gifts of the Holy Spirit. I see a move-

---

[1] Mark Hatfield, "An Economics for Sustaining Humanity," *Post American*, March 1975.

ment of evangelical social action, a movement of community, and a movement of church renewal.

But I look with fear at the possibility that our culture might overpower even these movements. The movement of social concern could end up much like the liberal concern of the civil rights movement, a movement of good works and legislation where energy left before much solid development or structural change took place. Evangelical social action in our day could end up in charity or in a very cheap form of conscience washing. One aspect of it that disturbs me deeply is the seeming inability of black Christians and white Christians to form any meaningful coalition.

The movement of Christian community, where more and more Christians are seeking to share their lives and resources together at deeper and deeper levels could very easily end up in groups of white, middle-class Christians talking themselves out of the loneliness and meaninglessness of the suburbs. It could end up as a new form of withdrawal from the realities of evil in our systems into a new form of communal materialism. Christian community is still a phenomenon enjoyed basically only by those people able to have the mobility and the leisure to "shop" around the country for a new life, a luxury which the poor and disenfranchised in our country have never been able to afford.

And the movement of church renewal could follow the institutional church's pattern of noninvolvement with victims in the poor, black communities of this country and result in the terrible stagnation that has been the fate of so many religious movements committed to inner growth without relevant outreach.

We need a quiet revolution.

But for me, hope and fear dwell together as I look out at the church today and see how what could be revolutionary might be just some more religious jive. Pope Paul said it for me. He was hosting a conference in the Vatican on church spiritual renewal and in one address he said something like, "This movement for our church is like opening up the windows in an old house. The Joy! The Life! But I admonish you, there are those in the world who make up the majority—they are hungry, thirsty, naked, without shelter. They will demand more than your joy."

There is, I believe, one key issue, which if addressed by the church today, would give meaning to each of these movements. The issue is this: "How do we as Christians relate our lives and our resources to the real needs of the human victims around us?" This issue could take the form of some specific questions too. Like, "How do we as Christians get rid of and replace the welfare system in America?" Or, "How do we as Christians preach the gospel in the Mississippi Delta?" Or, "How do we as Christians begin to minister in the hill district of Pittsburgh?"

How can we be part of a quiet revolution?

To me, our legitimacy and our identity as the church of Jesus Christ is wrapped up in our response to the victim in our world. As one author put it, "The gospel to the poor and the concept of the church are inseparably linked. Failure to minister to the poor testifies to more than unfulfilled responsibility; it witnesses to a distorted view of the church." [2]

If the church is to be the quiet revolution, it must face the poor in our society.

But how? Many of our communities are in a state of decay. And that decay threatens all America through crime, the rising cost of welfare, and the increased economic pressures the poor create. Traditional Christian and secular strategies have not worked in developing these communities because they have relied too heavily on cultural values rather than a sincere compassion for those living in them. Evangelism could be part of the answer. Social action could be part of the answer. But we lack a comprehensive strategy for community development because we have cheapened our evangelism to a smile and "Jesus Saves"; we have cheapened our social action to charity and welfare. We Christians have for the most part lost the sense of power that comes from being the Body of Christ.

The longer we worked in the community of Mendenhall, the more God unfolded to us the real power of the Body, that it's not just a group. As Christians coming together, cemented by our central unifying commitment to Christ, we began to see how we could be transformed into corporate power, how we could corporately give our lives in the direction of evangelizing or economic development or relieving human need or justice and make a difference.

We must relearn what it means to be a body and what it means to continue Christ's ministry of preaching the gospel to the poor. I believe there is a strategy to do this. We have seen three principles

---

[2] Howard A. Snyder, *The Problem of Wineskins* (Downers Grove, IL: Intervarsity Press, 1973), p. 51.

work that seem to be at the heart of how a local body of Christians can affect their neighborhood. We call them the three "R's" of the quiet revolution: *relocation, reconciliation,* and *redistribution.*

First, *we must relocate the Body of Christ among the poor and in the area of need.* I'm not talking about a group of people renting a storefront through which to provide services to the community. I'm talking about some of us people voluntarily and decisively relocating ourselves and our families for worship and for living within the poor community itself. William and Ruth Bentley, for instance, are leaders in the National Black Evangelical Association. Both are professionals. But instead of fleeing to the surburbs, they live over a storefront in a Chicago ghetto, where they pastor a church. That's relocation!

If we are going to be the Body of Christ, shouldn't we be like he was when he came in history? He didn't commute daily from heaven to earth to minister to us poor sinners. He didn't set up his own nice mission compound. No, the Bible says that "the Word became flesh and *dwelt* among us, full of grace and truth" (John 1:14). That's how we were able to behold his glory, because he dwelt among us.

And people will behold us and give glory to God if we dwell among them. In all of our stumblings at Voice of Calvary, I look back on this one principle and see how all the rest of what has happened has come out of it. From the beginning we were committed to living with the people in the same place they lived. In fact, we cut off all the other alternatives. Of course, like I said, there were times when I wanted to leave Mendenhall—but I couldn't. I was trapped, thank the Lord.

A living involvement with people turns poor people from statistics into our friends. I am not willing to lay down my life for a statistic. But I am more willing to lay down my life for my friends. Again, Jesus is our model.

One way this worked is with my kids, who experienced the same educational system that all the other kids we worked with had to go through. So my commitment in ministry to the education of children in the neighborhood was also a commitment to my own kids. I could not raise the educational level of my own children without dealing with the problems facing all the children in Mendenhall.

Relocating myself makes me accountable to the real needs of the people because they become my needs. A person ministering from within the neighborhood or community will know and be able to start with the real needs of those around them instead of forcing on the people what he or she has assumed their needs are. After meeting some real needs, you can begin to communicate through these "felt needs" to the deeper spiritual needs of a person.

When this happens the quiet revolution has begun.

Then *we must reconcile ourselves across racial and cultural barriers.* I hear people today talking about the black church and the white church. I do it too—it's reality. But it's not in Scripture. We should not settle for the reality our culture presents us with.

You see, the whole idea of the love of God was to draw people together in one body—reconciled to God. That's supposed to be the glory of the church! But we aren't manifesting the love of God today that can really move across racial and cultural barriers. What we do is to go on preaching the gospel within the limits of our own culture and tradition.

The test of the gospel in the early days of the church was how was it going to effect Samaria. I believe the gospel is being tested again today. To reconcile people across racial lines, black people, white people, all people, is to stage a showdown between the power of God and the depth of the damage in us as human beings. It's been my experience that the power of God wins and the result is a dynamic witness for Jesus Christ that brings others to confront him in their lives.

When reconciliation is taking place across cultural lines—between blacks and whites, between rich and poor, between indigenous and those who are new in the community—the quiet revolution is ready to spread.

The final result is redistribution. If the blood of injustice is economics, *we must as Christians seek justice by coming up with means of redistributing goods and wealth to those in need.* How well a ministry can begin the process of creating a stable economic base in the community determines the motivation of that ministry. Is it simply "charity?" Or is it really trying to develop people and to allow them to begin to determine their own destinies? It also determines the long-range effectiveness of a body's commitment to a neighborhood. For without an economic base there will never be a launching pad for ministry. A ministry in the poor community which has no plans to create economic support systems in the community is no better than the federal government's programs which last only as long as outside funds are budgeted. The long-term goal must be to develop a sense of self-determination and responsibility within the neighborhood itself.

It's at the point of redistribution that I begin to see a possibility for structural change to take place. What we need is a change created by Jesus Christ in our institutional behavior equal to the change that can occur in the life of an individual. And as we commit ourselves to just redistribution in terms of creating a new economics in broken communities, we can see how Jesus, through us, offers himself. The Body of Christ becomes the corporate model through which we can live out creative alternatives that can break the cycles of wealth and poverty which oppress people.

When this happens, the quiet revolution is winning the battle for the community.

If we take principles like these three "R's" and share them with our churches and reorient our bodies' objectives around them, I believe something wonderful would happen. I believe that the church and hopeful movements within the church will be turned face to face with the victims in our midst. I believe it would mean new life for the church.

I don't believe everyone in a middle-class, suburban church, black or white, will move to the ghetto. But I do believe that a body with these priorities will see itself totally mobilized for taking the battle of the gospel to the ghetto or any neighborhood of need. There will be the shock troops, the infantry who will be there in person. But there will also be the support troops, organizing the resources so desperately needed.

This would mean blessings of reconciliation across racial and cultural barriers, both for the "old" church and for those participating in developing a "beachhead." There will be the blessings of associating with the people for whom God has claimed a special love, the unique blessings of considering the poor (Luke 6:20, Ps. 41:1, Job 29:11–17).

And there will be the blessings of seeing God complete the love and faith which he has put within us. Just like John 3:16 is God's loving response to humanity, so 1 John 3:16–18 is the completion of that love in us as we reach out to others.

And there will be the blessings of fulfilled promises, like the one in Proverbs 29:13—"The poor man and the oppressor meet together; the Lord gives light to the eyes of both."

And I believe that if we follow principles like these into the black communities, into the poor rural areas, into the slums, then we will see the hopeful movements in the church take on real meaning in the lives of our people.

As we, by faith, were led from one work of ministry to another in Mendenhall, God's equipping hand ignited our concern through education and health care and cooperatives; ignited our sense of Christian community with returning leadership and developing disciples; ignited our gifts of evangelism, preaching, teaching, our gifts of service and wisdom. It was like lighting one corner of a pinwheel on the fourth of July. The fire spread to the others until the wheel was spining. All our works of evangelism, social action, economic development, and justice were on fire, turning and burning around the pivotal priority of preaching the gospel to the poor.

This could happen in towns and cities across the rest of the country—wherever Christians and needs exist together. What if the dynamic movements of the church today were ignited among people, preaching and doing the gospel with a special concern for the poor? I believe what we would see would be a church ministering to the hearts, bodies, minds, spirits of men and women, merging together in a unified ring of fire, like a pinwheel in motion, spreading the light of liberty, shining the light of justice throughout the land.

Let's come off of the hope, though, for a minute and get into some specifics. What if the churches began to relocate, reconcile and redistribute? What real effect could it have in the battle to make the gospel known in America?

I believe the welfare system in this country is one of the most wasteful and destructive institutions created in recent history. The dependence and exploitation it encourages, its inability to deal with the real, deep-seated needs of people is pitiful. In a speech he gave in the fall of 1973, however, Senator Mark Hatfield quotes some startling statistics that reveal the depth of the impact the church could have on our country and in meeting needs:

> Religious institutions could play an indispensable role in enhancing the renewal of community. For instance, if each church and synagogue were to take over the responsibility of caring for 10 people over the age of 65 who are presently living below the poverty level, there would not be any need for the present welfare program focused on the aged.

If each church and synagogue took over the responsibiliy of 18 families—a total of 72 adults and children—who are eligible for welfare today, there would not be any need for the existing Federal or State welfare programs to families.

If each church and synagogue cared for less than one child each, the present day care programs supported by Federal and State funds would be totally unnecessary.

Our religious institutions would be a natural focus of community activity directed toward meeting the human needs of one's fellow citizens.[3]

And as churches became those centers for community activity, what a witness, what a testimony, what an opportunity they would have among not only the needy (and primarily unchurched) people, but also to the world at large. It could be the most effective environment for evangelism ever seen on the face of the earth since the time the Master himself walked among the people healing, teaching, and calling people unto himself.

One other specific example would be our prisons. According to the latest statistics, there are as of 1975, 332,465 churches in America.[4] And I read in a recent *New York Times* story that there are 250,000 persons in prison today (1976), each one being maintained at a cost of about $17,000 per year. Not only that, but the crisis is mounting with 10 percent more prisoners this year than last. If every church in America would take responsibility for one prisoner, there would not be enough to go around!

These are only some of the battlefields for the quiet revolution.

I do a lot of speaking. And whenever I speak to students they always ask a question that gives away their feelings. It goes something like this: "Rev. Perkins, after living through and being active as a Christian in the struggle for equal rights, do you see another movement developing today?"

To me this question says something very positive, that there are many students on college campuses who wish deep in their hearts that they could have participated in the civil rights movement and are regretful.

The civil rights movement is over. But I would rather be standing at no other place in history than right now. There is among evangeli-

---

[3] *The Congressional Record,* vol. 119, no. 145, Monday, October 1, 1973, Senate.

[4] *The Yearbook of American and Canadian Churches,* 1976 ed.

cals a belated but genuine social concern. There are people moving toward developing church communities, not just for themselves, but for organizing their resources around areas of need. There are Christians seeking and searching for ways to develop the church as the Body of Christ and to equip the saints with the gifts of the Spirit for real service to people. With these trends, I believe that we are quickly moving to a position where we can begin to really preach the gospel in a way that makes reconciliation and love meaningful to all people.

The test will be to see if these trends are more than a movement. Don't hope for a movement! The civil rights movement died right on the brink of some real human development. We must have some people who will keep moving after the movement dies, after it is no longer popular to do what is right.

If we as Christians can see the issues of our day—the poverty, the racism, war and injustice—and if we can use the skills and resources that we get from our training at school or on the job, and if we can really be open to being equipped by the Spirit of God, then we will be used. We must lie on our beds at night and wrestle with how we can individually and collectively bring our faith from talk to power, how we can bring our faith and works to bear on the real issues of human need.

I believe that right now we are facing a most difficult time in history. We are discovering that old strategies have failed and that the new ones, or rediscovered ones, will not let us hold onto our old life-styles.

But I feel time slipping away. Just as people are beginning to look for these new strategies, I see the tide of concern going out again. I see that racism and self-interest are stronger in the society at large than the legislation which created integration, open voting, and various programs for relief. We have lived through a short lull in the fighting with the world that took place when people were forced to conform to laws of state. But the fact is that many times transformation has not taken place, and so I doubt the future.

I see it in the wind. As times get worse economically and psychologically, as people lose their jobs, times get tight and charity dries up, the Klan rises in Illinois, Florida, and Louisiana. But are Christians prepared? The fact is that we are at war with the world—not détente, not ceasefire, not a time-out, not peaceful coexistence—but war.

Do we see the battleline? Can black Christians and other oppressed Christians get beyond survival and blame? Can white Christians get beyond charity and the American dream? Can conviction be stronger than culture? Can we, like Zacchaeus, take responsibility for our past because of the presence of Jesus Christ in our lives? Can we pay our dues and move creatively ahead to claim the joy of overcoming past injustice? Can we move beyond racism? Can we seek partnerships with brothers and sisters of another race? Can we seek the confrontations that will come from these partnerships and let Christ provide each other with the culture shock necessary to deeply question our values, to seriously investigate our lifestyles, our motives, to become skeptical about any good which we find in our deepest selves? Can we be called to a brotherhood like the one described in Proverbs where "iron sharpens iron, and one man sharpens another" (Prov. 27:17)?

My hope is in Jesus Christ and the new life he can bring to a person and to a community. The people I work with and I have put our resources behind an alternative. But we cannot do it alone. We must create models that will break the cycle of poverty wherever it is. We must create models of health that will show the kingdom to the world. Not only do we need cooperative development and local leadership, but we also need supply lines, transports, shock troops and guerrillas, working as bodies in the system, organizing resources and skills around areas of need. We need God's people to declare a salvation that saves people from their personal sin and goes on to make them whole and healthy.

The world is tiring, but we are to endure. The world will become frustrated, but we can have hope. The world will withdraw, but we must strike. We are God's guerrilla fighters, his spiritual saboteurs. We must now go to battle in our communities armed with the evangelism, social action, economic development, and the burning desire for justice through which Jesus can continue to carry on his quiet revolution.

Appendix

DEMANDS OF THE BLACK COMMUNITY

Dec. 23, 1969

The selective buying campaign in Mendenhall, Simpson Co., was launched today, Dec. 23, 1969, primarily to secure employment in the business establishments in our town. We demand 30% of all employment in all business establishments as we are 30% of the buying population. We also urge and call for employment of Black citizens in city hall, court house. We call for police brutality to come to an end so that no more Roy Berry incidents will develop. We call for additional employment of Blacks on city police force. We call for Black deputy sheriffs at the court house. We call for Blacks on the school board. We call for complete school desegregation. We call upon reasonable men, Black and white, to help us in this move to bring justice and equality to Mendenhall and Simpson County.

WE DEMAND:

1. We demand 30% of all employment in all business establishments.
   a. We demand Black policemen on the police force.
   b. We demand Black employees in the post office, FHA office, ASCS office, food stamp office, welfare office, bank, Sup't of Education office.
   c. We demand Black deputy sheriffs and Black jailers.
   d. We demand Black recorders in J.P. court.
   e. We demand Black 30% of employees and voting-members of the local draft board.
   f. We demand Black members on the school board.
   g. We demand that all businesses with more than 3 employees have Black employees.
2. No Black person shall be fired for not buying in Mendenhall.
3. We demand desegregated recreational facilities and Black full-time city-paid personnel be hired as supervisors.
4. We demand that all personnel, including maids, be paid the minimum wage including premium pay for over-time.
5. We demand the closing of all back-door cafes.
6. We demand that police brutality and murder of Black people be stopped. We demand an end to all police harassment, shakedown, beatings, threats, insults, abusive language, threats of violence, illegal searches and illegal arrests.
7. We demand that police must obey the U.S. Constitution and Supreme Court orders. Persons must be legally arrested, advised of his rights,

rights to remain silent, rights to immediate bail, rights to phone call, attorney, clean and healthy containment.

8. Police, sheriffs, highway patrol must have sworn warrant for the arrest of any person, the search of any house or car.

9. We demand a court-appointed attorney be provided all persons arrested, from time of the arrest to the end of the trial.

10. We demand that police chief Sherman, officer Coleman, and officer R. T. Walker be fired and prohibited from holding any law enforcement position in the county.

11. We demand a complete remodeling of the jail and monthly inspections by the U.S. Dep't of Health.

12. We demand the establishment of a bi-racial Human Relations Committee to act as a police review board, to hear all complaints concerning police, sheriffs, and jailers. This committee will have power to make investigations and inspections of complaints, jail conditions, violations of rights, police misconduct, police headquarters; will have power to fire police, sheriffs, jailers and remove highway patrol officers from county beats.

13. We demand that all streets in the Black community be paved.

14. We demand that all charges be dropped against Rev. Perkins and Doug Huemmer and Roy Berry.

15. *We demand our freedom.* We demand the power to determine the destiny of our community. Black people will not be free until we are able to determine our own destiny.

Selective buying will continue until employment situation is corrected. Then, and only then, will the other items be negotiable. These can only be negotiated by the selected Black people chosen by the Black Community. No one person can negotiate these demands. *Final acceptance of a settlement lies with the Black Community.*